DECIPHERING ELIZABETHAN FICTION

DECIPHERING ELIZABETHAN FICTION

Reid Barbour

Newark: University of Delaware Press
London and Toronto: Associated University Presses

© 1993 by Associated University Presses, Inc.

All rights reserved. Authorization to photocopy items for internal or personal use, or the internal or personal use of specific clients, is granted by the copyright owner, provided that a base fee of $10.00, plus eight cents per page, per copy is paid directly to the Copyright Clearance Center, 27 Congress Street, Salem, Massachusetts 01970. [0-87413-450-1/93 $10.00 + 8¢ pp, pc.]

Associated University Presses
440 Forsgate Drive
Cranbury, NJ 08512

Associated University Presses
25 Sicilian Avenue
London WC1A 2QH, England

Associated University Presses
P.O. Box 338, Port Credit
Mississauga, Ontario
L5G 4L8 Canada

The paper used in this publication meets the requirements of the American National Standard for Permanence of Paper for Printed Library Materials Z39.48-1984.

Library of Congress Cataloging-in-Publication Data

Barbour, Reid.
    Deciphering Elizabethan fiction / Reid Barbour.
      p. cm.
    Includes bibliographical references and index.
    ISBN 0-87413-450-1 (alk. paper)
    1. English fiction—Early modern, 1500–1700—History and criticism. I. Title.
PR836.B37 1993
823'.309—dc20   91-51139
                                                                               CIP

PRINTED IN THE UNITED STATES OF AMERICA

For My Family

CONTENTS

Acknowledgments — 9

Introduction — 13
1. Greene Deciphering — 21
2. Greene Discovering — 43
3. Nashe and the Stuff of Prose — 64
4. The Fortunes of Nashe's Stuff — 82
5. Nashe's Empty Stuff — 100
6. Dekker and Narrative Cant — 127

Notes — 145
Bibliography — 165
Index — 173

ACKNOWLEDGMENTS

The manuscript of this book would have remained rough and crude without the herculean efforts of Joseph Summers and Victoria Silver. I feel fortunate to have studied with such brilliant and patient teachers. At the University of North Carolina, Anne Drury Hall offered both a careful reading of the manuscript and a daily fund of energy and wisdom. From Rochester to Chapel Hill, the following people gave support and friendship: Jon Baldo, John Bird, Jane Danielewicz, Mary Kemp Davis, Alan Dessen, Darryl Gless, Vicky Gless, Larry Goldberg, Raquel Goldberg, John McGowan, Jeanne Moskal, Susan Navarette, Roberta Schwartz, Nancy West, and Marjorie Curry Woods. Whatever the failings of this book, I am honored to dedicate it to my family—to my parents, my brother and sister-in-law, to my grandparents and my nieces, Ashley and Claire.

DECIPHERING ELIZABETHAN FICTION

INTRODUCTION

Readers of Elizabethan and early Stuart prose narrative have sought high and low for the terms in which to approach the volumes written by Lyly, Greene, Rich, and the others. They have mined the poetics of Sidney and Puttenham, and they have searched the rhetoric books for tropes and figures. Early and recently, scholars have measured Elizabethan prose narrative by such abstractions as "humanism," "idea and act," or the "novel"; and they have carefully excavated historical contexts for this prose. More often than not, their labors have yielded fruit from what many sympathetic readers of Renaissance literature consider forbidding trees.[1]

But critics of what some are content to call the pre-novel in England have overlooked a simple but essential approach to the volumes of prose written between 1570 and 1630; for the authors of this prose narrative have supplied their own terms—only some of which find their way into the rhetorics.[2] These terms and the strategies they represent ought to enter the modern reader's lexicon of Renaissance "key words." This book defines and traces the transmission of these terms as they are used, not just often but in complex and dynamic fashion, from one writer to the next. While "deciphering," "discovering," and "stuffing" may seem unusual at first to the reader equipped with "litotes" or "decorum," this triad marks the way into the designs and vexations of prose narrative as the contemporaries of Shakespeare saw them.

Rather than survey the many authors of prose fiction as Paul Salzman has,[3] I have selected three—Robert Greene, Thomas Nashe, and Thomas Dekker—for two reasons. First, they deploy the key terms over and over in order to define the enterprises of prose narrative. Second, they respond to each other—Nashe to Greene, and Dekker to Nashe and Greene—and to the conventions of the very terms that provide our focus: *deciphering, discovering,* and *stuffing*. Their responses are complex: they adopt and change the strategic terms, in sympathy, in antipathy, or more often in something between the two. In their relations, these three authors and their key terms show us something larger than the strategies of prose narrative: that is, the closely knit, though not monolithic or static, community of values exchanged and negotiated among the prosers. Thus, my "concordance" to prose narrative is more than a defense of the pre-novel; it affords a vivid synecdoche of Elizabethan and early Stuart cultures.[4] Greene, Nashe, and Dekker were searching for the identity, boundaries, and function of prose at their present time; and in this pursuit they mediated some of their culture's ultimate concerns.

The prose works of Robert Greene are a good place to start for several reasons. The sheer volume of his output has led readers through the years to delineate the stages in which Greene moved from pastoral romance to urban realism.[5] But Greene himself encourages his readers to find organization in each work and among his many works. At every turn, the devices of Greene's prose—even his epigraphs[6]—declare and affirm schemes of order in his career, but also in the narratives that result from that career. Although I will be focusing on the narrative schemes themselves, it is important to recognize that Greene's affirmation of order assumes at every level a simple creed: that the example of his life and the prevailing designs of his texts guide the reader to a stable meaning by way of specific generic performances.[7] I want to emphasize here that this is Greene's assumption, and that "Greene" himself, like all authors, is both created by and creative of the "determinants" of his culture.[8] Greene's assumptions do not exhaust his texts, nor do they fall in pure and simple form into the reader's hands. In effect, there is a difference between the Elizabethan ideal of the text that compels its readers to receive controlled meanings in narrative, and the exuberant activities and resources of the text itself.[9] But Greene appears to believe that his prose has, for the most part, stabilized the transmission of meaning from narrative to reader.

Greene's assertion of a stable prose does not have to wait for the twentieth century to be challenged: the creed is attacked and transformed by his earliest readers, Nashe and Dekker, who guide modern readers toward the instabilities or limitations of Greene's prose strategies. Accordingly, my treatment of the prose strategies, or what I call the "modes," in the work of three authors involves two ongoing activities.[10] First, I explore Greene's two main schemes—so-called "deciphering" and "discovering." This exploration anticipates to some degree the criticisms of Greene's prose conventions that Nashe and Dekker will unleash. But on the whole my first two chapters attempt to reinvent the strategies that Greene has called "deciphering" and "discovering" and that he performs in a variety of specific genres.

Second, I recreate the critical questions and transformations with which Nashe and Dekker respond to Greene's two major paradigms for Elizabethan prose. As they refashion the aims, strategies, and values of Greene's prose, Nashe and Dekker rewrite the past and the future of what they feel to be a rising star, a prose whose modes and genres are measured against the traditions of verse and drama. By now it should be clear that my title contains a pun: *deciphering* gives the Elizabethan name for the mode with which the book begins, but it also names the modern project of rethinking how the Elizabethans conceived prose narrative.

Whereas my readers might readily accept the value of deciphering the conventions of Renaissance prose fiction, some will object, no doubt, to my beginning with Greene, who seems at times a self-serving hack. It is more useful, I think, to pursue the power and meaning of the conventions that Shakespeare and many others found attractive in the works of Greene. As I have suggested, Greene's conventionality stems not just from the pressures of larger cultural forces on his work, but also from the ideal alliance that he assigns between the fable and its readers. Thus, Greene offers his modes and genres as trustworthy and nearly irresistible guides to the stable meaning that justifies the very existence of the fable. He is not alone in this maneuver: an ideal contract between fable and reader entails that decorum, or some other exhaustive principle of meaning, dominates narrative and reader alike. Such a principle connects Greene's prose to that of the many other Renaissance authors who believe that "rhetoric has the power to persuade audiences to truth and goodness."[11] This suasion requires that the most astonishing plenitudes of figure and event serve a unitary or systemic purpose. For example, a tale is not given license to mean whatever it pleases, although sometimes it is protected by the claim that it means nothing at all.[12] In Greene's prose, then, and in what some critics would call its "humanist" traditions, narrative may unfold innumerable events and circumstances, but it must offer in all of this fabling what the Elizabethans would call "convenience."

The Elizabethan notion of "convenience" edges us closer to the conventional assumptions of Greene's prose.[13] Recall Puttenham's definition of decorum:

> Now because his [speech's] comelynesse resteth in the good conformitie of many things and their sundry circumstances, with respect one to another, so as there be found a iust correspondencie betweene them by this or that relation, the Greekes call it *Analogie* or a conuenient proportion. This louely conformitie, or proportion, or conueniencie, betweene the sence and the sensible hath nature her selfe first most carefully obserued in all her owne workes, then also by kinde graft it in the appetites of euery creature working by intelligence to couet and desire, and in their actions to imitate & performe; and of man chiefly before any other creature

aswell in his speaches as in euery other part of his behauiour. And this in generalitie and by an vsuall terme is that which the Latines call *decorum*.[14]

For Elizabethan narratives, "convenience" proposes a deeply felt, if mysterious, ideal. To begin with, decorum is meaningful rather than merely functional: it ensures a "sence" that informs and regulates the "sensible." Ideally, this sense inhabits stable places or points in the narrative; and the status and location of these places or points determine how a narrative strategy—be it "deciphering," "discovering," or any other—proposes to constrain the narrative. Sometimes, a truth is assumed to subsist, whether or not the narrative does, and to fashion the existing fable from the vantage of a semantic center. At other times, the strategy ensuring narrative of its stable meaning is distributed into a sequence of noteworthy "points" whose positions are not so much central or essential as extruding and schematic, posterior to the narrative itself. So for Greene, "convenience" may be prior, central, and essential ("deciphering"), or posterior yet remarkable and exemplary ("discovering"). But whatever or wherever they may be, these worthy presences are "convenient" only if they allow plenitude yet guarantee stability in the signifying practices of narrative.

Closely related to the stable and present "sence" of decorum is its praxis; for the places function to guard the narrative from the errors that can vex both author and reader alike. They help the author to invent the fable, and the reader to understand it—a role that will not surprise the modern student of Renaissance mnemonics and rhetoric.[15] Thus, "convenience" is practical as well as true. For Puttenham, nature itself ordains the "louely conformitie," or "graft" by "kinde," between the strategies of a narrative and its stable meanings. Such "norms of integration"[16] between a semantic scheme and its narrative plenty contain and redeem what the Elizabethans would call a "continuate" or open-ended narrative. In sum, the sense and the sensible are given a mutual relationship: the "graft" between them restrains the manifold fable according to the sense, but it also needs that fable to represent and to explicate the sense. Even so, "sence" is clearly higher on the hierarchy of values.

As a theory of decorum, "convenience" resembles other Renaissance guarantors of "sufficient" meaning: commonplaces, Scripture, *topoi*, proverbs, Ideas, and custom.[17] To Greene and his contemporaries, a meaning is "sufficient" when the "sence" completely authorizes its rhetorical and narrative representations. Nashe and Dekker have two retorts to the conventions of Greene's prose: one, that he has mistaken the requirements of a "sufficient" prose (Nashe), and, two, that he has erred in assuming that human beings have access to a stable prose at all (Dekker). But, however they might transform the conventions of Greene's prose, Nashe and Dekker often begin with those conventions in very specific terms. We can argue Greene's aesthetic merits in prose; but a refusal to grant his importance for Elizabethan and Stuart prose narrative is belied by any cursory glance at Charles C. Mish's list of prose fiction published in the first half of the seventeenth century. In turn, Nashe and Dekker are important for the ways in which they challenge and reanimate the conventions of their time—all toward the end of defining the place, function, and identity of prose narrative.

The remainder of this introduction will survey the course of my six chapters. If Greene divides his prose according to three epigraphs, we can divide it according to the two terms that he uses so frequently as to turn them into signposts. These terms are "deciphering" and "discovering." Each term has established pretexts and contexts, and each features a "convenient" strategy for fixing in place the meaning of plentiful narrative. In turn, each is provocative in Greene's very complacency about his fables and readers: Nashe and Dekker are compelled to question or subvert their heritage from Greene, even as they receive, absorb, and transmit that heritage.

Chapter 1 considers the resources and genres of Greene's "deciphering." This, the more consistently romantic of Greene's two modes, assures its readers that essential truth transcends its incarnation in the figures and *topoi* of its rhetorical fables. In his early pamphlets, Greene represents—"deciphers" is his word for it—this prior truth, be it the nature of Fortune, the essence of Love, or the character of a protagonist. But there are paradoxes and problems that, to some extent, vex deciphering; these, too, are the subject of the chapter. The most important problem involves the rhetorical poetics of Greene's mode and its subordination of narrative.

In chapter 2, I turn to the mode that Greene promotes in the latter part of his prose career—"discovering."[18] Some radical changes in Greene's rhetorical poetics for narrative (deciphering) help motivate the advent of this second mode as a strategy better equipped for dealing with unruly narratives and a disorderly world. Indeed, deciphering has much less to say about the sublunary world in general as it hides behind mystery, abstraction, or even poetic surfaces. But discovering leaves behind the old rhetorical poetics and claims for prose a dramatic and social identity. This prose of discovery has new designs on plots and readers, but it has a new set of narrative and social problems, too. In pursuit of these schemes and their conflicts, chapter 2 will interpose theories of prose, drama, and power.

In these first two chapters, then, I give two lively terms a stage on which to act their parts. But the final four chapters, three devoted to Nashe and one to Dekker, take their cue from the uncritical character of Greene's prose—that is, from the blind spots of deciphering and discovering. What Bacon says about deductive syllogisms in some measure describes the quality of Greene's prose that vexed Nashe and Dekker: "[they are] most agreeable to the mind of man . . . [f]or the mind of man is strangely eager to be relieved from suspense, and to have something fixed and immovable, upon which in its wanderings and disquisitions it may securely rest."[19] Greene's modes are open to a series of charges: that they neglect the creative or even distortive role of the reader; that they fail to energize prose toward its destiny as a new and material force in the world; and that they dodge the skeptical objections to stability or purity in literary systems. Nashe and Dekker raise all of these issues in the process of reconceiving the nature and limits of prose narrative.

The career of Thomas Nashe basically spells a growing rivalry between poetry and prose for the office of preserving, but also fashioning, the social and political agendas of Elizabeth's England. I reconsider the peculiar relations between rhetorical conventions, Nashe's prose, and the world with my focus on the trope by which Nashe promoted his prose: "stuff." Nashe wants a prose that has material force and somatic presence in the world; and he hopes that such a prose can fill gaps, those in the official designs of the established powers that commission his work, but also those on the strange threshold between his prose and the world at large. But in creating his "stuff," Nashe becomes the rival to some of the traditions that he should protect. These traditions include the legacy of deciphering, which Nashe parodies, abuses, and replaces with his "stuff." All in all, the material and political world becomes a trap for this new prose and its author; with fear and trembling, Nashe must learn to get along in this trap (Greene's "discovery" helps here) and then to leave the world behind in "lenten" stuff. This escapism is the great irony of Nashe's career: that at long last he wants a hermetic seal for his fictions when he has objected to just this idea in the backhandedly political rhetoric of deciphering. What is more, he has to reckon with the impossibility of escape—that is, with the possibility that his prose is of the world whether he likes it or not.

In the last chapter, I will focus on the skeptical Dekker, whose prose extends Nashe's criticism of Greene's conventions by destabilizing the plots and narrators of discovering. Dekker's exposure of the elusive and unstable nature of discovery is best seen in his plague pamphlets and in his rewriting of Greene's coney-catching series. With a focus on wonder, cant, and disease, Dekker is motivated by his strong reading of Nashe to challenge the very basis on which Greene's later prose rests. In Dekker's prose, the hybrid and uncontrollable language of narrative mediates between (on the one hand) the conventions of Elizabethan prose and (on the other) the identity crisis in prose narrative that produced the novel. With Dekker, too, the state of prose is measured against the state of the world.

With Greene, then, we have the desire for a stable prose narrative; with Nashe and Dekker, though, we are thrust into the "inconveniences" of this desire. The picture of narrative afforded by a few key terms develops into a larger scene of cultural transmission from the sixteenth to the seventeenth century. In fact, the modern meaning of "convenience" (like that of deciphering) grows out of the Renaissance debate between praxis and idealism in the principle of decorum. In a recent article, Ann E. Imbrie has argued that the meaning of decorum shifts in the Renaissance from a strict and natural hierarchy of meanings to a functional concern with meeting the needs of interpretation.[20] Victoria Kahn has found in decorum the humanist's recourse from skeptical nightmares.[21] But, whatever the chronology or the motive of this mysterious concept, it shares the same concerns over the order of texts and their world that we find in "deciphering," "discovering," and "stuffing." I believe that prose narrative offers us one of the very best ways of getting at the Renaissance debate over the place and function of literature in the world; for the Elizabethans weren't sure what to do with prose. It was poetic and dramatic, but it was more, too. It claimed purity and stability for its plenitude, but it also accentuated the impurity or disorder that could encroach on such claims. There are many histories of this prose; mine is the study of a few terms that the Elizabethan and early Stuart prosers could not get off their minds.

It is one of many histories, but each must have its own "story." I should emphasize from the beginning those best intentions of which this book will almost certainly fall short. When we look at the past, we would like to think that we have dismantled the Renaissance tendency to allegorize *their* past. Thus, I will insist here that the Elizabethan modes are strategies rather than reified essences or necessary poles, that their story of affirmation to skepticism is not the only imaginable progress of their culture, and that the skeptical challenge to stable narratives cannot be reduced to an origin of the novel, although the proposals of Renaissance narrative tell us much about that dialectical genre—even that which James Joyce and Virginia Woolf knew.[22] In other words, I aim to be "critical" of these texts in two senses, attentive to their details and alert to their problems. What this aim really means is that I have attempted to give a stage to an otherness, but that my stage is constructed within the theater that houses our modern allegories of the Renaissance.[23]

Even so, my decipherings of Elizabethan and Stuart prose narrative have profited in great measure from Nashe and Dekker, who teach a twofold criticism. Although they take issue with the conventions of their "father" Greene, these two prosers never allow us to forget that convention is always already at work in their own prose. And so they are careful readers of those conventions, even as they change them beyond recognition or send them packing to Saffron Walden. In their prose, then, Nashe and Dekker lead us with a creative energy that invites questions of which the Elizabethans and Jacobeans had only partial notions. It should surprise or discomfit no one if our recoveries or reinventions of the Renaissance are partial, too.

1
GREENE DECIPHERING

The work of this chapter is to reinvent Greene's narratives of "deciphering" as they mark the first half of the author's own schematized career.[1] The term *deciphering* was in vogue with Euphuism in the 1570s and '80s, but Greene uses it in a variety of settings, from hermit's cells and country granges to Ovidian scenes of metamorphosis. Whatever the setting, though, Greene defines the narratives of deciphering in terms of an idealized rhetorical poetics. Four assumptions proceed from this subsuming of prose in a Platonized "poesy." First, as the OED records, *deciphering* does not refer to the interpretive act of a reader, but rather to the representational act of a narrator. Authors decipher if they emblazon something in verbal pictures, figures, emblems, or *topoi*. Second, that "something" so revealed in rhetorical "places" is some prior truth or ideal essence—some "Idea," as the Elizabethans would mean that word. Third, when deciphering calls a story into being—a story whose purpose is to display a prior truth at some length—the narrative cannot mean anything apart from that truth. This control over the fable entails—and this is the fourth assumption—a similar control over the reader: deciphering fashions and regulates its own proper reading. In sum, these are the promises of closure with which Greene underwrites the rhetoric of his early prose. His term for these promises is *deciphering*.

The Narrative Promises of Deciphering

In the Elizabethan search for the identity of prose, "deciphering" is subject to constant revision. Nashe, we will see, redefines it in order to explode the limits it sets on prose. But even Greene rings deciphering through a number of alterations. We will study these changes at length and position them in terms of Greene's other mode, "discovering." But no matter what the face or game of deciphering, Greene is committed to its narrative stability. And he is not alone:

Elizabethan apologists for poetry idealize their rhetorical practices in the name of "deciphering." In G. Gregory Smith's anthology of Elizabethan criticism, for example, Sidney uses the term for painting the general idea of the poet; King James, in the process of painting that ideal in verse; and Lodge, for any painterly image and its right interpretation.[2] A little closer to Greene's early prose, Lyly compares the deciphering of some "character" to the work of a painter: "[f]or as euery Paynter that shadoweth a man in all parts, giueth euery peece his iust proporcion, so he that disciphereth the qualities of the mynde, ought aswell to shew euery humor in his kinde, as the other doth euery part in his colour."[3] With nature's graft between the "sence" and the "sensible," deciphering reveals the hidden "qualities" according to their "proporcion" and "kinde." The poetry of its prose is, therefore, decorous and true in all its colors.

When readers come across the term *deciphering,* then, whether it be on a title page or in a tale, they have the promise of a rhetorical narrative whose figures and *topoi* are sponsored by a prior truth.[4] These same readers also have a paradox in two senses: in the romantic mystery drawn around deciphering, and also in the problems that Greene's narratives attempt to ignore or to silence. Some of these "paradoxes and problems" are simple—for example, the charge that deciphering, for all its claims to a prior truth, relies on style or "mere" language. We will see that Greene does reduce some decipherings to the game of stylistic imitation; but even so, he asserts that in lieu of some remote "mistical" truth, such stylistic exercises can still govern the course of narrative.

Indeed, its styles and elocutions are less paradoxical for deciphering than this very claim to contain the activities and purposes of a plot. Framing is one example of the ways in which the mode brackets and even retracts *narratio;* it is well known that Lyly and Greene sometimes enclose their tales in long moral appendices. But, aside from frames, or within the course of the main narratives themselves, Greene fashions other means for keeping narrative subservient to sense—for example, the symposia at which gentle lovers interpose a few brief instances between abstract definitions of some quality or precept. At times these gentles even debate the hierarchy of axiom over example. But they scarcely broach—and certainly do not challenge—the subordination of narrative to the *topoi* and emblems of its prior truth. Stories are summoned to "confirm" the essence and nothing more.

Let us say, then, that some lover sets out to decipher his affliction— the very nature of love. Greene's lovers often make it clear that, while it sometimes helps to "unfold" love in a tale, "love" itself transcends (or has no need for) narrative. I have introduced the key Elizabethan term *unfold* here, because it enables us to summarize what it is that Greene wants to achieve when he "deciphers." For the Elizabethans (as for Cicero), *unfolding* means both to tell in full and to explain.[5] This double sense is rectified in Greene's prose insofar as one (explains) censors the other (tells in full). For deciphering shares in the Renaissance desire to have plenty, but also to manage it. The term *unfold* takes us even further into this desire because it refers to acts both of narration and of interpretation. It just so happens that, in Greene's early prose, these two practices are equated: narration interprets the prior truth that in turn guards that "unfolding" from error.[6]

"Error" includes these: that the plenty of narrative or the differences in interpretation become too licentious; or that it be proved that truth relies on narrative representation as much as narrative relies on the patronage of truth. Indeed, the Elizabethans had a piece of wit for this latter paradox. A cipher, they would say, is only "zero" until it joins other numbers. Only then does it have value. Greene advances the idea that narrative is such a cipher; but sometimes his tales suggest that narrative is the other number. This explains why Puttenham must naturalize the graft between the sense and the sensible: it is better to value the conjunction of the two for their fruit than to fret truth's dependence on—or contamination by—its fictions.

In the next section, I will situate deciphering within the Renaissance love affair with copia. But while we can review the mode in terms of larger cultural events, Greene never addresses the social or political agenda of deciphering's governance of prose narrative. This is perhaps the biggest problem for deciphering: its idealism protects the rhetorical narratives from making any visible difference—or from finding any identity—in the world that is so important to Greene's "discovery" prose and to Nashe's "stuff." Much recent criticism of sixteenth-century literature has been devoted to the politics of copia. Terence Cave has explored the twin desires in copia for both a semantic anchor and an abundant discourse. Richard Helgerson and Lorna Hutson have posed Greene and Nashe against the humanist program for a copia that has ethical force in its very avoidance of prodigal expenditure. Their work is related to the more Derridean studies of the "endless work" of Renaissance romance. And although with differences between them, the "new historicists" have launched a compelling attack on the Elizabethan fantasies by which power is mediated in terms of courtly romance and a benign hierarchy. Thus, the Queen's ideal body, the *logos,* and the cornucopia of economy and language: all represent the centralized restraints placed on the same unfailing plenty that the dominant voices of Elizabethan culture promote.[7]

But what is so striking about Greene's career in prose is the way in which he orders it: this order includes—even hinges on—a conversion to social practice. Greene's reversals affect not just his attempt to define a discursive space for prose narrative, but also Nashe's, for whom prose at its best is materially present in the world. The force of Greene's and Nashe's redefinitions of prose narrative is felt most, I think, if we concentrate on the protective strategies of deciphering, the ways in which its narratives, emblems and *topoi* pose as shields around some transcendental signified. Even when Greene pares his mode down to language games, it is hermetic rather than worldly; yet worldliness is the price of the redemption with which Greene announces the prose of "discovery" in the later part of his career.

The paradoxes and problems of deciphering begin with Euphuism. It is the first of the fashions in which Greene offers a rhetorical prose that anchors its plentiful narratives and fashions its proper readings. Whereas some readers might think that Greene is a hack for playing to fashion, it seems to me that his fashions show those "strange Elizabethans" in some of their most revealing colors.

Euphuism and Deciphering

It is well known that Greene's early prose is Euphuistic, to which vogue he owes the term *deciphering*. For Greene, the alliance between Euphuism and his prose yields character essences and thematic "ideas" in a loosely Platonic sense. Thus, the hidden is revealed in the tropes and figures (*isocolon, parison,* among others), the balances and repetitions, all rehearsed many times by scholars of Lyly's *Euphues, the Anatomy of Wit*. Rather than list these figures and their sources yet once more, I will isolate among them the specific motives of Greene's deciphering.

Readers have debated whether Euphuism is stable in meaning or redundant in effect, whether it is imperiled by the proximity of its opposites or trite in its devotion to ornament.[8] Greene is only one of many Elizabethans who could write in yet also satirize the vogue of Euphuism. Clearly, the style favors all manner of "contrary contents," the Elizabethan term for binary oppositions; but in Greene's early fables these contents are steered toward a set of prior semantic essences.[9] I feel sure that some of my readers will resist such a highbrow view of Greene's prose—at least that part of Greene's output that did not attract the dramatic genius of Shakespeare. But it seems clear that "deciphering" grew out of the same cultural dilemma that helped fashion Euphuism—namely, the search for a semantic anchor among plenty. This pursuit inspired Erasmus's *De copia* as well. Greene's decipherer, like Erasmus's orator, must learn to say basically one thing in a host of ways. This one thing may be gnomic or forensic, opaque or clear, but its inventor must "deliuer a matter with more varietye . . . both plainely and by prouerbes and Metaphors."[10] Plenty must have its anchor and guarantee if narrative is to be "sufficient."

There are, of course, classical precursors for saying one thing in a host of ways. One figure in particular, *commoratio* or "dwelling on a point," was described by the *ad Herennium* in an image that suggests a semantic continuum within a closed though abundant text: the "point" runs through the discourse like blood through the body. Cecil W. Wooten has shown that Cicero learned the strategy from Demosthenes, both men attempting in times of crisis to convey, with ineluctable power, the clarity of a single position.[11] And the figure interested Geoffrey of Vinsauf among the other rhetoricians of the Middle Ages.[12] But when we turn to Erasmus, it is possible to detect some signs of what later critics would call the humanist *agon* between words and things. Erasmus hardly wavers in his program of copia; he shares in the sixteenth-century civic and religious justifications of verbal abundance.[13] But Terence Cave is certainly right about the divisive tendencies in Renaissance copia: "the impossibility of escaping from verbal appearances," Cave writes, "does not eradicate the impulse to stabilize them, to anchor them in a referent located outside their domain."[14] This desire for a sense continuum is everywhere in Erasmus's works, especially where the advent of the Reformation drives him, as Cave has it, to "clarify and make explicit" an essential sameness in many words.[15]

Janel Mueller's work on the sixteenth-century prose of counsel links this pursuit of a semantic continuum to the mystique of Euphuism. In general, a "schematic styling" aims to unite author and reader on the ground of wisdom, with a sound-sense continuum to "ensure the transmission of the message."[16] For the sixteenth-century humanists, this is all part of a "scripturalist" activity that harks back to the "sense parallelism for redundant material" (332) in Hebraic books of wisdom. According to Mueller, George Pettie's Euphuism shares in the desire to elucidate a message by its schemes and figures. But Lyly's Euphuism sharply contrasts with Pettie's in the dissimulations of Lyly's style. Mueller's point is this: while Lyly's devices, repeated over and over, encourage us to look for a central proposition in all this apparent balance and homogeneity, "the 'same thing' said in 'different words,'" any such proposition is elusive or nonexistent, and the style remains enigmatic (404).

Mueller explains this "frustration" in Lyly's style in terms of Thomas Wilson's religious agenda of considering one's audience to be hostile. This difficult state of affairs for the orator is described by reformed writers with reference to fallen humanity and "infected wit." A contract with the audience must be carefully and doggedly fashioned. To "erect" their wits, the orator (or narrator) must surprise the audience with equivocation, conjecture, and hyperbole (344–72). But, in attempting such an agenda, Lyly obscures the semantic continuum, offering "the coexistence of extremes in an identity or interdependency relation whose nature is never clarified yet constantly reaffirmed" (405). Thus Erasmus's exposition of the one matter in different words converts, in Lyly's prose, into a mystery that requires and even compels the reader's faith.[17] Now, Greene's early prose lacks a scripturalist agenda, but it adapts the patternings to its own designs. In the compulsive repetition and enigmatic suasion of Lyly's Euphuism, we approach the romantic motives of Greene's deciphering— what Arthur Kinney sees as Greene's designs on "wonder."[18] The strategy of Greene's mode seems to be this: even as the reader marvels at the relation between figure and narrative, that same reader will be swayed to believe in a semantic center.

According to the *ad Herennium*, it is impossible to "dwell on a point" in brief. This relation between copia and "harping" on a point is in part the subject of Lyly's later novel, *Euphues and his England*. The plot features a scene in which Euphues tells the lover Philautis an amorous tale; but the teller is always dwelling on a point that delays the union of the lovers. It is no surprise, then, that Philautis, here and elsewhere, identifies Euphues as a harper who will "harp on yt string which is burst in my hart, and yet euer sounding in thy eares."[19] Philautis would have all tales of love delivered with an emphasis on the chief events of the affair itself. He is in fact "so eger of an end, as one leaping ouer a stile before hee come to it, [that he] desired few parentheses or digressions or gloses, but the text, wher he him-self, was coting in the margant" (Bond, II.51). The lover wishes to be a finger in the margin, pointing with all his might to the notable events in the romance, and unconcerned with digressive or repetitious styles. On the other hand, it is Euphues who slumbers during the tales so absorbing to his companion, harping, we may be sure, in his dreams.

Between the heroes of *Euphues and his England*, two paradigms emerge for prose narrative, and they are analogous to Greene's deciphering and discovering. Each has very different designs on plots and readers, and each dominates a half of Greene's career.[20] Indeed, Greene is self-conscious about fashioning not just orderly plots and readings, but also an orderly life as the master narrative: his love of epigraphs attests to this desire. But Euphuism is the most compulsive of all Greene's strategies: it allows deciphering to promise access to prior truths; it offers a code by which to know wholes by halves; and it nurtures the errant reader in the commonplaces of proverb, *parison* and *isocolon*, and in the emblematic lore of bird and gem. Starting with Euphuism, Greene continues to invent new genres in order to affirm the promises of deciphering, and to protect it from the world of Nashe where decipherers are embroiled in the dirty politics of rhetoric and interpretation. One of its readiest escapes lies in its simple task of "depainting" characters.

Deciphering in Characters

In his study of classical and medieval conceptions of character, Warren Ginsberg reminds us that the ancients translated character types into words and actions according to what I have called, after Puttenham, "convenience." Thus, writes Ginsberg, poetry "must obey the rules of 'convenientia.' . . . Certain congruence [between a type and its representations] must grace the expression if the poet wants to avoid the groundlings' catcalls."[21] No one cared more about avoiding abuse than Robert Greene. It is clear that his early Euphuistic tale, *Mamillia* (in two parts, 1580/83), wants very much to "decipher" the "perfect pattern" of its characters according to stable and accepted rules.

The plot of *Mamillia* alters Lyly's focus on the essentially faithless woman. In Greene's fable, there is a triangle between two devoted women (Mamillia and Publia) and one essentially treacherous man (Pharicles). But Mamillia's nature is hardly disturbed by male treachery: her character offers not just the "common consent of all the Graces" but the perfect congruence between inner and outer beauty. This ideal of womanhood—whereby the sense and the sensible convene—is considered natural. The narrator declares that it is pointless "to discipher her excellent perfection, sith nature had so cunningly paynted out the portraiture, both of her mind and body, in such comly coulours."[22] The decipherer, that is, follows the restrictions of decorum.

So it goes with the treacherous Pharicles, the man whom Mamillia loves and loses to the whims of his fancy. As her "contrary contents," Pharicles is essentially false: his outsides and insides are deciphered in their perfect opposition to one another. Thus, the main characters join the other binary oppositions of the text, female and male, nature and nurture, and so forth. And there is plentiful harping on each, for example, in the narrator's digressions for and against misogyny. Often enough, the narrator and the protagonists register their desire to harp on a point. The narrator opines that, had Pharicles "rested on this point, in my judgement he had hit the marke" (54). Pharicles himself ends a meditation when "he rested upon this poynt." This "poynt" is sometimes private unto the lone character, but when the company gathers in the household of a sick friend, Pharicles "deciphers" on request the ideal pattern of love with a copious display of causes, effects, and other "places."

These decorous characters must be protected from any "inconvenience" whatever. This caution has a moral level: Mamillia will "avoyd al inconuenience, as her presence among the lustie brutes might have procured" (21). But the narrator wants also to avoid any indecorum in the progress of his tale. He wants a "sufficient" tale—Greene's term for a character or a fable that allows no error or incongruity. Thus, while the chaste Florion "sufficiently defensed his minde with the rampyre of honesty" (40), the narrator deciphers the "sufficient signs" of his fiction. His readers need not fear any unwarranted figure or color therein.

Even so, *Mamillia* hints at the conflicts that might arise between the constraints of deciphering and the plenitude of narrative. Thus, Pharicles laments his status as the "one particular, on whom *Cupid* wil shew his craft, & decipher his nature" (122). Here, the treacherous man resists the priority of the very essence, love, that he has defined for all to hear. Not only is Pharicles unwilling to be grafted to a type (the blind lover), but he wants others to forget his vicious nature, the false libertine. In this tale, Pharicles is alone in fretting about his character; but when Greene attempts more complex plots, we hear all the more about the differences between prior truth and example.

As the second part of *Mamillia* progresses, the plot intensifies: the three protagonists separate from each other; Pharicles travels to find social prominence, decadence, and imprisonment; Mamillia prevails over great opposition and saves her beloved from a persecution that most readers will wish on him. But "deciphering" asserts its control over the narrative—the "vnfoulding of [Pharicles's] infortunate life" (177)—in two or three key ways. First, the characters gather at a symposium to hear one of their company "decipher" (paint, define, reveal) some essence such as "love." Second, Greene follows Lyly in appending several moral epistles between one Lady Modesta and Mamillia; here again, a story is summoned only to confirm or to explicate a virtue. But in *Mamillia,* the mainstay of deciphering is character, especially Mamillia, who proves to "stand so much vppon these points" of beauty and virtue that her story is sufficient against the wiles of men and narrative alike (239).

Deciphering in Emblems, *Topoi,* and Symposia

"Character" is not the only place where Greene can "disclose the essence"; he invents other *topoi* and emblems in which deciphering can protect yet reveal its prior truths. In *Arbasto* (1584), Greene keeps some of the Euphuism but also translates its "contrary contents" into the emblems prized by a priestly hermit. These emblems serve to frame the tale with what we are led to believe is the tale's essential meaning.

The story begins with a traveling "I" whose ship is driven by a storm into Sydon. In lieu of autobiography, this "I" encounters a hermit's cell in which he finds and defers to a priestly figure among emblems:

> whereinto as I entered, I saw an Archflamin sitting (as I supposed) at his Orizons (for so was the priest of the goddesse termed) who being clothed in white satten roabes, and crowned with a Diadem of perfect golde, leaned his heade vpon his right hand, powring forth streames of watrish teares, as outward signes of some inward passions, and held in his left hand the counterfeit of fortune, with one foote troade on a polype fish, and with the other on a Camelion, as assured badges of his certaine mutabilitie.
>
> (III.178–79)

Lyly includes hermit's cells in *Euphues and his England,* but Greene emphasizes that these "outward signes" or "assured badges" regulate the sense of the narrative to follow. Arbasto's emblems claim a magical authority over the story forthcoming: although remote, they assume a central position in the progress of the tale.

The emblems are so comforting to Arbasto that he resists telling his story. They are safe and, it would seem, free from the world outside this "place"—free as well from any need to be "unfolded." Arbasto attends to the images of fortune with such a fixation that the "I" must use his best Euphuisms to abstract the story of this wise Eubulus. But the cautious old man, himself an emblem of fortune, is aware that the young man's deciphering might be a cipher: "the smoothest talke hath ofttimes the smallest truth" (182). Narration is so painful for Arbasto that he offers first a bald summary of his life. Before extending the fable "to vnfold the cause of these [his] suddaine passions" (183), the hermit needs more confidence in the power of his emblems. The "I" obliges in directing his gaze toward "what the picture of Fortune did importe" (179).

There is plenty to tell: Arbasto's own idyllic kingship, his brother's death by murder, national revenge, and a love affair with the daughter of his foe (the king of France). As the emblems and their cell fade from view, the narrator reminds his auditor from time to time that their meaning is ever-present. We are all reminded, that is, of deciphering, not just in the Euphuistic monologues, but also in the lover Arbasto, whose perfect image of his mistress is "particularly deciphered by a secret imagination" (191). What is more, the narrator has an access to events and thoughts for which Nashe's Jack Wilton would require a chink in the wall. Somehow, deciphering enables its agents to know the whole by way of coded parts; so, although Arbasto may apologize for intruding on the thoughts of others, he nevertheless holds the key to their nature and meaning.

But the hastening sequence of events exerts some pressure on Arbasto's "assured badges." Events not only multiply, but they grow sour or, to give Arbasto's word, "inconvenient." Thus, during a truce, the French king proves treacherous—he "commit[s] an inconuenience" (217)—and imprisons Arbasto. Myrania, one of three French princesses, rescues her beloved Arbasto by trapping and killing the jailor; this, despite the fact that Arbasto loves her sister, the scornful Doralicia. The end brings Fortune's worst: having found out Arbasto's love for Doralicia, Myrania dies from madness; Doralicia, in love with Arbasto at long last, dies from his rebuke; and Arbasto, caught between love and guilt, is expelled from his throne by his friend Egerio. Chaos has come again, as Walter Davis argues.[23] But in the hermit's cell to which our attention returns, the emblems of Fortune are enthroned over the chaos of the tale and of the world. We begin with the "assured badges" and return to them; for they translate the chaos of Arbasto's life into a stable, prior truth, the ritual silence of which comforts the weary hermit. Arbasto is an unwilling narrator, and he wishes in the end to protect his cell and to caress with his gaze the signs of Fortune therein.

Arbasto's emblems are magical and remote, although they claim an authority over the entire tale. In the fable itself, Arbasto sometimes finds it difficult "to decipher in coloured discourses" (229); but in the cell he has "convenient leysure." In a later narrative (*Alcida*, 1588), Greene returns to the magic of deciphering in different *topoi* (metamorphoses, fountains); but first, in *Morando, the Tritameron of Love*

(1584/86), Greene is much less mysterious about the way in which deciphering frames its narratives. Here, Greene affirms the power of his mode in two ways. He adapts Boccaccio's *Decameron* for its strict but not mysterious framing devices. Indeed, the gathering of friends at a court or grange has little to do with the rituals and emblems of a priest. But this very convening of friends permits the second move: in the symposium, the speakers "decipher" in one kind of discourse— a diptych joining narrative *exempla* to the commonplace definitions of some essence. In other words, Greene's symposium is very different from Boccaccio's insofar as the former makes narrative ancillary: stories, often reduced to thumbnail "instances," are said to confirm a truth and nothing more.

Greene follows Boccaccio in setting the scene for "convenient leysure." A man is murdered on the street, and his family and friends resort to a private retreat. But the novellas of *The Decameron* are restricted only by the topic chosen at the end of each day. Greene's *Tritameron* never allows narrative such open space; its participants do not aim primarily to tell stories. From the very beginning, Greene's analogies between prose and painting suggest a hierarchy of literary values that demotes narrative. In the preface, Greene segregates "bare talke" and "imperfect tale" in a famous legend of the painter Zeusis, who, "painting Triton, drew onely his face, the rest he hid with the tumbling waues of the sea. And I setting foorth Morandos discourse, shew onely his bare talke, the rest I rudely shadow with an imperfect tale" (III.48). This legend is commonplace, but here the division of talk and tale anticipates the division between essential definition and narrative confirmation in the speeches of the main text. In the symposium speeches, orators harp on a question (for instance, "whether it be good to love or no"), define the key term ("love") by commonplace and category (cause, effect), then confirm their answers with examples from history and fiction (varying in length from a few phrases to two pages). The logic of deciphering runs thus: painting the face of Triton commits the character's essence to representation; this face (or "talke") benefits from having a body (the "tale"); but tales, down in the "tumbling waues," have a hidden and unpredictable energy for all their secondary status (the "rest"); and so they must be trivialized to protect the "assured sufficiency" of the face. The tales, then, are unnecessary and merely interpretive, or (like the body of Triton) illusory, not really *there*. Only the face is clear and present.

In the narrative proper, Greene offers another analogy between painterly and narrative frames. Panthia, the widow of the murdered gentleman, has taken her three daughters (Lacena, Sostrata, and Fioretta) to the grange of her husband's friend, Morando. There, they find the owner accompanied by three young gentlemen (Peratio, Aretino, and Sylvestro). Just after dinner and prior to their symposium, Peratio notices a "Table most curiously painted":

> wherin both the sea and land was most perfectly pourtraied. The picture was of *Europa,* the sea of the *Phenicians* and the land of *Sydon:* On the shoare was a beautifull Medow, wherein stood a troupe of daintie Damosels: in the Sea a Bull, vpon whose backe sat a Dame of surpassing beautie, sailing towards *Candie,* but looking to the crew of her companions from whom by sinister meanes she was seperated. The painter by secrete skill had perfectly with his Pensill desciphered the feature of their faces, as their countenance did seeme to importe both feare and hope. (56)

This "Table," with its several panels, serves as an emblem of deciphering. The artist paints the "importe" of "contrary contents" (fear and hope) in the faces. In turn, such "secrete skill" oversees the division of the narrative into panels or phases where the women rush, stand, and retreat as a confirmation of the fear and hope in their faces. Not only does the *Tritameron* feature such a paneled discourse; but this painting leads Madame Panthia to one of the many conversations in which some essence is "depainted": "Honestie," she says, "is alwaies painted like a woman" (60).

Indeed, the *Tritameron* shows very clearly what is at stake in deciphering: the subordination of the "instance" to a prior truth. We will see that the characters themselves are aware of this subordination. But Victoria Kahn's work on Puttenham helps us to understand the decorum of instances more generally.[24] According to Kahn, Puttenham conceives decorum so that it ensures true order in the nature of things. But that same conception eludes theory or principle, and it relies instead on the utility of instances and practices. This conception means, among other things, that decorum has social constraints; but it also spells, in Kahn's view, a "resistance to the epistemological threat that irony may pose to ethics" (377). Greene's reader, Thomas Nashe, worries about unstable equivocations in the codes of rhetoric; but what about the speakers in the *Tritameron*?

To begin with, they all follow the same basic procedure in their answers to the questions of love. The courtly combatants launch into monologues that dwell on commonplaces and categories, then cite examples from history and poetry. But, in order to escape from the mere "supposes" of their definitions, the speakers redress one problem (abstract conjecture) with another, the imperfect and open-ended narratives of "manifest instance." The auditors even warn the speakers about the sophistry of inferring the general principle from specific cases. Tales must always serve the "principle," "axiom," or "nature."

Just so, the instance must only encapsulate the essence without admitting any unwelcome fable: it must, that is, confirm rather than compromise the prior truth, for example, the "principle . . . that men by their constitution are indued with a more perfect and stronger complexion then women" (103).

So, whereas classical oratory places *narratio* before *confirmatio*, Greene conflates the two: narration is confirmation. But Greene's speakers face the same dilemma as the humanist resource books for the copious orator. The instance, poised between precept and story, is both useful and generative: it serves but can have a life of its own. For Kahn, this threshold is critical: instances "do not simply 'fail' to illustrate general precepts, but in failing, succeed in questioning their subordinate status as mere illustrations of theory" ("Resistance," 379). Texts are, of course, more or less explicit about this so-called failure. But, even when they ignore the failure, they often follow the two escape routes outlined by Kahn for resolving the conflict between the utility and license of the instance. "One can," writes Kahn, "either reduce the examples to mere ornament and thus ignore them, or one can attempt to bring some kind of order to the examples by privileging one sort over another" (380). I am arguing that each of Greene's two modes, deciphering and discovering, takes one of these two routes: deciphering turns the instance into an ornament, and discovering elevates one narrative event over another.

The speakers in the *Tritameron* show very well how deciphering handles the narrative instance. Among them, Sylvestro is the most ardent decipherer. He knows the proper resources for "depainting" an essence: Socratic maxims, Pythagorean ciphers, enigmas, allegories, tropes, "certain pictures," Euphuism, Ideas, and astrological secrets. Only with these resources in place does he adopt the story from Boccaccio about a boor who is transformed by love. Sylvestro believes that rhetoric should persuade its audience but also obscure its essence: thus, he accuses his opponents of two failures, for telling imperfect tales (no "perfect pensill") and for floating on the surface of allegory like Boccaccio's famous lamb. But Sylvestro "decypher[s] the miseries and mishaps of Loue" (119) with such zeal that he falls in love with Lacena: "the vertuous disposition of the Ladie *Lacena* had insinuated so cunningly into the depth of his thoughts, that he found the libertie of his mind countermanded, with a fore conceipted impression of an after possessed content" (113). Quintilian tells us that such insinuation comes from dwelling on a point; but the irony is, of course, that Sylvestro has become the instance of his own definition, although he exceeds the others in demoting the instance.

Counter to Sylvestro, some of the auditors distrust the enigmas of deciphering. Madame Panthia asks that the company "leaue these needles Allegories that haue such an amphibologicall equivocation, and may admit such diuerse construction" (127). She appears to prefer a deciphering that is clear in its depainted colors, and she fears that the mode will become a "Chaos of confused precepts" (143), its essence unavailable to the courtly audience. But the opposite danger is that bare deciphering will become merely functional or occasional without the aid of mystery. There is the fear that its codes will convert into empty flourishes or interludes that serve only to fill space in the tale. These concerns about the status of rhetoric and about the errors of interpretation are but romantic intimations of the work of Nashe, where "deciphering" is politicized in terms of some very worldly practices. Indeed, Greene's characters debate the merits of precept and example in their own hermetic cell, far from the crimes of the city. And, in the end, they ward off the multiplication of instances that might yield "a thousand other examples."

Thus, the enlistment of stories to "prove these premises" can provoke "innumerable" tales: or so realizes Peratio, whose definition of Fortune according to maxims and poesies incites even the auditors to remember narrative cases. One character, Aretino, promotes the vitality of the instance. He objects to Sylvestro's fear of these "forward motions," and to the intention to confine tales to just a few. Aretino charges that the other "ment thus abruptly to break off his discourse," despite Sylvestro's insistence that "our meaning is not to exclude others altogither" (158–59). But, as the instances grow longer, everyone agrees that the "sure truths," "general and infallable Axioms," "premises," and "sacred essences" should rule the meaning of narrative. Moreover, Lacena leads the charge toward more familiar, less mysterious forms of deciphering—to Euphuistic speeches or to the "plain" meaning of even the "Misticall Enigmas." Hers is a faith in the contract between the inner sense and the outer code: "yet loue hath made me so good a scholler to prie into your precepts . . . if your inward intent follow your outward attempt" (167). Lady Panthia, also eager for clarity, interrupts the citation of instances in order to recall a "table whereon was pourtrayed the picture or counterfeit of Fortune . . . [w]inged she was, and standing vpon a gloabe, as decyphering her mutabilitie" (133). This "digression" returns the conversation to the "substance" of Fortune, and to the activity of "painting out her properties." Even Aretino harps on "one doubtfull point of Fortune" (139).

In the name of deciphering, then, the emblems and *topoi* of Greene's early prose affirm the truth "forepointed." They insist that narrative instances function to confirm the essence, and that this confirmation, while useful, is unnecessary. There is some disagreement about the license that the instance should have, but none about the basic hierarchy of values. There is also some ambivalence about the value of mystery: the strange emblem and the lucid figure both have their day. It appears, in fact, that deciphering requires both a remoteness and a proximity: it must rule over the meaning of narrative, yet from afar. There are a number of other works in which Greene depaints the *ethos* of a character or the axioms of a symposium.[25] But the motives of deciphering warrant a full-scale myth in Greene's *Alcida*.

The Mysterious Source

In *Alcida* (1588), Greene creates an unusual myth of origins, one with several components. Alcida is another hieratic figure to whom a traveling "I" defers. But she is also the human persona of an ancient fountain. Before turning into a fountain (though Greene suggests that she is somehow already so turned), Alcida tells three stories for this "I," each of which she prefaces by displaying some emblem located near her cell. Each emblem and its story reveal (decipher and confirm) the vicious nature of a daughter. Here, Greene invokes his Ovidian muse: if the story of each daughter begins with the emblem, each daughter turns into the emblem at the end of her own story. Thus, the emblem is the beginning and the end of the fable.

But there is another facet to the myth of origins. Greene also adapts the fountain *topos* in which an origin for all rivers is located in paradise. Alcida is such a "source" in several respects: she tells each story, she subsumes each story into the progress of her own life (the metamorphoses follow each other neatly in time, and they piece together her life for the "I"), and in the end she turns into the fountain whose name and identity she already bears. The stories framed in the middle have two "sources," then: the emblematic monument with which each begins and ends, and the "fountain Alcidian," or mother, to which each returns. This Ovidian "manner" gives deciphering a strange new frame for its stories—one that is both distant (the origin) yet so close (the emblems into which each story "turns"). In this myth of the fountain, Greene suggests that all stories derive from and return to some origin, and that this non-narrative origin determines the meaning of the stories. Thus *Alcida* is Greene's closest dalliance with the mythic gods that have approved his utopian prose.

Alcida begins, as does *Arbasto*, when the shipwrecked "I" finds the solitary Alcida and asks for her story. Given leisure, she agrees to tell it. Alcida's story consists of three emblematic tales, each of which adds another link to her life. Like Arbasto, she is careful about her narrative, and she laments that so many artists have wrought imperfect emblems: "ill haue those painters deciphered time with a pumice stone, as rasing out both ioyes and sorrowes with obliuie" (ix.22). Having replaced the pumice, she "enters into" her "narration," but she ceases after some exposition in order to escort her auditor to a first emblem: "to a marble piller, fashioned and pourtraied like a woman" (23–24). The statue holds tables inscribed with poems and pictures, the first poem combining an allegory of Nature with precepts and instances, the second concerning the peacock's narcissism. Here, Alcida suggests, is the "place" of the story's meaning. The emblem is closer to its story than Arbasto's cell was to his; it is not hidden away in some distant temple, but it lies further afield in the place where the daughter's life ended. The statue represents, in sum, what the daughter essentially was, and her story is unfolded from its base.

The mother derives the other two stories from emblems as well; and, in each case, the story ends with the daughter's metamorphosis into the emblem. In the second story, a grove provides the isolated ground where Alcida and her auditor witness the abstract vice of the story about to unfold. The grove, "between two hills, like the supposed entrance of hell," is a commonplace, and includes "a goodly Spring" (the source *topos*) as well as "Hierogliphicall Embleames" (55). The third leaves us with the silence that any return to the source implies. On the third morning, Alcida and our narrator walk to a field by the sea to which the latter's story will return. The emblem is a tomb, which, in its evocation of mortality, suggests the erasure of all stories and their *topoi*. So it is that the tomb stands "without any simbole, embleme, imprest, or other Hierogliphicall caracter" (87). It has only verses. The tomb epitomizes the protective mystery of deciphering: it signifies, almost without representing.

As before, the story explicates the emblem for the auditor: it clarifies the "barren place" with "what after thou shalt finde" (88). This daughter's inconstancy is added to the trivial wit of the second and the pride of the first; and in each case Alcida has complete access to the hidden thoughts, feelings, and words of the characters. As Greene's most mysterious decipherer, Alcida oversees the "sufficient signs" of her tale to such an extent that her first person "I" silently moves at times into the position of another character. She does not have to explain how she knows in any critical or analytical fashion.[26] Alcida doesn't need sources because she is the source: after her account of the third metamorphosis, she turns into the fountain that she has always been.

In addition to its myth and emblems, *Alcida* features songs and verses, some of which make no essentialist claims but serve only as a lover's interlude. I argue in the final section of this chapter that Greene protected deciphering from the world in just this way—by redefining it as the "mere" imitation of verse and style. Like Spenser, Harvey, and Sidney, Greene experiments in patterns of verse and style so that his mode pursues a more gamesome (if still functional) control over the direction of narrative. This humanist venture in *nugae* is the revised agenda of *Perimedes the Blacke-Smith* (1588), *Ciceronis Amor* (1589), and *Menaphon* (1589). Although the imitation of style and verse has no mystery and invites the charge of triviality, it adheres to the strategy of regulating prose narrative according to a rhetorical poetics whose romance is set at a distance from the plots of the world.

Style and Verse

In *Pierces Supererogation*, Gabriel Harvey uses *deciphering* to name the imitation of styles: "What greater impossibility, then to decipher the high, and mighty stile of young Apuleius, without a liberall portion of the same eleuate spirite."[27] In this section I contend that Greene's own deciphering approaches the "mere" decoration of prose in the imitation of style and prosody, and that, in this shift, Greene ignores the humanist dilemma exposed by Harvey's comment on the "eleuate spirite."

Take, for example, the prefatory poems to *Alcida*, where Greene is flattered as the proper company of Ascham, Cheke, and the other English Tullies. He also is the famous censorious bee "Searching the secrets" of "learned Authors." Such searching or gathering can be construed ideally: the secrets can be those "Ideas" (Plato's commonwealth, Tully's orator, and Baldassar's courtier) that Greene often cites in sequence. This searching is "humanism" seeking the pure source of truth behind all impure vestiges. But that bee also can represent the editorial humanist who wants to produce proper texts and whose interest in rhetoric and method tends toward the practical transmission of knowledge and civic prowess. These enterprises need not be mutually exclusive, but they can be if the source of all texts defers to an acceptable edition.

In Greene's day, the devotion to experimental verse and to stylistic imitation led some to disparage the humanist agendas.[28] But the values of word and thing are very difficult to sort among the humanists: no easy dualism between *verba* and *res* is fair to their designs. The pedagogues themselves warned against slavish imitation, and it is easy to misconstrue Ascham's notorious statement that "[t]hey be not wise therefore, that say, 'What care I for man's words and utterance, if his matter be good? . . . Ye know not what hurt he do to learning, that care not for words, but for matter; and so make a divorce betwixt the tongue and the heart.'"[29] For the Reformers, editorial humanism weighed in the balance of souls; for philosophers, the improvement of the vernacular meant the conveyance—the very possibility—of ideas.

But critics attacked the humanists, anyway. Barbara J. Shapiro has summarized the growing distrust of words as against matter, from Bacon's *Advancement* to Sprat's distaste for "'this vicious abundance of Phrase, this trick of Metaphor.'"[30] All of this criticism is common ground, and it needs careful modification. Closer to Greene's deciphering is Harvey's warning that "it is not sufficient for poets to be superficiall humanists"; they also must know the profundities of astronomy and philosophy. There is also the concern among Ascham, Gosson, and others that literature will become idle and licentious without helping the commonwealth to grow in wisdom and in power. We will see that some trivializing does attend the imitation of style and verse in Greene's prose: the characters admit—sometimes mockingly—that pastoral games and aristocratic jokes are the only stakes now. But Greene's experiments in verse and style pursue an order in variety no less than his rhetoric of the essence.

For Greene, style and verse are codes to be recovered ("deciphered"). These codes must be transcribed from one rhythmic pattern (classical quantities) or language (Latin) to another (English).[31] Both codes were controversial in Greene's day. Each had a classical standard behind it, but each was compromised: the Ciceronian period by slavish imitation, the quantity by novelty and obscurity. Ascham, however, authorized both for his "euphues."

Greene's interest in versification is announced in a letter adjoined to *Perimedes the Blacke-Smith*. Here, an admirer asks Greene to "annex" those sonnets once intended for the interludes in his narrative. We are told that the author omitted the poems because he feared the readers' disapproval. Thus, the letter suggests that the poems have no integral role in the meaning of the narrative, but that they are worthy nonetheless. "Found" among loose papers, the four poems offer two contrary readings of the Venus and Adonis story, portray a mistress, and celebrate (in shepherd's guise) the blacksmith's love for his wife. In this last poem, Greene gives his verse its most important setting, the Arcadian interlude, where quantity and meter can safely play.

If the blacksmith's tale annexes poems, Greene's tale of Cicero (*Ciceronis Amor*) aims at a perfect style, "coueting to counterfait Tullies phrase." Greene directs us to fasten on the surface of his text: "If I speake mistically," the author advises, "thinke tis musically."[32] There are some "misticall" gestures: such ideals as are fetched from the "fount of Alcydalion" (2) are "deciphreed vnder Tullies doome," and Tully himself concludes that "there is no fount but Alcydalion" (61). We still have some Euphuism in style and theme and some definition of "ideas." But Greene instructs us to replace any mystical prose with a musical style as we read his imitations of Cicero's epistles. He includes some verse as well.

The music of style and verse has to contend with a complex narrative of many threads. Indeed, the narrator confronts what for humanists amounted to the fullest of all biographies. Greene's narrator promises strands of Cicero's life that those "who dard sweete Tullies fancies once vnfolde" (A4r) have failed to recount. Within the story proper, there are other signs of a manifold plot. The story is twenty-three pages long before Tully is even mentioned. Given an already complicated love affair that eventually doubles, new characters continue to appear, their lives and changes becoming dominant in the story. For one of these new characters, Greene translates and adapts from the *Decameron* the story of a simpleton changed by love into a perfect gentleman. Replacing Boccaccio's romantic battles with the Roman civil wars, Greene vexes his tale with the duties of historical reportage; and the narrative features scenes in which characters "trace"—that is, they walk on and on without purpose or direction. The characters themselves tell stories, sometimes at leisure, but also when they need to conceal some slip of the tongue.

Greene's musical prose relates to this narrative exuberance in at least two ways. First, it shares the same tendency toward games, especially in the pastoral interlude. Throughout the story, Greene announces his stylistic play: for instance, he offers and comments on melodic periods. Composing Latin and English epistles for his characters, he discusses the style of his fiction with reference to the *ars dictaminis,* and to the sweet cadences of Tully's letters to Atticus. This interest in style converges with experiments in verse. Among the several English poems found in *Ciceronis Amor,* Greene writes and then translates a Latin poem, calling it the "new learnd poetrie." All in all, then, he situates his prose in the enterprises of Ascham, Harvey, Spenser, Sidney, and Stanyhurst.

But for all this play, Greene also gives style and verse a dominance over narrative that should not surprise readers of Walter Ong (who finds a male puberty rite in Renaissance Latin).[33] An example of how verse attempts to contain the plot appears in the pastoral segment of *Ciceronis Amor.* After a shepherd has told the love story of Phyllis and

Coridon in prose, he sings an ode that retells the story in a different order, with less conflict and more description (of the place, of Phyllis, and of love). But stylistic imitation also subsumes the narrative. Even when the plot becomes more eventful toward the end, the lovers' strife ends in the "harmony" of Tully's oration. Like the ode, the musical speech reduces and contains the story—the story, we are led to believe, provides the orator with something to stylize.

Greene clinches the nugatory play of style when he parodies the vogue with which he began—Euphuism. The most famous joke on Euphuism is played in *Menaphon, Camillas Alarum to Slumbering Euphues*. In this work we have a review of deciphering: emblematic cells, the fountain of Alcida, and abstractions "deciphered . . . in sundrie conceipted passions (figured in a continuate Historie)" (VI.3) Greene worries once again that his playful intentions will elude the reader; and so he advises that, where "metaphors are well ment" but unclear, the reader should "take a little paines to prie into [his] imagination" (7–8). But the biggest game is style. When the lovers, Melicertus and Samela, want to have their "doubts . . . deciphered," they find themselves in a parody of Euphuism. When Melicertus greets Samela with a list of epithets and similitudes, she mocks him for his "superfine" language, "learnd with *Lucilla* in *Athens* to anatomize wit" (82). To "speake none but *Similes*" (82) is as gamesome as the musical idylls; and both are pastoral insofar as Euphuism, too, is now the "Countrey Logicke" of "homely" shepherds (139). Euphuism is always subject to trivialization: even in Lyly, it is considered idle. But here, its demotion is part of a general strategy whereby narrative control is played out as a game at the surface of prose. And with Greene's apologies to the reader, we can see that this game is poised (like the rhetoric of essences) against the license of narrative and reader.[34]

Menaphon's narrative is full like Cicero's: it embeds several tales, and, in the main plot, one dominant character gives way to another. The best example of this latter shift is Menaphon himself, who moves from a central and sensitive role to a marginal boorishness—the reverse of the boor turned courtier in *Ciceronis Amor*. And one narrative strand defers to another: this deference happens when we pivot from Sephestia in her pastoral setting to the life of her child, whose story invokes the *Cyropaedia*, other *ab ovo* epics, and the fabulous annals of Arcadia. The word *unfolding* appears several times, as the boy's story—now with pirates, then with a king—is complicated in the manner of romance. Sometimes, the narrator is impatient: "[s]ufficeth at this instant to vnfolde (all other circumstance of praise laid apart) that *Eurilochus* being farre in loue with his extraordinarie lineaments, awaited no farther parley, but willed his men perforce to hoyse [*sic*] him a shipboord" (93). The narrator, unable to tell all, invites us to let the chief points suffice, an editorial strategy that concedes to the countless "circumstance[s]" at hand.

It is possible that Greene saw a manuscript of Sidney's *Old Arcadia* and that he admired its eventful "history" and its style. Indeed, scholars have noticed parallels between them.[35] For Greene, whatever his model, the play of verse and style functions "as a cypher to fill vp a place at the worst hand," to ensure "that there can be no *vacuum in rerum natura*" (115–16). While Greene does not sacrifice this prose to what modern critics would call the "transcendental signified," it is clear nonetheless that the surfaces of his prose, like the commonplaces of a prior truth, protect and serve the laws of nature itself. Its "cyphers," however, are too unworldly (though backhandedly political) for Thomas Nashe, who rivals "deciphering" with a material "stuff" for the filling of gaps. Even Greene, in his mode of "discovery," situates his prose in a coney-catching world that Arbasto and Alcida would not recognize or care for. Greene and Nashe refashion the identity of prose—mainly because its old rhetoric demands a total concern over narrative and reader, then offers nothing tangible or feasible in the way of implementing that control.[36] Deciphering is too "misticall" or too "musical" for the coney-catchers and Jack Wilton. It gives way to a prose that has new assumptions and promises.

But in *Menaphon*, the song is everything: as one song leads to another, the singers treat their lyrics as a recourse from sorrow or uncertainty. Their verses play lightly with echo and balance: "Nimphes I meane, whose haire was blacke/As the crow:/Like the snow/Her face and browes shinde I weene" (69). Like the hexameters in *Greenes Mourning Garment*, this verse is excellence "deciphered in such quaint phrases" (IX.153). As characters "wrap [their] joyes in folds of endlesse woes," songs are advertised as pastime, culminating in the rustic games with their poetic contests. Eclogues are peaceful exercises in which we see "who best could decipher his Mistres perfection" (VI.122). Even the command of war is awarded to the best versifier. In yet another work, *Orpharion* (1588?/1590), Greene's title names a rustic musical instrument, and its prose song wraps plot in a "musicall concorde."

Or so Greene proposes, apologizing in the preface to *Menaphon* for any indecorum in the mixture of styles. But the assumption that one can protect style from the "serious" work of meaning is as vulnerable as deciphering's sometime claim to control meaning altogether. Nashe, who wrote his own preface to *Menaphon*, was left with the task of repudiating the decipherers. Greene, on the other hand, staged a new mode, "discovering," as an escape into the future where prose is redeemed by having a dramatic and social identity. In sum, he dramatized his own career so that he might divorce the old prose, with the old self, and embrace the new.[37]

2
GREENE DISCOVERING

Deciphering never disappears altogether from Greene's prose, but he prefers the word *discovering* in the latter part of his career.[1] The word appears very often, usually with some form of *notable,* and signals a strategy radically altered from *deciphering* in its assumptions about plots and their readers.[2] Even with its altered strategy, *notable discovering* still pursues the most important agenda of deciphering: a control over narrative and its interpretation. But Greene is interested in a different kind of control, an aggressive one that regulates the society in which his readers live.

My argument about the mode of discovering will proceed in four related stages. First, I will offer some preliminary definitions of *notable discovering* and its strategy for controlling narrative, reader, and society alike. The second stage will explore one facet of this strategy—the ways in which discovering aspires to an idealized drama and its grammar of plot. With Greene pursuing an analogy between drama and prose narrative, we see a marked contrast with deciphering's imitation of rhetorical poetics. But we also see the more clearly defined social conservatism of discovering, for Greene's theater of prose is a forum in which officials declare their upper hand over the radical energies of drama and, indeed, of the kingdom.

Having detailed the narrative assumptions of discovering and their analogy with drama, I will reconsider Greene's rogue pamphlets and the peculiar stance that they assume as social guardians. This third part also will show how the social agenda of discovery exposes Greene's prose to a number of attacks. The fourth stage of the chapter will argue that Greene's conversion plots are Christian and romantic versions of discovery. As such, these narratives pursue the mode's grammar of plot, its orderly theater of prose, without all the ill-fitted social trappings of the coney-catching pamphlets. As with deciphering, then, Greene fashions an identity for prose that, he hopes, will allow for plenty yet minimize the restive activities of narrative.

Preliminary Definitions

When I say that Greene's "discovery" plots are interested in "control," most readers with any knowledge of Greene's life and death probably will respond that the prodigal son certainly needed some.[3] And, indeed, Greene offers the story of his life as the master plot for discovery. But discovery guards other kinds of plots as well—among them, criminal exploits and romantic conversion narratives. Rather than explore those kinds here, I want first to sketch the strategies of the mode in general. When Greene claims to "discover" the "notable" or "notorious," he proposes in sum the following narrative stabilities: the exemplary value of one event over less important events; the exceptional yet typical value of one tale or anecdote over others of less "note"; and the reader's careful attention to such notorious events and tales. The narrator or author does not create so much as mediate the powerful conventions of discovery; in other words, its patterns are assumed to be inscribed in, and underwritten by, the very nature of things.[4] As such, the patterns of discovery are models for the ideal society as well.

Modern readers need one proviso if they are to understand the patterns of discovery. Greene's term refers to a mode of representation, not (as we might have it) to the act of an audience. For *discover*, the modern reader should substitute, more often than not, something akin to *reveal, uncover,* or *represent*. In other words, discovery leads readers and does not mainly refer to the act of finding. To this extent, the new mode resembles the old, deciphering, which also subordinates reading to narrative. In both cases, the ideal story fashions its own interpretation.

But the two modes diverge when it comes to their ideal modus operandi. With discovery, Greene boasts that he is stronger than the coney-catchers, but he no longer offers a total control over narrative, if by *total* we mean that every event is overseen by some prior Truth. In his discovery plots, Greene readily admits that the manifold details of a narrative and its even more scattered readings cannot be exhausted. Plots and readers must be allowed to roam, just as surely as crime is always with us in the rogue pamphlets. But Greene is not thwarted by the plenty or the many: time and again, he gives a clear if modest account of what discovery can restrain in plots, readers, and their society. The key to his aim lies in the word *note* and its cognates: Greene is always promising to discover the "notable."

In the English Renaissance, *note* indicates a privileged sign or token. For Greene, the *notable* can be defined more precisely as a discrete narrative event. In the simplest terms, such an event, isolated or outstanding from the others, is exemplary; in more complex terms, the discrete and notable event is both typical and exceptional. It differs from the essential, rhetorical places of deciphering insofar as the notable event is considered posterior to the narrative itself—one in a scheme of narrative points that have some elevated value in teaching or attracting the reader who might otherwise stray among details of less import. The readers, in effect, cannot pass up the notable: it stands out from the story and blocks their way. They must attend to it. But *notable* describes more than one event in a network; it can refer to one tale among many, or one kind of plot among others. In all cases, though, discovery edits narrative to a basic grammar, reducing plots to a few chiefly delightful and instructive events that emerge from (posterior to) the plenty of narrative itself.

The reader's role in this editing is subservient but crucial. The reader learns to expect, and thus to master, the plots and events that have a typical yet exceptional value. Greene assures his readers: see one scheme and you've seen them all; see one crime and you remember any. But what seems to be license for the readers who can now read on their own is, in fact, restraint because the readers are trained according to the grammar of notable discovering. Thus, the mode narrows the field of possibilities for reading narrative. As we will see in the next section, its editorial work relies on an analogy between the plots and genres of drama and its own. As his prose aspires to and intersects with the resources of drama, Greene asserts its control over the irregular or disorderly energies of Elizabethan society, among which might be numbered the prodigal life of the author himself.

Dramatic Plotting and Notable Discovery

In their several genres, Greene's prose discoveries aspire to an idealized drama. Greene finds the reductive analogy between drama and prose narrative attractive for a variety of reasons. In its plot designs, for example, discovery thrives on the kind of discrete and remarkable event that Aristotle called *anagnorisis* in Greek tragedy, or Donatus the *nodus* in the comedies of Terence.[5] With these models in view, Greene's mode aims for plots that are edited down to a schema of key events—like scripts that tend toward synecdoche, "rules of notice," emphatic "nowness," and pared dialogue, the most basic constituents of plotting.[6] Other facets of Greene's work show his interest in the dramatic plotting by which Nashe was impressed: after all, Greene is famous in the history of drama for his double plots and for a curtailed actor's texts of *Orlando Furioso*.[7] Some of the discovery pamphlets even take place in and around theaters. But there is more at stake in this analogy than the stability of prose narrative according to the most purely schematic outlines and accents of plot. The aspiration toward the discrete and remarkable units of drama is motivated by a desire to direct not just the plot but the audience and its values. Toward this end, Greene could trust his readers to notice two related links between "discovery" and theater practices: recognition scenes and discovery spaces.

Terence Cave's book on recognition scenes suggests how unstable discovery can be for the Renaissance.[8] For this very reason, it can teach us about Greene's ideal of a stable prose. Cave's study, which spans virtually all of Western literature, reconsiders some familiar sixteenth-century notions of recognition. For Greene and his contemporaries, a chief instance of the recognition scene was the conversion plot; this was a Christianized version of the romantic *cognitio* and catastrophe popularized by the commentaries of Donatus and Evanthius on Terence.[9] In fact, Evanthius gave the name *conversio* to the reversal of fortunes motivated by the recognition of some token of identity.[10] But it is more important for Greene's prose that the Renaissance commonly associated the *cognitio* and *conversio* with the Aristotelian drama of *anagnorisis* and *peripeteia*. Both pairs contribute to Greene's prose of discovery, for both entrust their plots to the stabilizing presence of discrete and exceptional events—to what Elizabethans would call the "notable."

Cave follows Renaissance commentaries as they debate the nature of recognition. For example, Renaissance theorists argued the intentionality, agency, and objects of discovery, usually with some passage from Aristotle in mind. Do audiences, characters, or narrative structures discover? Are people, deeds, morals, or objects discovered? Is discovery natural or contrived? Are discoveries made by means of tokens or syllogisms? All these questions, and the interplay between commentaries, new genres (romance, novellas) and Aristotle's *Poetics*, made "perhaps half a century" of the Renaissance "the heyday of the recognition scene" (83). Greene's prose was written in these years, although it avoided many of these issues.

Cave's study is useful for discoveries in Elizabethan prose, not just in exploring Greene's resources in Renaissance terms, nor just in detailing the importance of English dramatic structure in the multigeneric history of recognition scenes, but also in pointing out that, despite Castelvetro's use of prose fiction to illustrate the key terms, most commentators "overlook this particular gold mine."[11] English prosers, I am arguing, did not "overlook" the relation between their narratives and drama. Greene and others confess their faith in the discovery scenes that lead the audience by way of notable events (or "notes"), reversals, conversions, and other pivotal and discrete units of plotting. The notable unit is there in the plot for Greene, and not dependent on his audience. The audience is secondary, at least until the schemes are indelible in their minds. Only then does he allow the reader to participate in finishing the tale, and in retelling it and others like it.

Thus, Greene's ideal of a stable "discovery" is grounded in a structural feature, in a narrative event, or in a character's momentous recognition of some bygone event; and his overall emphasis on the logic of the plot is both Aristotelian and "in the mainstream of commentary and translation" in the Renaissance (Cave, 71). What is more, Greene's plays prove that he would in fact call the "recognition" scene—Castelvetro's *riconoscenza*—by the name *discovery*.[12] In *The Scottish History of James the Fourth*, James is a reprobate who has tested the patience of his virtuous wife, Dorothea. Greene signals the *anagnorisis* and *peripeteia* of the play when the vicious king is reunited with his wife in a pivotal moment of amazement and amendment ("Tis kingly to amend") whereby fortunes reverse ("Thy foe is now thy friend"). This scene is effected when Sir Cutbert presents Dorothea to the king: in the original stage direction, probably from Greene's foul papers, we are told that "hee discouereth her."[13] The "hee" here includes James, but also Cutbert who uncovers the queen; this double reference matters because it exposes another link between Greene's term *discovery* and the theaters of his day—the "discovery spaces."[14]

In regard to Greene's prose, discovery spaces are spatial versions of the temporal recognition scene—and both are designed as discrete or accentuated theatrical units. First of all, discovery spaces are "notable" just because they depend on stage directions. In general, Elizabethan stage directions approach Greene's prose discoveries in advancing parts for wholes. However stage historians may disagree about the specific meanings of stage directions for plays produced in the Curtain, Rose, Globe, or Swan, they tend to concur about the reductive function of these directions. Alan C. Dessen likens their role to synecdoche and italics, both of which describe the idealized units in Greene's prose discoveries. In each case, an emphatic part stands for the whole as a means of directing the attention of the audience. As the prologue to *Henry V* tells us, the signs of Elizabethan drama guide the imagination through a kind of shorthand; and the selection of marks is so conventional that the audience can fill in the rest.[15] Greene supposes that his discovery pamphlets work the same way: he reveals a scheme of notable points to his audience, and then he trusts them with the rest of the plot or with other plots.

One direction instructs some prop or person to be "discovered" in a bed, in a study, or in a grave, among other such locations. Some researchers, devoted to an evolutionary approach to the proscenium stage, imagined an "inner stage" to be the place of discovery.[16] Others would emphasize the "as if" facet of many such directions ("discover as if in bed"), still others the thrusting out of props and persons onto the stage.[17] For Frances Yates, the stage design—including the discovery space—is notable as a cosmic mnemonics. But most students of the Elizabethan stage basically accept the conclusions of Richard Hosley's work on this stage practice.[18] To summarize a vexed issue, Hosley has concluded that the "discovery space" consisted of an alcove in the tiring-house, covered and revealed by double doors or curtains over those doors.[19] *Discover* means, then, to reveal a prop or person in that space by opening doors or curtains, so that the emphasis, with however many exceptions to it, lies on the "disclosures . . . of a player or object invested with some special interest or significance."[20]

The discovery space, like the recognition scene, is problematic. One can question just how "special" these "disclosures" were or were meant to be, ponder which seat in the theater would permit spectators the best view of the space, and debate the extent to which *discovery* refers to the audience, both in the play and in the theater. Greene's contemporaries raise all these issues, some of which—for example, the one concerning agency—converge with the problems of *anagnorisis*. But in Greene's prose, discoveries—from stage practices to the traditions of Aristotle, of New Comedy with romance and tragicomedy in its wake, and of the novella—conspire to assert stable, if wondrous, plots against the burgeoning lowlife of crime.

Greene's prose has other affiliations with Tudor drama besides those related directly to the word *discovery*. The word *notable* also evokes the stabilizing conventions of dramatic plotting. We need only remember Minturno's term for the recognition scene, *agnitione,* and the familiar *cognitio,* to see the motive of the pairing, "notable discovery."[21] More curious and intricate are the generic relations between the discovery pamphlets and drama, especially those which derive from the novella tradition. With the novella, for instance in the influential *Decameron,* we have tales, jests, and quips that are praised for turning on points (acted or spoken) of wonder or mischief. Boccaccio's narrators prize the sudden strike or the pivotal turn of events in their tales.[22] But more than this, some Renaissance commentaries associate such tricks and reversals in the *Decameron* with Aristotle's *anagnorisis* and *peripeteia*.[23] All in all, generic kinship can be traced between the novella, jest books, interludes, the drama, and the coney-catching pamphlets.[24] This network extends from specific vice figures and plot reversals to the general creed that a tale should be the "recipe"—or the basic outline with its indispensible ingredients—of something worth telling.[25]

The analogy between drama and prose narrative allows the typical yet exceptional units to be several ("point to point") or single and culminative ("among the rest, one").[26] But however the "notes" are graduated, they offer to guide the reader through the byways of what Elizabethans called a "continuate historie." The notable events are marked, as it were, by a finger in the margin: this event, the invisible finger points out, is chiefly instructive and delightful among the variables of the tale. In the coney-catching pamphlets, the narrator marks the place with a variety of stage directions: he shifts tenses, repeats a key word, announces chief members of a sequence, omits or summarizes less important strands, and addresses the reader. Even as readers are sent away to retell the same tale or to tell others much like it, they have in their possession, or so Greene's discoveries promise, a menu of priorities and values. But Greene also is explicit about his social conservatism in the rogue pamphlets: poised against the coney-catchers, the drama of discovery aims to censor and preserve the order of a society that extends beyond the boundaries of pamphlet and theater.

The Coney-Catching Pamphlets

Greene's rogue pamphlets have seemed problematic to some readers who find in them egregious self-advertising or a delight in crime that nullifies instruction.[27] These accounts of Greene's output are useful so long as they do not dismiss his prose as just so many attempts to put food on the table. Even so, they miss the narrative and social agenda of notable discovery; for whatever Greene's intentions, his coney-catching pamphlets profess specific designs on both plot and the world at large. Greene "discovers" crime in a number of pamphlets: *A Notable Discovery of Coosnage, The Second Part of Conny-Catching, The Thirde Part of Conny-Catching, A Disputation Betweene a Hee Conny-Catcher, and a She Conny-Catcher,* and *The Blacke Bookes Messenger* (1591–92). The title of the first is but one of the innumerable times that some version of the phrase *notable discovery* appears in these texts—so many, in fact, that Greene leaves no doubt about its importance for naming a set of strategies and devices for isolating the typical yet exceptional event.[28]

As the self-elected agent of discovery, Greene assumes the somewhat ill-defined position of a constable who was once himself among the criminals. Such an office permits him to translate the multitude of criminal activities into short paradigms and tales, all to signal the notable points in the crimes. Thus, Greene aims to show us that transgression is "full of Peripet[e]ia,"[29] and that for this very reason it can be mastered by the hapless but honest reader.

The watchman prefaces all strategies by situating his tales in an urgent context. Crime, he says, is proliferating in the city and throughout the kingdom at the rate of a plague. It threatens to affect each and every citizen; and so each must learn the constants in the complex formulas of crime. But these formulas have both a real and a narrative form. Consequently, the lessons about social practice are also lessons about its representation in plots. To regulate society and narrative alike, Greene's pamphlets, maps for reading cozenage, must uncover the notable at every level: in the selection of tales, and in the emphasis of narrative events within single tales. Once the reader has mastered the signs for the notable event and tale, he or she can wander around in the plenty of narrative or in the endless streets of London with the assurance that the map will guide and protect. Greene claims all the more credit for the map because his own life is blessed with a discovery—namely, the conversion by which he has left a life of crime.

Few strategies can hope to match the energy of the rogues, but Greene entrusts his reader with two: the taxonomy and the tale. The taxonomy—what Greene calls the "laws"—is somewhat unusual and needs a word of explanation. Rather than tell one instance of a crime, the "law" attempts to epitomize the genre of a crime in a single formula. This formula has variables, but it also features constants on which the watchman or bystander can count. These constants can, therefore, be "discovered" as the notable events in a hypothetical "performance" of the law. Take, for example, "Barnard's law," which the reader can easily locate in the table of laws "wherein is discouered the nature of euery terme" (*Notable*, 37). The crime depends on some victim being lured into an alehouse where he will lose money to three rogues—the fast talker who brought him there, a supposed "landed man," and a country boor. Right away, Greene would have us notice the analogy between drama and prose: each participant is given a name, like a part in a play; and only the required actors are included.[30] Lest the victim turn the tables, a fourth rogue plays the part of a quarrelsome drunkard who enters, only to provoke alehouse warfare at just the right moment.

Greene considers some of the variables as such—the conversation of the "taker-up," the amount of wine requested by the players, the character of the victim, and so forth. Like actors who take their play on the road, the rogues work to prepare against all adverse fortunes that might arise in the performance. But Greene's point about discovery is that the mastery of constants and the minimization of variables permit the watchman to reduce the trick to a brief scheme of notable events for the hapless reader. In other words, the law provides the potential victim with a dress rehearsal in which the key or pivotal points in the crime are surveyed.

At first, these laws serve Greene's narrator better than would tales; for laws, like promptbooks, outline the actors, props, and basic actions of the crime. The "highly schematized" laws acquire almost the force of logic in what James A. S. McPeek has called their "passion for order even in disorder."[31] Even though Greene's later pamphlets offer more tales than laws, the laws still provide a general reference for the tales, and they therefore support those tales as notable discoveries.

Whether or not laws are more orderly than tales and jests, the latter prevail in Greene's second and third coney-catching pamphlets. In one way, tales are simpler than hypotheses; tales decide from the outset whether the victim is naive or sophisticated, so that the discovery need not consider the effects of the variables. Thus, despite the joke about long-winded raconteurs who forget part of the tale (the end), the tales can simplify matters by specifying, for example, that the victim is Welsh and so, according to stereotype, unable to express himself. But, no matter what the specific circumstances of the tale, the narrator insists that each one is a "note"—that is, a curt and schematic outline of the crucial points in the crime.

If the watchman has his way, the series of pamphlets will teach the reader the notable events in many crimes—the careful setting of the stage, the turn of the trick, the reversals and the discoveries of the victim. But the reader also should detect the recurring devices by which the narrator italicizes the notable events. Among these "rules of notice" is the extension of recognition scenes so as to emphasize the vivid here and now. This increase in what Gérard Genette has called "duration" occurs especially when the trick is clinched and the victim recoils from his "present Discovery" of the deed (for instance, in the tavern scene in Barnard's law). Although this delay conflicts somewhat with the mode's *rapiditas,* Terence Cave has found at least one commentator who is interested in gradual discovery scenes.[32] Greene quickens the pace in the same scene, however, when he embeds dialogue, fragmented stage directions, and directives to the reader in his haste to consolidate the schema of the crime.

Instructions to the reader are, in fact, one of the most common signals of the notable in the rogue pamphlets. The narrator often tells the reader what to imagine—"imagine the connie is in the tauern" (*Notable*, 22)—but even more commonly informs the readers when they may venture on their own to unfold the denouement or to retell this tale and others like it. This relation with the audience, one that allows their freedom yet dictates its boundaries, is conventional in the tradition that gave rise to Greene's pamphlets. So it is that Greene often leaves his reader to "suppose" or to "imagine" the rest of the story or some other less notable feature.[33]

Readers can be trusted with supplying the rest of the tale when they have grasped the fundamental "notes" of each crime. Again, this is conventional. The author of *A Manifest Detection* shows how the significance of many tales can be reduced: how of "a few examples instead of infinite, that might be rehearsed, this one universal conclusion may be gathered, that, give you to play [the games of rogues], and yield yourself to loss."[34] Not just the lessons, but also the plots are reducible: as Luke Hutton's Zawny declares in his rogue pamphlet, he can refrain from telling more stories because "[the rogues] keep one order almost, in performing them all" (*Judges*, 291). So, too, Greene's narrator urges his readers to believe: once they have witnessed in laws and tales the discovery of chief points in typical plots, readers will have a mastery over all possible crimes. And if all goes well, these same readers will not mind their own restraints, thanks to the justice of discovery and the order it keeps.

Beyond its instructions to the reader, discovery uses some very simple devices for marking the notable event. Sometimes, the watchman accentuates the notable by stating what is not notable: "[t]hough it was no maruel to see him so liberall, because indeede hee was a good companion" (*Thirde Part*, 35). But one of the most common accents is the shift between past and present tense. Often, just before a scheme is executed, or when a victim recognizes the trick, Greene switches to present tense: for example, in one tale, "[n]one are nowe vp but poore Margaret and her counterfeit coosen" (19). While examples of this practice can be multiplied, I do not mean to imply that this technique is original with Greene, or that he has systematized it.[35] My point is rather that such italics are congruent with the aims of discovery. Like discovery spaces or stage conventions, verb tenses in this prose concur with the narrator's commitment to elevating some events above all others.

Whatever the format or device, Greene's discoveries aim to reduce narrative to its most basic constituents. They do not intend to tell all. Perhaps Greene's faith in the analogy between a regulated drama and his prose led him to write dialogue in another rogue pamphlet, *A Disputation Betweene a Hee Conny-Catcher, and a Shee Conny-Catcher*. For good measure, though, he appends to this dispute the autobiography of an "honest whore," the "Shee" of the title. Her narrative of repentance coincides with several others in Greene's later prose; we will return to their importance for the discovery mode, its analogy to drama, and its social agenda. Between dialogue and *conversio*, however, the essential point is that Greene is searching among various resources for the most persuasive *reductio ad notas*.

Even more indicative of Greene's reduction of narrative to its most basic constituents is his promised index, *The Black Book*. The book itself is advertised as "notorious": it will be, we are told, the biggest and last discovery of all. But it is so precisely because it offers the utmost reduction of narrative; for the black book promises to be a quick reference work, a listing of criminals and their vital statistics. In such an index readers would have access to crucial information in a minimal format. This book might be dangerous in two respects, as an endless list (a common concern in discovery pamphlets) and as a relatively blank page on which the readers might project their own tales. In the case of *The Black Book*, however, Greene's discovery is vexed not so much by the openness it admits, but by the very impossibility of its own reductive task. Greene's *Black Book* was, in fact, the utopia of discovery; the pamphlet never appeared, and it is entirely possible that Greene never wrote it. If utopia did not exist, Greene had to promote it as the elusive ideal toward which discovery, in some measure, must always aspire.

Indeed, the narrator's ideal theater of prose is not so safe as he might wish. The "laws" as performances, the tales with their recognitions and reversals, and even dialogue: the analogies between criminal narratives and drama are believed to play into the narrator's bid for the upper hand against the rogues. Even so, the theater is a dangerous setting for watchmen in search of a stable prose and an orthodox society. Greene laments just this point in his repentance narratives; but the point is more subtly made in the few coney-catching tales set in a theater. One tale in particular opens the way for the criticisms of the mode that were, in any event, forthcoming from other pens. In this tale, a rogue is distracted "because a merriment was then on the stage" (*Thirde*, 38), and so she fails to receive the purse that is passed to her. The mistake creates an opportunity for other rogues to rip her off. Although the good crime and its orderly narrative are comparable to the planned spontaneity of a dramatic production "performed as is before rehearsed," the rogue is overwhelmed by the energies of the theater itself—energies that she has not factored into her own performance. She is entrapped by the "merriment," even before she can be reduced by the narrator to a formula. But there is a further irony here. The rogue errs in part because she wants a better seat whence she "might best beholde the play" (38). The contingencies of a viewer's position are, however, precisely what the narrator's discovery seeks to demote. Conservative discovery is not prepared to admit so much freedom that the stable power inherent in the "notes" of the performance is questioned. Greene would allow some degree of liberty in plots and in readers, but he would minimize their license.

Greene's actual readers had a variety of critical responses to his discoveries. According to one group, stable discovery is simply the official pipe dream performed with an eye to duping the people. Their pamphlets expose the political biases in the selective editing that the watchman stages. Greene's narrator, they declare, finds "notorious" or "most prejudiciall" only those crimes that he or his patrons do not commit; meanwhile, the real crimes go unnoticed. This opposition suggests that, while the rogues win their living with marked cards, the cultural cards are marked at a much higher level and with a different winner. What the official declares to be natural is in fact, they say, a policy that relies on labor and contrivance. So say the defenders of coney-catching, whoever they might be. But there is other opposition from noncriminals—from moralists who declare that the discoverer's fascination with roguery spells lurid voyeurism. Both criticisms turn Greene into the criminal (some modern critics would agree with Renaissance preachers and the narrator of *A Manifest Detection* on that score).[36] Further, there are the skeptical critics, who rewrite the rogue pamphlets in order to show the instabilities in any claim to isolate or to objectify a discrete and "notable" event in narrative, free from all other events and from the biases of the narrator. Thus, Greene's watchman stands charged in his own theater on different counts, on account of political interest, decadent pleasure, and shaky epistemology.[37] To this critical audience, the "notable" is either contrived by the official, or dangerous and unavailable to him.

Greene is forced to admit that the theater of prose serves as a battleground between the hydra-headed critics and his officer of the law. But the latter continues to promote the stable and unfailing merger between instruction and delight in a grammar of plot, which, like Aristotle's, is designed to stave off skepticism in several ways: a "discordant concordance," surprise by design, an insistence on the typical nature of plots, and the allowance of completions by the reader.[38] No matter what his critics might say, Greene insists that his notes are all "confirmed," not contrived—that their truth and power adhere to the naturally exceptional (though typical) events and fables.[39]

For Greene, then, discovery and its controlled performances can tame even the most infamous of criminals by the way in which it renders them notorious—exceptional, but therefore memorable in typical and orderly schemes. The case is best illustrated with Ned Browne, whose "most notable" life is recounted in Greene's *Blacke Bookes Messenger.* Because Ned refuses repentance, Greene sequesters his story from that of any converted rogue: "the Methode of the one is so far differing from the other" (1). Ned's tale may lack this "passion of great importance," but it does have a final *peripeteia* in Ned's suicide. According to Ned, though, it is his endless series of marvelous exploits that earns his life the title of "notorious." In fact, he raises the chief narrative dilemma for the discoverer: how can one unfold the "whole course of life" (2) from the egg, yet focus on the discrete wonders of that life? Ned alternates between the "all" and the "notable," as each prank is supplanted by the next, bigger one; but at times he struggles to organize: "I liued wantonly, and therefore let me end merrily, and tel you two or three of my mad pranks and so bid you farewell" (17). Yet, the pranks become parentheses in the overall narrative: the rogue must work to convert his jests into episodes and then back again. And, while another narrator instructs us, after the suicide, to "note a wonderfull iudgement of God shewed vppon him after his death" (32). Ned has made any negotiation between the typical, the exceptional, and the manifold a difficult task indeed.

The labor of discovery can make the narrator weary, as it does in Greene's *Disputation:*

> But amongst all these blythe and merry Iestes, a little by your leaue, if it be no farther then Fetter-lane, oh take heed, thats too nye the Temple, what then, I will draw as neare the signe of the white Hart as I can, and breathing my selfe by the bottle Ale-house, Ile tell you a merry Iest, how a Conny-catcher was vsed. (79–80)

But the discoverer needs more than rest. In disposing of the monstrous opposition, his erstwhile companions, Greene would also deflect what Cave has called the ideological tensions of "recognition"—namely, the "perpetual threat of imposture on the one hand and arbitrary law and coercion on the other" (*Recognitions*, 15). Whatever Greene's audience might suspect about the hand that they are dealt or about the dealer, his converted narrator relies on the belief that the cards are marked by the Almighty, whose creative hand underwrites the stability of all "notes infallible."[40] No dismissal of Greene—especially not the one that devalues all this prose as the product of a hack in search of his next meal—erases the forceful terms in which he chose to serve himself, if that is in fact what he was doing. For in the theater of his prose, the author directs on stage between the powerful conventions and urgent oppositions that to some degree invented him.

The Power of Discovery

That the drama of prose discovery would offer social and moral stability is not very surprising in an Elizabethan culture that believed that God had inscribed "notes" in the very nature of things. There is, they would say, a *punctum saliens* in any egg, and falls, crucifixions, and conversions in the pilgrimage of Christianity. In history, Renaissance people saw heinous sins, the Last Judgment, and a network of intersections in typology. Greene, we should recall, wrote a "looking glass" play. If a drama had special "knots" in its fable, the theater of the world featured them in the tail of Pisces. Thomas Browne admired the microcosm precisely because it was typical and exceptional as a synecdoche of the cosmos. And there were new outstanding features on the stage of the world, the ones Galileo saw on the sun and moon, although critics challenged him to prove that these spots and hills were real, not just projections.[41]

It would seem natural to Greene's readers, at least to most of them, that a narrative reveals its salient points—each in exemplary isolation but also as part of a network of signs. But naturalness, especially when it is so forthrightly enforced by guardians, is the best friend of ideology; and I want to reexamine, for a moment, those curious bedfellows, notable discovery and the policing narrator that Greene claims, however absurdly, to be. Recently, in Renaissance studies there has been a great deal of talk about ideology, nature, and power—for instance, regarding Elizabethan theater, cartography, and closets of curiosities. Indeed, each of these forms—the synecdoche of theater, the grid of a map, the proto-museum—has some bearing on notable discovery.[42] But I want to focus a few terms of cultural theory on the perennial question about the coney-catching pamphlets—that is, about the conflict between delight (the rogues) and instruction (the officials). It is not enough to say that the narrator risks compromise when he delights in the crimes against which he must warn us. Greene's own contemporaries knew that the very fabric of social order was at stake in the far-reaching strategies by which Tudor London sought to categorize and systematize roguery. So, given the theater of discovery and its claims to regulate crime, we might rephrase the dynamic between Greene's pamphlets and the hostility to them in a series of questions, such as this sequence: How can notable discovery promise to encase the criminal opposition? To what extent does the discoverer fear his own reliance on the spontaneity and luck of that opposition? Is criminal opposition alive and well in the coney-catching tradition, or is that opposition nullified by official policy and its unofficial narratives?

For Greene and his fellow pamphleteers, the "unthrifts" amount to a "plague" in an otherwise lawful city. As such "ulcerous impostumes," however, they offer the city and its officials an optimal chance to demonstrate their ability to control disorder. Or so might say Michel Foucault, who has written that plague tests the power grid of the city and, indeed, tightens that grid.[43] Such an official test concurs with Greene's exhortation to the city officials that they police the restive kingdom. His own texts, Greene assures them, provide the model. According to Greene, readers must think of the network of notable points as a grid, beneath or in which disorder lives but from which disorder cannot escape, and to which disorder can do no lasting harm. In similar fashion, Greene's "laws" tidy up prose narrative, but they also dodge the Elizabethan legal dilemmas of ranking the idle according to various criteria—physical welfare, for instance, or patronage.

Divisions between the worthy and the criminal get especially vague, however, when it comes to drama. Plots can create and maintain order, or they can escape the bounds of theater and authority; players can be classified as unthrifts, or patronized as servants.[44] As we have seen, though, the potential for opposition exists not just on the stage but also in the performance of coney-catching.[45] There is the venerable tradition of rogue literature in which the criminal culture either thwarts or criticizes the officials.[46] And Greene's own position—he claims to know both cultures from the inside—indicates the dangers of compromise, although Greene denies any such perils beyond the criminal threats on his life. Even so, critics then and now have remarked that he profits from the very criminal energies that he would restrain.

As a student of the Renaissance and a cultural theorist, Michel de Certeau helps us with the peculiar status of notable discoveries inasmuch as his ongoing critique of Foucault (the favorite of new historicists) articulates both the power of an official grid and the eloquence of its opposition. De Certeau's work has, I should say, a limited utility for my purposes, for it is the eclectic summation of a general theory of opposition. What motivates my recourse to modern cultural theory is the fact that both Foucault and de Certeau have examined Renaissance patterns of domination in terms so crucial to the novella and coney-catching traditions.

In one article, de Certeau has explored Montaigne's "Of Cannibals" as a critique of the colonization of the exotic—an issue that resembles discovery and its usurpation of the marvelous from the criminals.[47] More to the point, de Certeau argues in another essay that the layout of modern cities features "a finite number of stable and isolatable elements, each articulated to the other."[48] Lest we think that those "isolatable elements" have nothing to do with Renaissance "notes" in their urban environment, de Certeau reckons that such a "concept of *city*," designed for the "exhaustion of all data" by "univocal strategies," dates back to the sixteenth century. In both periods, the spatial concept of the city ensures that the "innumerable anomalies" of everyday life—walking, acting—are "transposed into points that create a totalizing and reversible line on the map."[49] For the Elizabethans, I would argue, this "totalizing . . . map" reappears in the notable discoveries of prose, unfolded beneath the vigilant eye of God and queen.

What all this means for coney-catching will be clearer, I hope, if we look at de Certeau's "On the Oppositional Practices of Everyday Life" for definitions of *strategies* and *tactics*.[50] Dominant networks of power operate spatially by way of "strategies"; these latter depend upon entrenched *loci* or notable bases from which the status quo projects itself over everyday life. De Certeau suggests that Foucault's emphasis on "strategies" neglects the incessant activities of opposition. In response to Foucault's omissions, de Certeau argues for the vitality of what he calls "tactics," carried out by the weak within the spatial networks of domination.

De Certeau describes tactics in terms reminiscent of the coney-catching tradition. Tactics are temporal, not spatial. Although people may oppose the status quo even without knowing it, tactical opposition requires in any event a brilliant or skillful use of time within the spaces of power. Thus, "oppositional practices" occur when people seize an opportunity, turn a "trick," or cultivate an unarticulated artistry, all part of the novella and coney-catching traditions. Indeed, de Certeau declares that tactics are a "nodal point in all the practices of daily life"[51]; that is, the tricks of the people work as temporal nodes against the spatial nodes by which the status quo regiments and controls the unfolding of time.

In the narratives devoted to the urban life of the sixteenth century, the conflict between "laws" and roguery amounts to that between strategies and tactics. Greene's strategies purport to enclose those well-timed tricks that, he must confess, innovate within the grid with an irreducible energy and variety. If Greene's discoveries mark the apex of conservatism in prose, Dekker's plague and coney-catching pamphlets, with their emphasis on the uncontrollability of epidemics and on the elusive language of cant, show the force of the opposition. But in each case, the coney-catching tactics are said to proliferate within the grid of notable discovery, reducing the conflict to at least two possibilities: that the stability of notable discovery is always threatened from within, or that the mode always encompasses that threat. Greene professes the latter option, no matter what his texts imply.

If nothing else, the voices of opposition help Greene to capitalize on the urgency of the moment: now, he says, is England's pivotal point between order and chaos. At such a moment, he can afford to represent only the chief stratagems and their noteworthy points of law. As A. V. Judges said long ago, Greene brags about his close relations with the criminals in order to heighten our interest in his "discovering the inconvenience that grows to man."[52] But the moral commentary on the "lamentable case of England" recalls a more complex network for discovery: the analogical "looking glass" dramas, one of which came from Greene's own pen. These looking glasses, for example, between cities past and present, offer a loose typology with notable points of comparison. But they also help the narrator insist that policing is required throughout "lamentable . . . England" as surely as it is needed throughout history.

Stephen Greenblatt has recently discussed the Elizabethan "attempt to understand and control the lower classes" in coney pamphlets.[53] Less recently, the compiler of rogue literature, Judges, remarked that an increase in Elizabethan policing motivated the spate of coney-catching pamphlets in the last decades of the century.[54] Excessive pleasure is only one target in policies aimed sometimes at alternative societies, be they the Indians in the colonies or the vagabonds at home. By promoting his own orderly tales and arresting attention, Greene's discoveries emulate and represent official policy, no matter what the wishes of the government. His strategy against the rogues depends on a narrative control that admits yet circumscribes freedom in text and in readers alike. No doubt more could be told—no doubt some problems (for example, economic ones) have been deemphasized. But the discoverer has mapped the prominent points of the story, along with some crucial variations. So the urgency of the world demands, for narrative must be saved from roving, and readers from vagabondage.

Thus, Greene's prose is resilient in its confirmation of order. It resists the charge that the coney-catchers, tricked into believing the naturalness of contrived values, are the real conies after all, and that their tricks cannot prevail in the logic—or beneath the providential eye—of discovery. If Greene wrote *The Defence of Conny-Catching*, the usurpation of "tactics" is clinched. But in any case, his later prose strives to dramatize itself without giving too much voice to the catcalls, too much stage to the criminals, or too much license to the fable. So it is that, in the schemes of his discoveries, Greene mediates some vital and deep-seated conflicts over the unfolding of truth and order in the Renaissance. These conflicts define prose, its contexts, and its author's self-presentation; for Greene's own redemption is always the master narrative behind his notable discoveries.

The Drama of Repentance

The laws and tales of crime are not Greene's only pattern for discovery. His prose also stages the dramas of *conversio* and *cognitio,* where the greatest emphasis or accent falls on the Christian and romantic conversion of some reprobate. At the same time that he is chasing urban rogues, Greene is also writing long romantic tales about Francesco and Isabel, the upshot of which is this action: the man leaves behind his virtuous and patient wife to visit the city, is corrupted by courtesans and wits, discovers his folly when the rogues turn their "trick," and then repents. For all the embedded and doubled plots of this fable, the event of conversion lays claim to the same ineluctable power that Hardin Craig finds in the conversion of Dekker's protagonist in *The Honest Whore*.[55] In Greene's *Groats-Worth of Witte* (1592), the *conversio* allows Greene to perform two tricks of his own: to elevate his own life as a model for the repentance of the errant prodigal, and to remove his discoveries from their troublesome social contexts by baptizing them in the rites of spiritual justification. The author would edit his own life, and then edit out society altogether. Even so, Greene has his mind set on the power-yielding relations between prose and drama, the failures of which motivate the romance of discovery.

At first, *Groats-Worth of Witte* concerns itself with the repentance of a fictional character, Roberto. But Greene interrupts the fiction in order to explain that he is Roberto after all. This intrusion, offered as a notable event itself, confirms the analogy between the parable and Greene's career, and it italicizes the narrative moment of conversion from vice to virtue. More than ever before, Greene's discovery attempts to direct the reader's judgment, as the author forces his way in to dictate how this *cognitio* should be read. The paradox of discovery is made perfectly clear, too: in the course of admitting or even thrusting more narrative strands into the text, Greene insists that the readers attend his pointed directions.

But Greene's insistence on his own spiritual conversion leads him to offer more than a final "discouer[y] . . . [of] youths pleasures" (6). His confessions take up the rivalries and conflicts of a playwright in Elizabethan society—that is, the frustrations of being a crafter of plots, one whose schemes are abused by performers and audience alike. Greene laments that actors can be mis-readers who fail or refuse to follow the shorthand of the "notes infallible." The fictional Roberto has to suffer the roguery that surrounds him in the city and its theaters. But it is Greene who has the groats-worth of wit to offer his readers about plots and their place in the theater of the world. And his advice begins with the intrusive way in which he breaks into his plot and redefines his audience.

As he mourns the demise of his life and career, Greene's address to his audience narrows cautiously, from "Gentlemen" (already partial) to "those Gentlemen his Quondam acquaintance, that spend their wits in making plaies" (43), and finally to specific playwrights who he feels will understand the warnings so mysterious to us. According to Greene, some readers (Harvey, the players) simply cannot be trusted to unfold his repentance scene aright. By narrowing his audience to certain playwrights, Greene suggests that his prose, like their plays, should control its reception. For drama, too, is assigned the task of revealing the notable to the people, although it is lamentable to Greene that drama—its plots and their interpretation—can both serve and thwart the representation of acceptable values. These values, presumably natural and typical, are ignored by the upstarts who leave true discovery as a grave and thankless burden to the old guard of playwrights.

For the older prodigal son, however, God is the only important auditor because God has created all things and apportioned their significance. The regenerate Greene feels that the final judgment is at hand, at least for himself, although for God, perhaps, the notable points of human history are flattened. In any event, Greene tells his narrowed audience that he is weary, and he seems ready to commit the world to his opposition, to the rogues who have maintained that all estates are implicated in the fall of humankind—that no crime is more notorious than another in any pure sense. Certainly, any attempt to delay God's own discoveries is vain, as Greene laments: "Defer not (with me) till this last point of extremitie; for little knowst thou how in the end thou shalt be visited" (44). Rather than defer the notable, Greene seizes the plot and makes his own demise the groats-worth of wit. In typical fashion, Greene defers instead the uncertainty that presses us to question discovery: How can we isolate the notable? How can we avoid merely projecting it? How can we know when the divine jury is ready to judge us? We need only remember Faustus—Greene's address to Marlowe makes this connection easy—to realize that such uncertainty has much to do with the imperfections of reading the notable, with the important page turned too quickly, or the celestial tokens misapplied.

The worst of the upstarts, though, is Shakespeare, whose dramas explore the problems of discovery with a complexity and energy that Greene clearly resents.[56] For Greene, an uncritical commitment to the stable effects of the notable simplifies the definition of prose narrative, even as it involves far-reaching analogies and conventions. As an escape from his own social and dramatic confusion, Greene confesses his sins many times, as if to ensure their notoriety. At last, however, the author becomes his readers, having realized that there is too much to unfold:

> for mans time is not of it selfe so short, but it is more shortned by sinne. . . . Wel, my hand is tyrde, and I am forst to leaue where I would begin: for a whole booke cannot contain their wrongs, which I am forst to knit vp in some fewe lines of words. (47)

Sin shortens one's life, but the act of shortening the tale expresses the needs and limits of the sinful world. The narrator can "knit vp" the most important strands of the tale, but he is also "forst" to admit that the end is also a beginning: wrongs will continue, and so will their telling, in private, undetermined, yet (it is hoped) with memorable notation.

Groats-Worth of Witte is, above all, a prayer to the authority behind all controlling schemes. In advertising his notoriety, Greene affirms the stability of the "notes infallible," and he so wants us to believe in them that he restages the trick time and again. But if his intrusion into the plot aims to remove prose discoveries from the theater of the world into the city of God, it manages even so to evoke the everyday concerns of those Elizabethans who lived by the shape of their plots.

Among these authors are two of Greene's earliest readers, Nashe and Dekker, who spent their careers redefining prose in the shadow of Greene. Their complex response to Greene's prose is the subject of the rest of this book. In his attempt to free prose from rhetorical poetics, Nashe asserts the material presence and force of his own prose. His idea of a material prose requires more than finding vents for an extraordinary fund of verbal energy. Nashe also confronts the conventions of the prose that precedes his; his "stuff" (as he calls it) imitates but also rejects the traditions of deciphering, while it uses the drama of discovery in order to negotiate a new set of narrative and cultural problems.

Dekker, however, cannot believe in the stability of Greene's discoveries. Whereas Nashe attacks deciphering, Dekker rewrites the coney-catching pamphlets with daimonic agents and canting rogues. At a more general level, his plague pamphlets convert the "notable" into the "wonderful" and therefore render it elusive to human designs. The pamphlets situate the "wonderful" beyond human control or interpretation; writers and their conventional tokens have no ultimate authority over fables, never mind the cosmos. And each strategy for narrative, unstable in itself, is so involved in the others as to question the purity of literary systems in the name of hybridity and slippage. Dekker's criticism of Elizabethan prose serves many purposes—among them, to unleash prose from its constraints, but also to praise the divine mystery and authority behind all schemes. But Dekker also admits the power that the earlier prose has over his own: his skeptical prose and all of its aims gain impetus from Dekker's reading of Nashe.

These critical revisions of Greene intersect with the skeptical enterprise that, according to Terence Cave, revalued the contrivances of sixteenth-century plots, and rejected the discovery plot above all others. In turn, criticism of the *anagnorisis* ushers in the formation of new cultural and narrative ideals in the seventeenth century, although these are enmeshed in the old terms and paradigms.[57] That these ideals have something to do with that genre we call the "novel" is a story told at length and well by others.[58] In the following chapters, I aim to explore instead the strange and complex ways in which Nashe and Dekker rewrote the ciphers and notes of their predecessors and, in doing so, transformed the identities and boundaries of prose.

3
NASHE AND THE STUFF OF PROSE

Thomas Nashe never cared much for "decipherers." The word appears a handful of times in key contexts in his works; and with rare exceptions it names either literary or political activities that he despises. Decipherers, he declares, pretend that their tropes and figures are innocent when, all the while, their rhetorical tools are both weak and mean. When they are not writing, decipherers read texts according to some malicious topical bias. It will take three chapters to lay out the dimensions of this antipathy for the word that Greene prized so much in the earlier part of his career. For Nashe's position between Greene and Dekker is complex and transitional. He wrote an admiring preface to *Menaphon* but also challenged Greene's fashions in prose. And Nashe passed on a style to Dekker that the latter used to subvert Elizabethan conventions all the more. It is no longer possible to dismiss Nashe as a commercial hack failing at someone else's game.[1] What is more, his game in prose—his own "mode," we might say—is fundamental for understanding the other games in the Elizabethan pursuit of prose narrative.

I will proceed in the following stages. In this chapter, I will lay out Nashe's master trope for prose—"stuff." Critics have discussed the ways in which Nashe's prose seems corporeal or material to them. But I want to focus on Nashe's own conceptions of a somatic prose, which would include the insistence that his writings are virtually present in the cloth, organs, and metals of the world. *Lenten Stuffe* is only the most obvious use of the trope, and it involves a late, revised apology for Nashe's career. In this first chapter, however, I will review those attributes of prose which Nashe attaches to "stuff," and the problems that result from them.

But the next step of the chapter is more slippery. The question arises, what did Nashe hope to do with his "stuff"? I will argue that the agenda of Nashe's prose leads its author into a trap from which he cannot escape. While he pursues a prose that will have a material force and somatic presence in the world, that prose is caught between its legitimate commissions (by prelate or patron) and the very real threat that it poses to those same authorities. Nashe fights as best he can to find a space for his prose in the aftermath of Lyly, Greene, and the other mediators of convention. But, whereas the task that Greene sets for his prose is easy and complacent, the goals of Nashe's "stuff" are vexed and irreconcilable. When he wants his prose to fill the world, he fears that it cannot; when he wants it to escape the world, he fears that his first wish is true with a vengeance. Here begins the search for scapegoats: the decipherers, the Harveys, the stuffer himself.

The fears and triumphs of "stuff" are the subject of the next two chapters, in which I spend time with four works: *The Unfortunate Traveller, Christs Teares Over Jerusalem, Have With You to Saffron-Walden,* and *Lenten Stuffe.* In the present chapter, I will sample from the early works for illustrative purposes, and then offer an extended reading of *The Terrors of the Night.* All in all, the three chapters will argue that Nashe's career in prose is the site of a struggle between the conventions that we have traced in Greene and the skepticism that will lead Dekker to rewrite the prose of discovery.

Of Stuff and Stuffers

Nashe is clear about what stuff is not. He despises a half-baked prose that scarcely can be distinguished from the rhetorical schemes and tropes of a Petrarchan sonnet. Such a prose is absent from the world, without force or body. Lorna Hutson has recently discussed Nashe's rejection of the conventions aligned with the humanist literature of counsel; I will focus on the conventions that Nashe associated with "deciphering," in which empty rhetoric and malicious interpretation intersect with humanist concerns.[2] But Nashe's break from convention is partial and vexed: it begins with a lukewarm response to Euphuism and an ambiguous participation in didacticism.[3]

What stuff is and what its presence in the world entails are harder to discern. In fits and starts, Nashe stipples his early works—the prefaces to *Menaphon* and to *Astrophil and Stella, The Anatomie of Absurditie, Pierce Penilesse His Supplication to the Divell*—with praise for the qualities of the prose that he himself hopes to write. His prose must be inventive in a new and active sense—not just a search through the "places" of oratory. It must be spontaneous or "extemporall," a roughshod version of the Augustinian grand style—sometimes secularized, always Marprelatanized—and with an admiring glance cast back at Aretino.[4]

Indeed, the stuffer does more than "invent"; he "vents" the materials of his prose, a word that with *expedition* becomes a key metaphor for Nashe. For stuff must be economical: it must be vented into particular spaces like the agile boats in Hakluyt that "vent" by entering and supplying the channels of the New World.[5] It has its sails out (or its feet "with like expedition") in search of vacancies to fill, unlike some static, harping prose that "stand[s] talking all this while in an other mans doore" (III.333). We will see that inventing and venting—as both the source and the goal of prose—cause problems for Nashe. But these tropes also describe the most triumphant moments of his extemporal stuff.

"Venting," after all, is ambiguous when it comes to the source and supply of materials. The ships provide a material wealth to the New World that they have not created (the same double sense invades "inventing"). I will be arguing that the nature of stuff—its body and presence—is and must always be in question in the political arena where the proser's service to his commissioners and his freedom in the zodiac of his own wit are so tightly bound. But it is important, first, to add the ingredient of "stuff" on which all the others (spontaneity and invention) are predicated: that is, the strange materiality or incarnation of prose.

Critics have responded in various terms to the somatic prose for which Nashe has so much praise and so many boasts. Perhaps the best critical effort has been Neil Rhodes's "grotesque," which attributes a radical incongruity to the proto-Falstaffian materiality of the style.[6] Everyone notices the wild puns, coinages, and nonce words—all of which Nashe materializes with the trope of money in *Chrsts Teares*. One of the chief ways in which Nashe signals the material nature of his prose involves his famous catalogues of stuff—fabric, grease, excretion, gold, beer, sedge, paper. More often than not, these stuffs are clustered in wordplay, metamorphosed in image, and spatialized in terms of the vast, diminutive, plenistic and airtight.

Take, for instance, the portrait of Greed, whose house and rooms Pierce finds guarded by Famine, Lent, and Desolation:

> and in the inner part of this vgly habitation stands Greedinesse, prepared to deuoure all that enter, attyred in a Capouch of written parchment, buttond downe before with Labels of wax, and lined with sheepes fels for warmenes: his Cappe furd with cats skins, after Muscouie fashion. . . . But of al, his shooes were the strangest, which, being nothing els but a couple of crab shels, were toothd at the tooes with two sharp sixpennie

nailes, that digd vp euery dunghil they came by for gould. . . . On the other side, Dame Niggardize, his wife . . . [with] an old wiues pudding pan on her head, thrumd with the parings of her nailes, sate barrelling vp the droppings of hir nose, in steed of oyle, to saime wooll withall. . . . The house (or rather the hell) where these two Earthwormes encaptiued this beautifull Substaunce [gold], was vaste, large, strong built, and well furnished, all saue the Kitchin; for that was no bigger then the Cookes roome in a ship, with a little court chimney. . . . It were lamentable to tel what misery the Rattes and Mise endured in this hard world; how, when all supply of vittualls failed them, they went a Boothaling one night to Sinior Greedinesse bed-chamber, where finding nothing but empines and vastitie, they encountred (after long inquisition) with a cod-peece, wel dunged and manured with greace (which my pinch-fart penie-father had retaind from his Bachelorship, vntill the eating of these presents). Vppon that they set, and with a couragious assault rent it cleane away from the breeches, and then carried it in triumph, like a coffin, on their shoulders betwixt them. (166–68)

Nashe delivers Greed, not by system but by the sheer matter (merchandise) and force (venting) of his stuff. He wants us to believe not just in the somatic presence of his prose, but also in its protean nature. One word can become any other, one image any other. His very muse and wit are related to Proteus. As we will see, Nashe's prose stuff has every reason to claim a radical changeability, not just within the conventions of language but also between the realms of language and the world.

Because Nashe, unlike Greene, is so prone to talk about the performance of "stuffing," his early works repeat their praise for the qualities we have enumerated so far: the extemporal invention or venting of a somatic prose that is elastic as well as material.[7] Nashe is not timid: he announces an especially powerful stretch of prose, or promises an incredible venting of matter. In fact, "stuff" is often a promise or, we might say, a hypothesis. This, I believe, is crucial for getting at the cultural pressures that are written across Nashe's inventions. "Put case," he asks us, "to shewe how I can raile, thus would I begin to raile on [Harvey]" (I.195). He begs us to imagine one invective that "shall rattle through the Skyes, and make an Earthquake in a Pesants eares" (195). He also puts case, "if I were to paint Sloth" (209), and "if I would raunge abroad, and looke in at sluggards key holes" (209). In sum, one of the strangest metamorphoses of Nashe's prose takes place between the "is" and the "would-be."

But the supposition of prose stuff converges with analogies that also suggest the quasi-materiality of Nashe's productions. For instance, Nashe compares his language to spirits of the night in all their shapes, sizes, and realms. This analogy dominates *The Terrors of the Night;* in the earlier works we must provide the link between the two. Although they "may be toucht, wounded, or pierst" (234), the protean spirits consist of God knows what: "they are creatures incorporall, yet can they take on them the induments of anie liuing bodie what soeuer, & transform themselues into all kind of shapes, whereby they maie more easilie deceiue our our shallow wits and senses. . . . yet are they flexible, motiue, and apt for any configuration" (234–35). So, too, stuff can and must assume ever new shapes and innovations:

> Should we (as you) borrowe all out of others, and gather nothing of our selues, our names should bee baffuld on euerie Booke-sellers Stall, and not a Chandlers Mustard-pot but would wipe his mouthe with our wast paper. Newe Herrings, new, wee must crye, euery time wee make our selues publique, or else we shall bee christened with a hundred newe tytles of Idiotisme. (192)

Nashe pursues a prose that is "flexible, motiue, and apt for any configuration"—one that is expeditious. But, like its hypotheses, the ghostly nature of stuff renders that prose both a shocking presence and a quasi-materiality. Stuff has a body, but the nature or the reality of that body is elusive: it moves between the "mere" language on a page and the "real" formation of the world. Stuff, like the world, has many realms and is always changing.

The hypothesis and the numen: but stuff also resembles the wits of its producer. This is the most dangerous of the analogies because it attaches the quasi-somatic nature of prose to a human agent who is subject to punishment. Great writers will travel in the zodiacs of their own wits if imagination will "make a ladder of cord of the links of their braines" (180). But the worldly and political status of "stuff" makes this continuum between wit and prose a vexed and troubled one. Thus, Nashe claims miracles in his prose, and he credits these spectacles with a material force and presence. But there is something tentative about their habitation in the world. As Leonard Barkan has said about the pagan gods and metamorphosis in the Renaissance: "To characterize the pagan gods as demons is to place them in a realm of phantom, imagination, sleep, dream, and immateriality—and to sanction the existence of such a realm within God's purview."[8] For Nashe, stuff can be a good dream or a bad, depending on the "sanction" that its strange materiality receives.

The Commission of Stuff

None of the ingredients mentioned thus far can make "stuff" without the apparatus and the fire of its political motives. For Nashe's somatic and extemporal prose is conceived in part according to its hired purpose—to fill the spaces vexing some patron. In the name of both public and private interests—for instance, the orthodox church or the Carey family—Nashe's "good merchandise" is sponsored, its daring delivery licensed. But commission also ensures the anxieties of Nashe's prose, not the least of which derive from the too many facets of the world—material, spiritual, and institutional—and from the official ideology of an Elizabethan golden world that refuses any decentralized repair. If the official version of the world requires and receives new work, that work must be sanctioned and somehow natural. There can be no vacuum in the formations of nature and society; and there can be no perverse or "singular" contrivance in the stuff that contributes to the fullness of the world.

It might help to get at the motives of "stuff" if we notice the conspicuous absences in Lorna Hutson's excellent study of Thomas Nashe "in context."[9] For all the good readings that her book includes, Hutson offers no extended discussions of those works for which Nashe sought patronage: *The Terrors of the Night* and *Christs Teares*. Nor is there much on the Marprelate controversy. Hutson has a good reason for this omission. She wants to situate Nashe in the contexts of a humanist program of reform that swept economy, morality, and literature under the same need to use resources with utmost providence. According to Hutson, England underwent a crisis of resources in the middle of the sixteenth century, which led to the official insistence on discovering, creating, and hoarding supplies wherever possible—and sometimes where it was not thought possible. Once these resources of language, virtue, or material wealth had been secured, then the English were warned in sermon and treatise not to spend—to save always for the future. But what may have been necessary for England's survival went too far, Hutson concludes. It turned into an impersonal and possessive front for the powerful and prosperous who translated bankrupt didacticism into land and money. Nashe, she believes, devoted his career to the ironic ridicule of this front.

Hutson's argument is a compelling one: Nashe values an older conception of festival, one that celebrates the transient and spontaneous expenditure of the here and now, one in touch with the rhythms of the seasons. This commitment to festival permits Nashe to write an ironic and improvisatory prose, a prose with no didactic purpose and with no deference to the future. His is a popular prose in the deepest sense of that term, but it is also somehow medieval and even classical in its traditions. Yet Hutson's muted but important agenda here is not so much historical as theoretical: for she finds in Nashe's prose the freedom of a carnival. Somehow, Nashe has escaped from ideology: somehow, his prose can turn the literature of counsel into the pleasures of irony and subversion that one would have lived in the medieval countryside: "[f]undamentally, all Nashe's writings challenge this identification of eloquence with persuasion and providence by conceiving festively of time and of human endeavour and refusing to acknowledge the humanist conception of time and personal talent as being investments in a patriotic enterprise" (123).

Hutson gives us the tools with which to rethink both the shadow of humanism and the so-called empty contents in Nashe's prose.[10] And I agree that Nashe's prose implies a freedom extempore—that it even declares this freedom from time to time. But Hutson has used Bakhtin to free Nashe too much. Even freedom, say, in *Lenten Stuffe* is entangled in the ideology of official humanism and patronage in the age of Elizabeth. Hutson has factored out the anxiety and the drama of Nashe's prose, although sometimes she revises her totalizing claims to include variety in "all Nashe's writings," or even a quiet anxiety in the real straits of the proser's life.[11] She needs to account for those recent studies that have sought to correct what is too naive about the Bakhtinian festival. For that festival can be appropriated by the very offices and agendas that Hutson would have Nashe subvert.[12] The only patronized work that she discusses—*Summers Last Will and Testament*—is attributed to a patron, Whitgift, whom admiring biographers credited with a true understanding of festival and its free dispensations. But we need to put the problems of service back into Nashe's "stuff." Hutson is right to defend Nashe against the charges of incompetence at someone else's game; yet, his brilliance in refashioning humanist prose is fretful and servile as well as indecorous and free. The master plan of "stuff" and the changes in that plan are tied in a knot where the commissioned and autonomous Nashe are bound together.

When Nashe was hired by the prelates to defeat Martin at his own game, it was clear that this lowbrow proser was meant to serve as a stopgap in an emergency. The guardians of the established church—also the protectors of learning, government, and morality—wanted to minimize the damage already done. They saw "*Diuinitie* wyth a scratcht face, holding of her hart as if she were sicke, because *Martin* would haue forced her, but myssing of his purpose, he left the print of his nayles vppon her cheekes.[13] But the officials wanted to prevent any further damage or, indeed, to deny that the damage was really already deep. The new prosers would supply a kind of cultural salve: their prose could fill the ruptures caused by the subversives, and act as "Dawbings . . . Cementings, Wrinkle-fillings, and Botchings up." This demand for a stopgap against the sieves created by the raucous prose of Martin is part and parcel of Nashe's conception of prose as a quasi-material stuff. For his prose began with the commission of filling every hole in the institutions, the body and soul of the Elizabethan "settlement." Stuff is patchwork, and as such it must fit any finite space with a brilliance and a plenty that have no limit or end. Stuff must be restrained and circumscribed, like Terence Cave's cornucopian text, but it must be real and present—not just rhetoric or language. Herein lies the force of the metaphoric venting; for, like those voyages of discovery and supply, Nashe's stuff is only conditionally authorized. It must work or perish.

However, the brilliant presence of stuff—the stuffer's boast, as it were—calls attention to the defective status quo. This is a problem, and it explains why the status of venting and of stuff must remain elusive or ambiguous. The proser must perform two feats at once: he must supply the materials with which to salve the "scratcht face" of the status quo, but minimize or even erase altogether the signs of his work. He must serve, but then act as if the damages and the repairs never happened. Nashe's position is thus more subtle and vexed than Greene's watchman; for Nashe's stuff is both authorized and unclaimed. Nashe knows and proclaims the miracles of his inventive wit: such pride seems almost necessary for the production of a forceful and somatic prose. Yet, he is constantly deferring to and running from figures of authority. His prose is everywhere worried about fathers and mentors—and he often denies any substantive role in the reparation of values or truth. However, denial runs cheek by jowl with an insistence on the force and presence of stuff. As Stephen S. Hilliard has shown, Nashe must always struggle with his own "singularity."[14] Locked in this struggle, the career of "stuff" dramatizes the Elizabethan search for the most fundamental identity and status of prose.

So stuff must be thrust into the world, but from an elusive source: its source in the wits of the author must elude us because the stuff of the world should always already be there—created and sturdy. Part of what we can gather from this agon is the authorial and festive freedom for which Hutson argues so powerfully in Nashe. But there is more to the problematic of stuff than its liberation in folly. For the stuffer is a servant and even a victim of the same conventions and powers from which his prose offers some escape. Moreover, his efforts to escape from responsibility or from punishment may range from self-effacement to an exile in Yarmouth; they may lead him to call his own prose nonsense or a ghostly dream. But, whatever the strategy, or however "quasi" the body of his prose, Nashe's career in stuff is always marked by its commissions. This fact does not preclude an endogenous and festive power in Nashe's career: it deepens and confirms that power.

Thus, stuff must remain a mystery, for all its boasting. Just what is this stuff, this language of prose that seems so real and tangible? Is it of and in the world, really here with us? If so, the producer has to worry about its origins in his own wits. Or is it only language after all, as empty of a body as Petrarchan catalogues? If so, the stuffer must fear that his job is ill done, that his stuff is only promised or merely ghostly. The paradox of stuff is irreducible. Where Nashe desires its presence in the many realms of the world (social, moral, material), he frets that the dream of his prose fades into thin rhetorical air. But where (in the end) he advertises its trivial absence from serious affairs, Nashe fears that his prose can never exit from the world and the conventions of duty.

It is the strange and difficult task of stuff that determines in large part Nashe's lifelong ambivalence toward the humanists (such as Ascham) and the poets in prose or verse (such as Sidney or Greene). Nashe is locked in a rivalry with these cultural heroes, and this rivalry leads him to such a variety and complexity of response because he is hired to preserve their cultural traditions in a language that they cannot approach, approve, or understand. His attitude toward Greene is especially mixed up; that toward Sidney, more deferential but also self-serving.[15] His defenses of the learned traditions for which Ascham stands do not end with *The Anatomie of Absurditie*.[16] But, as Hutson has shown so well, Nashe is most powerful (and funny) when he is assailing the bankrupt or inert conventions spawned by the pedagogy and didacticism of the reformed schoolmasters. One of the ways in which Nashe makes these complexities manageable involves "deciphering."

In *The Unfortunate Traveller*, Nashe will pose his muse, the lusty *bona roba*, against the Petrarchan muse of decipherers who empty their prose of any solidity by preferring opaque and ethereal tropes, figures, and emblems. Even in *Pierce Penilesse*, he has no time or interest to "decypher at large" a picture of Roman gluttony because some other laureate "who, for a man that stands vpon paines and not wit, hath performd as much as any Storie dresser may doo, that sets a new English nap on an old Latine Apothegs" (199). Here, we see the first rebuke of the old static harper, who paints or dresses verbal pictures with faded colors and heaps of tropes. The decipherer creates no "liuing bodie" or no gigantisms of "a belly as big as the round Church in *Cambridge*." There is, however, another kind of decipherer for Nashe to attack, although the second is related to the first. In *Pierce Penilesse*, but also in the later works, decipherers are readers, "mice-eyed" in interpretation. These readers mangle texts with topical allusions that are chosen according to political interests. "*Sed caueat emptor,* Let the interpreter beware," warns Pierce; "for none euer hard me make Allegories of an idle text" (I.155). With Jonson, these politic readers get the name of "decipherer" in Nashe's works.[17] As the problems of stuffing intensify, these simplified fools and villains, the decipherers, become the scapegoat of the stuffer who wants most of all to avoid his own demise—his own forced absence. Let us proceed, however, to a work that is relatively free of victims: to *The Terrors of the Night*, a text in which Nashe's patchwork in the daimonic realms of the world serves a family's interests.

A Little Night Stuff

I am arguing that the peculiarities of Nashe's quasi-somatic prose can be studied in terms of the contradictions between his commission to fill gaps in the body and soul of the status quo and the endogenous invention of that prose. We can focus the questions arising from "stuff" if we look at Nashe's *The Terrors of the Night or, a Discourse of Apparitions* (registered, 1593; published, 1594). Nashe's interest in spirits began, we have seen, in *Pierce Penilesse*, where he delves into demonology. In that text, Nashe initiates his lifelong fascination with voids and sieves—images that appear in one form or another in many of his texts. Often, the sieve is a sign of the hapless nightmare or impoverishment into which Pierce (or Jack Wilton) has fallen. Some holes are demonic: "I do not doubt (Doctor Diuell) but you were present in this action, or passion rather, and helpt to bore holes in ships to make them sinke faster" (I.185). Some are simply vicious, like the lechery that "hath more starting holes than a sive hath holes" (216). As a *vacuus viator,* Pierce is truly picaresque (as Harvey recognized), insofar as Lazarillo's motto says that "where one hole is closed another opens."[18] There are foolish vacancies—Harvey is one such inflation of nothingness.[19] But the ultimate sieve is Pierce's last resort—hell itself.

Such images of gaps and holes confront the narrators of nearly all Nashe's works. But I want to focus on the one political void of *Pierce Penilesse* because it prepares us for the role of the stuffer in *Terrors*.

Pierce links idleness and sedition, and he asserts that work fills the vacuities of a commonwealth. To prevent holes in the nature of things, the authorities ought to allow for stage plays, honest rivalry, and, indeed, for war, which vents the "wastes of people." It is hard to gauge how much of this assertion is mockery—certainly some of it is, as Hutson claims. But Nashe's own stuffing is a vocation that often poses as faith in the powers that rule. So, whereas Nashe's prose comprises "higher matters" in contrast to the "light toyes" that simply keep other people busy, his enterprise always straddles the line between serious, remedial work and trivial play. This straddling explains why Pierce invokes faith toward the end of his treatise: "Nor doo I affirme [the other cures for spirits] to be vnfallible prescriptions, though sometime they haue their vse: but that the onelie assured way to resist their attempts is prayer and faith, gainst which all the diuells in hell cannot preuaile" (239).[20] With stuff, work must be faith and leave no trace of itself—no fictive bronze in the "Golden World" (191) of the Elizabethan establishment.

Hutson has argued that *Pierce Penilesse* is for the most part mockery, although she concedes some traditionalism in Nashe's approach. But the same cannot be said for *The Terrors*, which critics have dismissed for its confusion. As C. G. Harlow has shown, two families, the Cottons and the Careys, had vested interests in this pamphlet's account of dreams and spirits.[21] In the process of working through the many theories of dreams and spirits in the Renaissance, Nashe manages to raise the most basic questions about the nature of his own prose, and about the void that it is asked to fill in silence. What is stuff? How can it be present in the world—its body, numen, and social formations? How can proud, extemporal stuff account for its presence when it is no longer authorized by its onetime patrons?

The preface to *The Terrors* reminds Elizabeth Carey that this work has been necessitated—imposed on Nashe—by some acquaintance. The motive appears to center on the strange, potentially bewitched, visions of a dying "Gentleman" in a house where Nashe has stayed. The stuffer, in essence, must account for the dreams: were they real or melancholic? But, as Nashe at once affirms and denies the numinous dream, he likens the materials of his language to dreams and spirits, all elusive in regard to their makeup. To the skeptic, dreams materialize only to the extent that they derive from the poor digestion of some legume or piece of meat.[22] To the believer, dreams are not just real or true, but somehow present—even *there* in the room like a daimon. Just so with prose stuff: Nashe suggests that his verbal leviathans—his thick locutions—shift between the physicality of things, the daimonic presence of visions, and the airy nothings of a nominating fancy. What is more, the skeptic and the believer disagree about the remedial function of the dream. To the former, the dream signals the state of the body or the cathexis of the mind,[23] whereas the latter credits the dream with some miraculous intervention. But at the same time, Nashe's treatise on the dignitary's dream either redresses the needs of one family and, by extension, his own needs, or it ensures the numinous presences to which dreams and daimons contribute.

Dreams become, then, the perfect analogue for a quasi-material prose: for both are problematic in their substance and in their production. The worst vexation for both visions and "stuff" is the devil. Satan can enter into dreams, of course, but he also possesses qualities that are the mirror image of Nashe's ideal prose (hence the irony of Pierce's supplication to the devil). The devil is flexible: "nimble and sodaine . . . in shifting his habit" (I.349). He creates vents in order to fill them: "The wrinkles in old witches visages, they eate out to entrench themselues in" (349). The very thickness of evil spirits stifles a hypothetical audience: "In *Westminster* Hall a man can scarce breath for [spirits]; in euery corner they houer as thick as moates in the sunne" (349). In fact, devils leave no vacuum with all their cramming:

> What do we talke of one diuel? there is not a roome in anie mans house, but is pestred and close packed with a campe royall of diuels. *Chrisostome* saith, the aire and earth are three parts inhabited with spirits. Hereunto the Philosopher alluded, when he said, Nature made no voydnes in the whole vniuersall: for no place (bee it no bigger than a pockhole in a mans face) but is close thronged with them. Infinite millions of them wil hang swarming about a worm-eaten nose. (349)

Here, then, we have a demonized version of that ideal to which Nashe's prose aspires until *Lenten Stuffe* relocates his inventive prose in a void. But, as Nashe edges toward the connections between spirits and prose, he leaves the devil—whom faith can make "vanished"—for more anonymous and potentially benign spirits.

In regard to apparitions, Nashe insists (with the "credit" of the gentleman in mind) that "[n]o, no, they are spirits, or els it were incredible" (350). But he also reduces spirits to the flimsy "bubbels" of a superstitious imagination. The bubbles of the dreamer are figured in more material terms: dreams are the "bubling scum or froath of the fancie, which the day hath left vndigested; or an after feast made of the fragments of idle imaginations" (355). While Nashe conflates the leftover thoughts of a day and the residues of the metabolism, he takes a step toward language, the "fragments of idle imaginations." Indeed, "fome" also names Harvey's idle words in *Strange Newes*.

The stakes for the dreamer also are at issue for the stuffer: the nature of the product and the place of its production, in the mind or outside the mind in the very nature of things.

Dreams may be materially present in the room, or they be the foam of an overwrought imagination. But Nashe makes a firmer connection between these dreams and his own prose when he reports the prodigies of "Island" (i.e., Iceland). The subject of his inventive digression seems empty: "how come I to digresse to such a dull, Lenten, Northren Clyme, where there is nothing but stock-fish, whetstones, and cods-heads" (360). The herring is destined to become a major trope for Nashe's prose. But the lenten quality of the fish is not so important here as the surreal nature of the prose that has invented these materials as the stuff of a barren land:

> I care not much if I dream yet a little more: & to say the troth, all this whole Tractate is but a dreame, for my wits are not halfe awaked in it: & yet no golden dreame, but a leaden dreame it is; for in a leaden standish I stand fishing all day, but haue none of Saint *Peters* lucke to bring a fish to the hooke that carries anie siluer in the mouth. And yet there be of them that carrie siluer in the mouth too, but none in the hand: that is to say, are verie bountifull and honorable in their words, but except it be to sweare indeed, no other good deedes comes [*sic*] from them. (360–61)

Thus, the prose is a leaden dream that is "extraught" from the world in several respects. The play on fishing expresses the frustrations of the Elizabethan writer in a patronage system; but it also invokes the soteriology of works (fishers of men, St. Peter's catch of "good deedes") that is troublesome for the patronized stuffer. For Nashe has a job to do: he must resolve the mystery of the particular dream that has vexed his hosts. This is to say that Nashe's prose—its status halfway between sleep and waking—must either declare the dream empty, celebrate its reality, or create that reality with the stuff of his verbiage.

The anxiety of the oneiro-critic whose own productions might be criticized is everywhere apparent in the text. There are analogies between death and dreams: "as when a man is readie to drowne, hee takes hold of anie thing that is next him: so our flutring thoughts, when wee are drowned in deadly sleepe, take hold, and coessence themselues with anie ouerboyling humour" (370). Then, there is the recurring motif of the master and the servant, a relation that in Nashe's works spells humiliation for the former or pain for the latter. For the servant, dreams mitigate pain, although only for awhile: "He that dreams merily is like a boy new breetcht, who leapes and daunceth for ioy his pain is past: but long that ioy stayes not with him, for presently after his master the day, seeing him so iocund and pleasant, comes and dooes as much for him againe, whereby his hell is renued" (356). We see the schoolboy once again "with his hoase about his heeles, ready to be whipt, to whom his master stands preaching a long time all law and no Gospel, ere he proceed to execution" (373). For all dreamers, night can summon the stuff of punishment and torture: "a man should be rosted to death, and melt away by little and little, whiles Phisitions lyke Cookes stand stuffing him out with hearbes, and basting him with this oyle and that sirrup" (373). Sleeping can be like unfortunate travel, where the "wearie traueller . . . layeth his fainting head vnawares on a loathsome neast of snakes" (345).

These images of anxiety recur throughout Nashe's works, and they often condense the key elements of stuffing. There are vents in the world and in the body that can drain us. The stuff in those vents, like the materials in our pillows, can make matters even worse: for we can "stuffe . . . our night pillowes with thistles to encrease our disturbance" (373). But the vents and the stuff of our dreams can also save or repair us:

> Sooner [the devil] will pare his nayles cleanly, than cause a man to dreame of a pot of golde, or a money bag that is hid in the eaues of a thatcht house.
> (Heere is to be noted, that it is a blessed thing but to dreame of gold, though a man neuer haue it.)
> Such a dreame is not altogether ridiculous or impertinent, for it keepes flesh and bloud from despaire: all other are but as dust we raise by our steps; which awhyle mounteth aloft, and annoyeth our ey-sight, but presently disperseth and vanisheth. (368)

One of the traditional notions about dreams holds that they supply us in sleep with what we lack in our waking hours.[24] But prose stuff itself is required to provide such a thatch against despair, emptiness, and the devil. For this reason the prose dream has its own share of anxieties. Its materials might not suit the remedial task at hand, or they might slip from the author's control: "Come, come, I am entraunced from my Text, I wote well, and talke idely in my sleepe longer than I should" (361). Much of this fear concerns the stuffer's need for authorization and boundaries: "I feare I haue strayed beyond my limits: and yet feare hath no limits, for to hell and beyond hell, it sinkes downe and penetrates" (376). Fear and triumph alternate in the images that mediate for Nashe between authority and endogeny. He courts but also criticizes his humanist masters; and he seeks but also excoriates patrons. Nashe serves, then runs from the officials of the Elizabethan government.[25] But in the commission of *Terrors*, the analogy between the dreamer and the stuffer brings the vexations of service to the fore.

Nashe insists, to begin with, that his "sources" are authoritative. The Church Fathers have his respect, although the standard dream lore gets an impatient and dismissive citation. There are oral authorities: we see the boy Nashe absorbing endless stories: "I haue heard aged mumping beldams as they sat warming their knees ouer a coale scratch ouer the argument verie curiously. . . . When I was a little childe, I was a great auditor of theirs, and had all their witchcrafts at my fingers endes, as perfit as good morrow and good euen" (369). But his most eager appeal is to his patron, Carey, whose virtues Nashe even offers to "decypher" (375). In the final section of *Terrors*, the family servant reinvents the dream, whose mysterious origin is of interest to the Cottons but also perhaps to the Careys. The skeptic in Nashe claims at one point that "there is no certaintie in dreames," but he offers at another some exceptional assurance of their truth: "I confesse the Saintes and Martirs of the Primitiue Church had vnfallible dreames" (372). As the proser begins his task, dreams are no longer just a metaphor for his stopgap prose; for that prose is caught in the middle of a dream whose "credit" Nashe must record, supply, or suspend. And it is more likely that he will have to do all these things at once.

Not only the interests of gentle families are at stake. We see Nashe's own interest in filling the vents of his new patron's world when he celebrates its hermetic seal: "Through him my tender wainscot Studie doore is deliuered from much assault and battrie" (375). The protected servant has, therefore, the leisure to recreate what may be "true apparitions or prodigies" in his own forceful prose. That his prose mediates the dream of the honorable friend is crucial: Nashe can invent the material in a hypothesis (a challenge to "put case"), or just reflect the daimonic world as faithfully as Camden's "last repollished Edition of his *Brittania*" (374) conveys the artifacts of the world. For Nashe, stuff wavers on the line between the idealized realms of fact and fiction, the world and the wit. Duty requires that the stuffer be humble—he will not "underprop" the dream or "take vpon [himself] to determine" its status (378). But he also must satisfy the gentle family and himself. And so the prose must be his and not his, a somatic presence and an airy nothing. His stuff, that is, refigures the problem of the gentleman's apparitions.

Nashe prefaces his account with praise for the dreamer's credibility and "strong faith" (380). In the dreams, too, the old man conquers the devil in a battle for the dreamer's soul, even though the devil can produce unreal dreams out of the errant faculties of the dreamer. But whatever their source, Nashe gives the dreams all the qualities of good stuff: they are gigantic, metamorphic, and forceful in their entrance to the dying man's room. Thus, we see global mouths and "whole shelues of Kentish oysters" for eyes (379). And the dreams come into the room from outside—they appear as corpulent presences external to the dreamer.

Despite the "perfect ease" in the dreamer's faith and in the presence of the dreams, Nashe defends his own role in the recreation of this faith and presence. Has the stuffer filled empty dreams with the body and power of his language? Or has he merely represented the already full and forceful presence of the dream? His answer is careful: "God is my witnesse, in all this relation, I borrowe no essential part from stretcht out inuention, nor haue I one iot abusde my informations; onely for the recreation of my Readers . . . heere and there I welt and garde it with allusiue exornations & comparisons" (382). Any "stretch out" material was only trimwork ("welt and garde") and unimportant to the validity or redemptive quality of the dream. But "invention" cuts two ways for Nashe, toward the gathering of commonplaces ("allusiue . . . comparisons") and from the author's own venting wits. Nashe has not exactly clarified the status of his work.

He proceeds, however, to make explicit his patchwork on truth:

> If the world will giue [the dream] anie allowaunce of truth, so it is: For then I hope my excuse is alreadye lawfullye customed and authorized; since Truth is euer drawne and painted naked, and I haue lent her but a leathren patcht cloake at most to keepe her from the cold: that is, that she come not off too lamely and coldly. (382)

We are a long way from the mysterious and rhetorical colors of Greene's deciphering. One wonders, though, how far it is between truth's "patcht cloak" and divinity's "scratcht face" in the Marprelate controversy. Nashe is careful enough to make this proviso a matter of representation—of how truth will "come off." He would expedite the reception of an otherwise hobbled truth. But he does not explain whose fault it is that truth "come[s] off" so weakly—the reader's, the author's, or truth's own patron. What exactly is the servant lending, and to whom?

The ventings of the stuffer are perhaps safest if he simply gains our faith in his tale: "Are there anie doubts which remaine in your mynde vndigested, as touching this incredible Narration I haue vnfolded? Well, doubt you not, but I am milde and tractable, and will resolue you in what I may" (382). Our digestion will be aided by the "tractable" stuff of his prose—for stuff is nothing if not flexible and solvent.[26] The proser would not only ease our digestion of the dream; he would fill our pillows with a material that will allow us to "haue a good night, and sleep quietly without affrightment and annoyance" (384).

But, although his readers may rest well, Nashe's mode of prose keeps him busy in the pursuit of the strategies and claims by which he can defend "stuff." In two other works, Nashe dramatizes good dreams and bad. The strange homily of *Christs Teares* has some kinship to *The Terrors;* and, indeed, both works address the Careys. In *The Unfortunate Traveller,* Nashe unleashes a nightmare of torture for his stand-in, Jack Wilton. This latter work best illustrates one of the darkest aspects of stuffing for hire: the need for scapegoats. That the proser might prove a scapegoat results from the proximity between faith and works, fact and fiction, service and subversion. But, although the stuffer must fear his own exile or demise, he has some favorite scapegoats, too. For Jack Wilton, it is the deciphering Surrey. For Nashe, it is Doctor Harvey whose claims to under-prop the status quo with "works" are presumptuous, but whose poetic style resembles nothing more than a sieve:

> Nor do I altogether scum off all these ["inkhornisms"] as the newe ingendred fome of the English, but allowe some of them for a neede to fill vp a verse; as *Traynment,* and one or two wordes more, which the libertie of prose might well haue spar'd. In a verse, when a worde of three sillables cannot thrust in but sidelings, to ioynt him euen we are oftentimes faine to borrowe some lesser quarry of elocution from the Latine, alwaies retaining this for a principle, that a leake of indesinence, as a leake in a shippe, must needly bee stopt with what matter soeuer. (*Strange Newes,* I. 316)

In chapter 5, I will take a long look at the strategies by which Nashe foists his own fears of presumption and leakage onto Harvey. As Nashe defines and then redefines good stuff, he can always attribute bad stuff to the doctor. Harvey claims too much cultural importance for his words, and in any case his prose lacks the malleable form and somatic presence of Nashe's animated stuff.

But the author of good stuff can sympathize now and then with Harvey's need for "desinence," which G. Gregory Smith glosses as a proper boundary.[27] For stuff, with all its spontaneity and abundance, needs closure, too. Although Nashe never ceases to brag about his expeditious style, he fears losses: "If my stile holde on this sober Mules pace but a sheete or two further, I shall haue a long beard. . . . O it is a miserable thing to dresse haire like towe twixt a mans teeth, when one cannot drinke but hee must thrust a great spunge into the cup, & so cleanse his coole porridge, as it were through a strayner, ere it comes to his lippes" (292). The work of stuffing can leave one weary and compromised: no wonder that *Terrors* ends abruptly with a prayer for closure in the final judgment.[28] He suggests that such an event is notable for being a seal against or an end of anxiety rather than the very epitome of and prelude to the damnation of souls. Whatever the case, the final sentence epitomizes the creed behind responsible stuff: "Thus I shut vp my Treatise abruptly, that hee who in the daye doth not good woorkes inough to answere the obiections of the night, will hardly aunswere at the daye of iudgement" (386). For Nashe, "stuff" is the proser's answerable style.

But the answer is not simple: its soteriology of both faith and works entails that stuff cannot afford to be clear about the origins of prose. Nashe seems always to be debtor and lender at the same time. For this reason, he is especially ambivalent about his literary heritage: both strongly committed and resistant to "influence." As Harvey suggests, Nashe's biggest problem with influences is Greene. He defends the prodigal Greene and even claims to have learned plotting from him, a lesson in discovery to which we will return in the next chapter. Indeed, when it comes to extended "histories," discovery offers "stuff" the same kind of escape into narrative control that it lent to Greene's coney-catching and repentance pamphlets. But, as we will also see in the next chapter, Nashe's lukewarm reception of Euphuism and his disdain for "greene colours" are part and parcel of his most reduced scapegoats, the decipherers, whose idea of a sufficient prose is superseded (Nashe believes) by the force and presence of his material stuff—the verbal leviathans and thick words. The decipherers have sold out—to politics, to pleasure, to convention. Even so, this scorn for the decipherers brings with it a considerable irony: that in the end, as the stuffer tries to empty out his prose and to situate it outside the world, he faces the possibility that stuff is closer to the paradoxes and problems of deciphering than he could ever admit.

Lorna Hutson has poised the festive Nashe against the humanist "preoccupation with the depletion of resources" that gave rise to literary, moral, and economic reform.[29] Such reform affected the idea of copia, and so the idea of deciphering. But the sieves and materials of stuff are more fully implicated in this context than even Hutson suspects. For the nightmares of *The Unfortunate Traveller* and the offering of a redeemed stuff in *Christs Teares* are all part of a madcap dream that thrusts prose into the constitution of the same world that Greene's idealized mode would govern in absentia. Nashe, however, cannot so carelessly maintain the obvious distance between golden worlds and leaden.

4

THE FORTUNES OF NASHE'S STUFF

In the previous chapter, I have argued that the master trope of "stuff" epitomizes the peculiar demands of commission and convention on Nashe and his newfangled prose. With quasi-materiality claimed for and retracted from prose, Nashe breaks from "greene colours" and plunges into what Lorna Hutson has described as the double bind of Elizabethan writers. On the one hand, they are required to profit the Church and State; but on the other hand, these same authors are censored and punished for their strategies—which strike the authorities as too ambitious or presumptuous.[1] With *The Unfortunate Traveller* (1593–94) and *Christs Teares over Jerusalem* (1593), the strange fortunes of the stuffer take a decidedly narrative turn. Each text poses as and relies on some chronicle of events, yet each unfolds its "reasonable conueyance of historie" against the nightmarish backdrop of a city filled with vents: the trapdoors through which Jack Wilton falls, the crevice through which he views a rape, and the sieve of desolation in Jerusalem.

Nashe and his stand-ins, Jack and Christ, have essentially two responses to their bad dreams. Both narrators want to save their tales from the pitfalls and frustrations that affront them. To this end, Nashe and his surrogates invoke the strength and presence of a material language that might seal the holes and gaps of irony and transgression. But any cursory reading of these texts also reveals that their endless catalogues of stuff amount to the gore and the mire of a world shot through with irony and transgression. Stuff needs help. I will argue that it gets that help from the plots of discovery, ranging from jest books and coney-catching to repentance narratives.

Critics have never quite known what to make of Jack Wilton's jests and conversion to "honesty." Nor have they tied these discoveries to his critical awareness of narrative.[2] "Theres a further path I must trace" (II.210); "[i]ost a little neerer to the matter & the purpose"

(207); the "notorious" point or "principall subiect pluckes me by the elbowe" (266): these and many other remarks show us a Jack who has a keen sense of plotting. When Jack describes the knights of a tournament, he obeys the basic criterion of notable discovery when he announces that "I wil rehearse no more, but I haue an hundred other: let this bee the vpshot of those shewes, they were the admirablest" (278). Thus, the aggressive Jack competes against the other servants of Church and State—the orators or the poetizing Surrey (all decipherers). But he relies, as does Christ, on discovery to redeem and escape his chronicle of torture and vanity. There is, however, one further irony in the narratives of stuff: that the "notes" of discovery have been invented by the stuffer himself, and they require the same kinds of defense that his extemporal and incarnate prose demands. The most explicit apology for the materials of prose accompanies a preface to the second edition of *Christs Teares*, the first edition of which brought the wrath of public officials on Nashe's head.[3]

If Jack comes to serve the very patrons of Europe whom he has plagued and rivaled, his prose can be said to create the very discoveries—the controlled and moralized plan for the fable—that he has wished for in the face of violence and doubt. It is no wonder that Jack, Nashe's most brilliant stuffer, deals with his fears of being unstuffed by taking easy shots at the empty and absent colors of deciphering. With Christ, the complicity between a material and a discovered prose receives the troubled blessing of a vexed savior who is made present in the text by way of *prosopopeia*.

Against Deciphering

Jack Wilton tells of a European culture in the combative and violent flux of revision. Events lack an anchor in any clearly defined community of values, while history unfolds in unstable, macabre sequences. Even the Anabaptists, such easy prey for the satirist, elicit an apology from Jack when they are slaughtered. Indeed, the massacre, like so many other events, seems irreducible and vexed; no simple gloss is available to explain the disembowellings, rapes, and murders that interact with the trivialized political and cultural landmarks of the narrative—its parade of kings, magicians, and learned men.[4] What is worse, Jack expresses a desire for closure to which he has no access: "as good [to end] now as stay longer" (241). The page to Henry VIII seems as intricately bound to his nightmare as are fact and fiction or lies and truth to each other.

For all his lies and games, Jack worries at times about his status as the narrator responsible for shaping and explaining this European history. He is a young "practitioner in diuinity" who suspends history so that he may debate the questions of his faith "a little more grauely than the nature of this historie requires" (234). At the same time, he disclaims any supporting role in the defense of the Church: "farre be it my vnder-age arguments should intrude themselues as a greene weake prop to support so high a Building" (236). Moreover, he imagines the many ways of punishment for the overzealous: we see schoolmasters flailed and schoolboys gelded.

In sum, Jack Wilton has the hilarious task of explaining the inexplicable, and then of mocking or refuting those cultural heroes or overdoers who have asserted their interpretations by the sword or by the word. Thus, the page's narrative task approaches the nightmarish position of an author much like his own, Thomas Nashe.[5] Both are extempore and ludic historians in the middle of rampant political opacities and social instabilities. And both are threatened with punishment. Much like his author, Jack Wilton survives because he can fashion a clear-cut rivalry between the inventors of a material, forceful prose and the jaded decipherers of an empty, absent rhetoric.

Like Nashe, Jack Wilton severs deciphering into two kinds. The first amounts to malicious (if dull-witted) misreadings that serve the interpreter's political interests. When Jack outwits a would-be intelligencer who practices "two-handed Interpretation," he claims a victory for the simple proser: "what neede the snaile care for eyes, when hee feeles the way with his two hornes, as well as if he were quicke sighted as a decypherer" (221). Such a usage never figures into Greene's lexicon; but Jack associates deciphering with a myopic and politic reader.

The second kind of deciphering in *The Unfortunate Traveller* is closer to Greene's mode of representation. Time and again, Jack competes against orators and poets whose rhetoric is ineffective—empty, absent, or insincere. Jack's triumph over these decipherers—and he uses that word, as we will see—depends in part on his own verbal powers. Early in the tale, he celebrates his own extraordinary venting: "Here let me triumph a while, and ruminate a line or two on the excellence of my wit: but I will not breath neither till I haue disfraughted all my knauerie" (225). For the transition between the English and European segments of his fable, Jack purveys the various stuffs of the sweating sickness: fat women wipe off their chins, cooks melt into "kitchin stuffe" (228), hair drops off to become the cheap matter for glovers "to stuffe their balls with" (229). For the most part, however, Jack asserts his forceful, corporeal prose by way of three sets of rivalries: between a Ciceronian orator and one Vanderhulke, between Jack and Surrey, and between a romantic tournament and a merchant's banqueting house.

Cicero gets rough treatment in Jack's narrative. He is summoned by the magic of Agrippa on the charge of forensic duplicity; but more generally, his legacy has been inherited by the "discontented" studies of the humanists whose failures are everywhere apparent.[6] At Wittenberg, Jack hears an orator who is devoted to Tully's style. His speech is woefully pompous and derivative; its periods rely on "choice" invention because it searches the "places" for its every phrase: "there is a choise euen amongest ragges gathered vp from the dunghill" (247). The orator wins fulsome praise from the politic members of the audience, but Jack only mentions the oration, leaving it forever absent from his tale. The deciphering of styles, he suggests, shows not just a love for Cicero (we might pun on Greene's *Ciceronis Amor*), but a desire to succeed in a trivial courtly politics. Perhaps these decipherers are not so far from the two-handed interpreters after all.

By contrast, a second speech, delivered by the gigantic Vanderhulke, is quoted in its bulging, somatic prose. The speaker himself boasts a trapdoor mouth, oyster eyes, and a beard replete with "strawe, haire, and durt mixt together" (247). Above all, the tavern-haunting orator despises emptiness: like a good fellow, he will fill a "plaine emptie Canne" with drink (248), or the empty air with grotesque and cumbersome words. This stuff gratifies—a far cry from the previous speech, or from the Lutheran debate that Jack excludes because its "masse of wordes . . . heapte vp agaynst the masse" has "nothing to make a man laugh" (250).

The second rivalry adds more complexity to the rivalry between good stuff and all pretenders. Jack is both a servant and a foil to the earl of Surrey, and he gets into trouble when he goes too far with their switched identities. Indeed, their exchange of identities brings us closer to the ambiguous status of the lowly proser who is hired to seal the established order from any damage wrought by the Marprelates or Harveys. But the vexed relations between earl and page are channeled into a more innocent and literary rivalry. For Surrey is a Petrarchan poet whose idealized verse is challenged by Jack's sexualized prose.

Gordon Braden has argued that Petrarchan love poetry requires and even prefers the absence of its putative subject, the lady.[7] In *The Unfortunate Traveller*, Jack charges Surrey with just such a desire for Geraldine's absence. When Surrey abandons his beloved in England in order to visit her home country, the earl carries his devotion to an absent mistress *ad absurdam*. Jack does not hesitate to contrast this strange fashion with his own sexual desire. Desire affects language, too. For Surrey, poetry is a "second Mistris" for whom he feels "especiall affection," and who supplies the poet with "the plaister of absence" (244). But Jack contends that this verbal "plaister" is itself an empty surrogate for his own sexualized and material language. Surrey's muse is an absent and idealized angel, whereas Jack's good stuff is inspired by the *bona roba* who is present in the room. Surrey's verse shows a "supernaturall kinde of wit," one "conuersant in the heauen of Arts" with a "Paradized perfection" (242). But Jack knows that "earth is earth, flesh is flesh," and that "plaine dealing" wins the day over "those nice tearmes of chastitie and continencie" (245).

Jack's own aesthetic is clarified when his master concocts poems to the absent Geraldine in images of "[a]ll soule, no earthly flesh" (254). Her breasts, Surrey warbles, toss his spirit out of this world of turmoil. In fact, Surrey transforms the courtesan Diamante into his Petrarchan mistress, and then he awards her with "body-wanting mots" (271). At this stroke, Jack concludes that Surrey "was more in loue with his own curious forming fancie than her face; and truth it is, many become passionate louers onely to winne praise to theyr wits" (262). When Jack's own prose wins the favors of the *bona roba*, he leaves us to conclude that good stuff yields gratification ("it doth me good when I remember her" [261]) and material profit (she "made vp my market" [263]). The servant derives a mutual relation between the fat of Diamante and the body of his prose: if he produces a sexual prowess from prose, Jack also finds good verbal stuff in sex, since Diamante has "metall inough in her to make a good wit of" (261). And "stuff" has energy and movement as well as "metall": for it is Surrey who harps in composing "euery thing vnder the name of his loue" (262). "Could no man remoue him," Jack declares; and he proceeds to dismiss a grave old man's Euphuistic diatribe against travel with the same impatience.[8]

Surrey's romantic tournament in honor of Geraldine clinches the parody of deciphering. One by one, the knights parade by Jack, each bearing an emblem that serves to "characterize" some quality. Among them is the image of duplicity: "His horse was harnessed with leaden chaines, hauing the out-side guilt, or at least saffrond in sted of gilt, to decypher a holy or golden pretence of a couetous purpose" (274). If this blazon seems politic, the others are opaque at best, silly at worst, and they lead Jack into the slough of interpretation: "What his meaning was herein I cannot imagine" (276). Only the decipherers might know for sure.

By contrast to the rhetoric of romance, Jack celebrates the artificial plenty of a banqueting house that belongs to a merchant. Not only is the owner a venter of goods; his house is crammed so full with materials that it leaves no gap or vent: "Forsoth ye tail of the siluer pipe stretcht it selfe into the mouth of a great paire of belowes, where . . . it coulde not stirre or haue anie vent betwixt" (283). Jack exposes the "inrinded" mechanics and the "intrailes" of this upstart paradise; and he revels, too, in its replacement of an incorporeal poetics. Failing any "body-wanting mots," the house features "bodies without soules, and sweete resembled substances without sense" in its "seconde part of the gorgeous Gallerie of gallant deuices" (282-83). As if this were not enough to make the house a stuffer's Eden, it has two modes of operation. Jack takes a peek behind the scenes at the machinery, but he also confesses that this merchant's garden maintains its plenty as if "by inchantment." Any proser who must supply as if by magic would find pleasure in this house.

The banqueting house shows how faith can be works, and works faith, in a perfectly stuffed text of the world. It is not surprising that a theological debate over "works" makes it way into the travelogue. Jack complains that the Roman Catholics perform deeds of charity to the shame of "vs protestants": "if good workes may merite heauen, they doe them, we talke of them" (285). This remark warrants some doubt about the motives of works, for all their simple power: "Whether supersticion or no makes them vnprofitable seruants, that let pulpits decide; but there you shall haue the brauest ladies, in gownes of beaten golde, washing pilgrimes & poore souldiers feete" (285). Rome is, of course, no perfect image of heaven, "of which *Mercators* globe is a perfecter modell than thou art" (285). The works that one finds there might very well be flawed.

But there is no corruption in the banqueting house: "No poysonous beast there reposed, (poyson was not before our parent *Adam* transgressed)" (284). The stuff of this garden is a sinless remnant of the unfallen world. Jack, however, is faced with one nightmare after another—with the most fallen of all worlds. He cannot remain in the garden. Here, we find the point of the rivalries between the best of all stuffs—material and forceful, but troubled by rape, treachery, and impasse—and the absurd decipherings of orator, poet, and knight. Jack is a survivor who must bracket the problems of faith and works and simply forge ahead in the morass of European culture. Like Nashe, Jack is a working proser who can only hypothesize (or "recall") an ideal stuff. But this ideal, however compromised, is certain to triumph over a deciphering whose notions of a sufficient discourse are weak and irrelevant in the fashionings of a culture. For the fallen world in which Jack must work and survive is none other than the world that commenced from the Cloth of Gold and Henry VIII, the first of "vs protestants." It is the past, present, and future—the fact and the fiction—of a church and a state whose Elizabethan government was presumed to be settled and established—the best of all possible nations. In this light, we must consider not just the horrific stuffs of disembowelled and violated bodies, but Jack's attempts to exit from his narrative and to return to the Tudor fold.

Falling in a Fallen World

Jack's travels are a stuffer's nightmare. There are the disembowellings—potential and actual—which lend Jack an uncanny sense of his most basic materials or "intrailes." And then there are the holes and vents: Jack lands into prison, falls through a doorway, and views the "sad spectacle" of rape "thorough a crannie of [his] vpper chamber vnseeled" (295). The world resembles a sieve: thus Jack vanishes through the "cellar doore of a Iewes house . . . being vnbard on the in-side, ouer head and eares [he] fell into it, as a man falls in a shippe from the oreloope into the hold, or as in an earth-quake the ground should open, and a blinde man come feeling pad pad ouer the open Gulph with his staffe, should tumble on a sodaine into hell" (303). If some vents open, others surfeit: "death araid in a stinking smoak stopt his nostrels and cramd it selfe ful into his mouth that closed vp his fellows eyes" (286).

Among such extremes of vacuity and plenty, Jack's narrative task makes him weary and anxious: "Hauing worne out the anguish of my fal a little with wallowing vp & downe, I cast vp myne eyes to see vnder what Continent I was" (303–4). So the traveler must climb out of one hole after another to locate as best he can the point to which his tale has unfolded. But sometimes he just wants to exit from the tale altogether, for instance, with the rape of Heraclide: "Coniecture the rest, my words sticke fast in the myre and are cleane tyred; would I had neuer vndertooke this tragicall tale" (292). Jack's desire for closure makes him impatient with details: as he looks for cunning schemes by which to escape from his tormentors, Jack resorts to such narrative shortcuts as nonce phrases ("such & such") and indirect discourse (to make "short worke" of what he "heard" [315]). He begins to rein in his tale at will: "[n]ot too much of this . . . at once" (309); "[s]pare we him a line or two, and looke backe" (306); "[m]arke the ending, marke the ending" (310). And he defends the vents that help his narrative: "such & such consultation through the creuise of the doore hard lockt did I heare betwixt them. . . . [d]enie it if they can, I will iustifie it" (314).

Thus, Jack pursues a control over narrative and reader alike. To this end, he develops an interest in those plots that are prevalent in Greene's discovery phase: the jests at the beginning of the tale, the coney-catching stratagems with Zachary and Zadoch, and above all the repentance and conversion of Jack and Diamante. All of these facets of Jack's narrative point toward a complicity between stuff and discovery. As the *bona roba* is transformed into the honest whore, so, too, Jack's verbal stuff looks to discovery for closure and release from the somatic nightmare of his travels, with bodies stuffed and unstuffed in their violation.

Jack has devoted his verbiage to filling up the seemingly endless "conueyance" of events in his fictive history. His recourse to discovery is the main, though not the only, response to the stuff of a manifold narrative. At times Jack is flippant: as a guide to the attractions of Rome, he forgets details because he "did not beholde with anie care hereafter to report" them (280). He cuts strands of the story with the same feckless abandon: "That theame was quickly cut off, & other talke entered in place, of what I haue forgot, but talke it was, and talke let it be, & talke it shall be, for I do not meane here to remember it" (269). Even the author, Nashe, repudiates the "vein" of manifold narrative—the "continuate subiect of wit" (III.320)—in his preface.

But when his travels bring pain and torment, Jack can hardly pretend not to care about the details. And pain for Jack always involves the basic materials of his body. He is compelled to imagine his own anatomy. In a dark chamber where he awaits his demise, Jack can feel how every sensation bores a hole in his body, and how every flea pricks his flesh. He dreams of wound-closing medicines, but he wakes to the imminence of ulcers, bloodthinners, and slices. Venting his fears, Jack prays that his soul will find no vent: "a pimple rose with heate in that parte of the veyne where they vse to pricke, and I fearfully misdeemed it was my soule searching for passage. . . . [f]ie vpon it, a mans breath to bee let out at a backe doore" (308). He can fill the space only with images of the stuff at hand: parings, excrement, and other bodily matter. As Diamante, the *bona roba*, is Jack's muse, so his body turns into a master trope for the narrative from which he would escape.[9]

We often see Jack in prisons from which he longs to escape; and sometimes this desire finds some cranny through which he can survey the space beyond the prison. Thus, the "travailer" projects himself out of his traps in anticipation of the stratagems that will free him from the stone walls and iron bars. But these stratagems join other resources of discovery—conversion, repentance, narrative editorial—in helping Jack to fashion a moralized closure to the endless rambles of his travels. The finale is a sticking point for modern readers of

Jack's tale. These readers are not convinced by the chiliastic ending—which includes the honest Jack and Diamante, the confessions of Cutwolfe, the invocations of a providential Last Judgment, and the tying of loose ends, "like the three brothers that went three seuerall wayes to seeke their fortunes, & at the yeeres end at those three crosse waies met againe, and told one another how they sped" (316). But the discomfort caused by such plotting should not blind us to both the comfort and dis-ease it offers Jack.

Indeed, *The Unfortunate Traveller* covers the ground of Greene's discoveries, from reductive jests and tricks to conversion and repentance. But discovery, we recall, fought for its difference from mere desire or projection. The same fight pertains to stuff. We have seen the stuffer insist that his material prose is already out there in the world—not merely a product of his own wits. Nonetheless, this same stuffer is inspired by the extemporal and vital production of his prose—what might be called his "ventings." Stuff and discovery begin to converge in strange and complex ways. Discovery can allow Jack to escape from the slough of his narrative, with a moralized closure in tow. But discovery has much the same subversive baggage as stuff. Both kinds of prose must fashion narrative as if narrative were always already fashioned. Perhaps for Nashe, discovery is yet another product of the stuffer. After all, the Jack who generates catalogues of "intrailes" is the same Jack who invents jests and escapes through the final conversion to honesty.

In the end, Jack returns to England in the exhausted "triumph" of marital honesty and narrative closure. He announces his faith in God's own notable discoveries—"[s]trange and wonderfull are Gods iudgements"—and in the tale itself, which should "adde to [our] faith" (320). But this final creed is as "vnsearchable" as Jack's future in Tudor England. When we hear that Cutwolfe's mind is "as great as a gyants" (320), we know that his execution replaces Jack's own—Jack having resigned his spontaneous and presumptuous wits to God and king. As Jack arrives in the golden kingdom of Henry VIII, the endless supply and unpatched botchery of the Tudor settlement are just beginning, ready for those rifts to be opened by the marprelates and unthrifts. Perhaps Jack can no longer be numbered among the unthrifts, however incredible his conversion may be. But it is no wonder that the work closest in time to the doubt and violence of *The Unfortunate Traveller* is *Christs Teares*. This pamphlet has all the complexities of a historical narrative, but it justifies its labors to repair England in the name of Christ's reparation of souls. Such an aim proves to intensify the problems of stuff so much that Nashe is led to a forthright defense of his material words.

Patching the Temple

Christs Teares has been scorned (for the most part) and applauded (in one case) for the fustian with which it personifies Christ and rants about desolation. Aggrandizing its own rhetoric, the work writes large the claim that words can assume a remedial presence within a degraded status quo.[10] By turns, Nashe announces and retracts his contributions to the healing of a city for which he will soon renounce all responsibility in *Lenten Stuffe*. But this game of hide-and-seek does not conceal the fundamental duties of Nashe's prose. His work must redress the "word-dearthing" vacuities of sin and misery (II.69). Words must find passage into every soul—must "peirce vnawares into the marrow and reynes of my Readers" (15)—and then supply or cement that passage with the healing salve of judgment and redemption. From Mar-Martin to preacher, the proser believes that his incarnate stuff is perfect for the vents of transgression.

Vents abound in the images of *Christs Teares*. The savior's own tears, eyes, and heart look for passage:

> So penetrating and eleuatedly haue I prayd for you, that mine eyes woulde fayne haue broke from theyr anchors to haue flowne vp to Heauen, and myne armes stretcht more then the length of my body to reach at the Starres. My heart ranne full-butt against my breast to haue broken it open, and my soule flutterd and beate with her ayrie-winges on euerie side for passage. (37)

The temple itself "was no more a prayer-prospering House, but a pudlie Vault of dead-mens bones and cast-out bodies kneaded to durte. . . . Her hie roofe was mingle-coloured with mounting drops of blood, that seemd, by soking into it, to seek for passage to heauen" (66–67). Hunger drives human tongues outward, too: "Their watry wesands were like to leape out of theyr mouthes for meate, and in theyr crawling vp to seeke passage, readie to haue beene seazd on by their iawes for sustenance" (69). The escape from hunger requires yet another passage; preparing to eat her child, Miriam frees him as well: "but one gappe broke ope [in the child], [his] entrance is made [into heaven]" (75). Between perdition and redemption, the vents of the city open everywhere, their seams unable to contain the gruesome stuffs of Jerusalem.

The bodily stuffs of Jerusalem are as ubiquitous as the vents. Moreover, Nashe suggests an analogy between the materials of the city and a language that might cement the passages in temple, soul, and narrative alike. Thus, the "young imperfect practitioner . . . in Christs schoole" compares his words to a "handfull of Ierusalems mummianizd earth" (9). This verbal "earth" is composed of glutted images ("bodies kneaded to durte" [67]), polysyllabic stock ("sacrificatory," "abhomination vnremissible" [66]), and the motivic words that link one paragraph to the next (for example, "stoniest," "astoniest," "stones"). With hyphens ready at hand, Nashe at once predicts and opposes the vents of desolation: "[since] you haue founded your Pallaces on the sands of your owne shalow conceits . . . the raine wil rough-enter through the crannies of theyr wauering, the Windes will blow and batter ope wide passages for the pashing shoures" (47).

Even so, the young scholar must deny the importance of his "owne shalow conceits" for the work of salvation. It is not enough that he invokes the patristic tradition and denounces the atheists who attempt to fill the supposed absence of God with their own "plenty and aboundance" (120). The narrator proceeds to hide himself behind the *prosopopeia* of Christ. As we will see, this figure is hardly safe, although Nashe declares that "[o]ur best methode to preuent this excluding [of God], or seperating from Gods presence, is heere on earth (what soeuer we goe about) to thinke we see him present" (170). The proser's best security is humility, and so Nashe denies the readiness of such young men as himself for divinity:

> Our Fathers are now growne to such austeritie, as they would haue vs straite of chyldren to become old-men. They will allowe no time for a gray bearde to grow in. If at the first peeping out of the shell a young Student sets not a graue face on it, or seemes not mortifiedly religious, (haue he neuer so good a witte, be hee neuer so fine a Scholler,) he is cast of and discouraged. (122–23)

Such youth are merely crammed with "grosse full-stomackt tautology," and with "Scripture . . . thicke and three-folde . . . so vgly daubed, plaistred, and patcht on, so peeuishly speckt & applyde, as if a Botcher (with a number of Satten and Veluette shreddes) should cloute and mend Leather-doublets & Cloth-breeches" (123–24). The temple, rent by sin and desolation, cannot depend on their texts, even the ones "plaistred" with scripture.

But Nashe also must decide the extent to which his stuff is indebted to the best of all fillers, the word of God. An analogy to fabric shows how the proser can debase the Bible: "Scripture we hotch-potch together, & doe not place it like Pearle and Gold-lace on a garment, heere & there to adorne, but pile it and dunge it vp on heapes, without vse or edification. . . . Out it flyes East and West; though we loose it all it is nothing, for more haue we" (127). Nashe's own stuff served as ornamental finery in *The Terrors;* but here, such a function for Scripture is posed against the careless dispersal of its resources. The expense of God's word resembles nothing more than the sieve of avarice, whose "Cart . . . is [so] ouer-loden or crammed . . . [that it] hath a tayle that will scatter" (105). And something more seems at stake in the loss of Scripture: for it is a model for the incarnate prose that Nashe invents and thrusts into the desolate holes of the city.

Against the loss of his own stuff, Nashe asserts that Scripture is the "last seale to confirme any thing," the "corner stone, to close vp any building" (127). Even those key words—"stoniest" and "gather"—derive from the Bible and therefore "close vp" the edifice of Nashe's own text. A biblical phrase can fill the vents of desolation because it is supremely full: "If but one lyne . . . included all this, what doth the whole Scripture include? Not a peece of a lyne in it that talkes of the Lake of fire and Brimstone, but by a hundred thousand parts more importeth" (79). Politic decipherers must beware of such a language because it amounts to a "ball of Wild-fire round wrapt vp together, which burneth not but cast foorth, a close winded clue, conducting those that deale vnaduisedlie with it, into the Minotaurs Laborinth of payne euerlasting" (79–80). By contrast, the earnest reader is fed with the "power and authoritie" of the saving word (19).

In a preface to the second edition of *Christs Teares,* Nashe defends the unconventional language with which he has lamented the transgressions of the city. But his most radical italics for good stuff are formed by the extended *prosopopeia* of Christ. The stuffer frames the passage with hypothesis: to begin, "[t]he more to penetrate and inforce, let vs suppose Christ in a continued Oration thus pleading with them" (21); and to end, "[h]eere doe I confine our Sauiours collachrimate Oration, and putting off his borrowed person, restore him to the tryumphancie of his Passion. . . . [n]ow priuately (as mortall men) let vs consider howe his threats were after verified in *Ierusalems* ouer-turne" (60). The narrator is something of a Proteus throughout his tale: "Heere begins the *desolation* Christ prophecied . . . [l]et me suddainly waxe olde, and woe-wrinckle my cheekes before theyr tyme, by describing the deplored effectes of theyr sinnes within" (65). But the most urgent new persona is Christ, whose quasi-presence offers to stop the leaky vessels of sin and misery: "Not the least hayre of my body, but may it be as a pegge in a vessell, to broche bloode with plucking out, so in the droppings of that bloode *Ierusalem* will bathe herselfe" (54). With the soul of a city on the line, Nashe gives us yet another hypothesis in which the stopgap is both here and not here.

Thus, the figure giving voice to Christ promises an astonishing but elusive guarantee of incarnation in the text and the world at large. What is more, theories of *prosopopeia* clarify this peculiar trope for the corporeal stuff of Nashe's prose. For instance, deconstructive critics argue that *prosopopeia* most summarily figures the absence of a transcendental signified from all language. Language, they claim, defers the presence of truth or self and resists any simple mimesis of nature; the world itself writes the ghostly absence of language. For Paul de Man, *prosopopeia* merges with Saussure's and Riffaterre's "hypogram" in proposing to emphasize "'a name, a word, by trying to repeat its syllables, and thus giving it another, artificial, mode of being added, so to speak, to the original mode of being of the word.'"[11] But, says de Man, the cosmetic "giving face" of this figure "implies that the original face can be missing or nonexistent."[12] The "hallucination" of an original face is comparable, moreover, to the undecidability of dreams (the sleeper dreams that he or she is awake)—to, that is, the "hypothesis of dreaming."[13] The desire for presence leads the critic—in this case, Riffaterre—to require the "actualization" of the anagram as a "confirmation of the phenomenality of language." In other words, there is no anagram on "gold" in "right holding" because the "g" in "right" is silent. For de Man, the reversal of this error toward figuration spells the "dismemberment" of the hypogrammatical word, the rhetorical overthrow of "semantic determination," and, in sum, our inability to refuse "the textual inscription of semantic determinants within a non-determinable system of figuration."[14] Language is always already giving face to the (absent) face "beneath" the text.

Without invoking de Man, Jonathan V. Crewe exposes the ways in which Nashe's "unredeemed rhetoric" betrays its linguistic claim to truth or even to a subject.[15] As Crewe remarks, Nashe is inevitably a pawn in our own debates about status of language; and *Christs Teares* is perfectly suited to a dismantling of logocentrism. But de Man's theory of *prosopopeia* can also serve as a pawn for recovering Nashe's specific dilemma about the quasi-materiality of his "stuff." I have already argued that Nashe likens his words to the undecidable presence of dreams, hypotheses, and spirits (so de Man, on the "phantasms of dismemberment" [37]). And like Riffaterre's hypograms, Nashe's logocentric motifs are dispersed throughout the text of *Christs Teares*. With *prosopopeia*, Nashe wants to materialize the presence of the *Logos*—if not of Christ, then of words approximating the phenomenal force of Christ incarnate. But such a desire for incarnation is problematic even for those Renaissance allegorists at the top of the literary hierarchy, never mind the lowly servants who write a marprelatanized prose.

Abraham Fraunce can speak for the rhetorical handbooks on what one modern scholar has called the purest form of allegory, the "personified abstraction."[16] According to Fraunce, *prosopopeia* "is a fayning of any person, when in our speech we represent the person of anie, and make it speake as though he were there present."[17] Whether "imperfect" (brief) or "perfect" ("fully and lively," [G2v])—and Nashe uses both for Christ—this figure underscores the "as if" of the added face, and acknowledges only a quasi-presence. The original can be inanimate ("dumme and senceless," [G5r]) or fictive; but, in any case, the allegory is a "fayning." When Nashe gives voice to or puts on the person of Christ, he intensifies the basic questions about stuff: about its uncertain status, and about its remedial place behind yet also in the world. Thus, the great irony of Nashe's stuff is not simply that the *Logos* is always already absent; presence and absence are much more vexed for him than that. The irony of his career is that the anxious position of the stuffer leads him, in *Lenten Stuffe*, to eschew presence (of the world in language, of language in the world) and to embrace absence with all his might, only to realize that the world is inescapably figured in his texts. The world clings to the soon-to-be banished books that he has written. In sum, then, Nashe cannot quit the culture in which he writes; his nightmare becomes the recurring dream of presence, not of absence. When he boasts a somatic prose, he must fear its absence; but when he proclaims its absence in lenten stuff, he must fret its tenacious presence in the England of Elizabeth. As Paul de Man himself writes: "[t]his does not mean that fictional narratives are not part of the world and of reality; their impact upon the world may well be all too strong for comfort" (11).

When the narrator "suddainely" transforms himself into the persona of Christ, he credits stuff with some elusive substantiation. His own language is presumed to mingle with and, in some measure, to create the scriptural "cornerstone" on which is prose is founded. Nashe has insisted that scripture provides the textual cement; but *prosopopeia* suggests—with dreams, daimons, and hypotheses—that stuff is both present in and absent from that cement, or that stuff has somehow turned into the face of Christ. As usual, Nashe displays his ambivalence about prose in his treatment of good works. At first he is prepared to celebrate verbal deeds: "If in your bodies you haue done no good works, of God you shall receiue no good words. . . . [t]he words of God are deeds; he spake but the word, and Heauen & Earth were made" (104). But if the proser imitates God in creating

"Bulwarks raysed vp against the deuill," he adds a brief reference ("Good deedes deriued from fayth") and a marginal note ("[i]t is not my meaning in all this discourse of good deeds to seioyne any of them from Fayth") in order to diminish the saving value of works (104). Even Christ rebukes himself for failing to convert the people. The Savior vents his feelings in powerful words, but he is not heard; his one cross is not enough, for "thy sinne exceedeth my suffering" (35). Christ admits, too, that his words only defer the death providing the means for salvation. As he becomes the scapegoat for the world, Christ is unsure about the force of his own prose.

But Christ makes room for other prosers when he welcomes their tears: "Hee that can weepe with more soule-martirdome then I, let him take vppon him to wash (in my stead) the earths Ethiopian face" (54). Such weepers will be needed all the more when the Savior is no longer present; but his surrogates, including the inventive author, risk a sinful pride in being "Luciferous passionatiue-ambitious" to attempt the "full blast of this *desolatiue*-Trumpet" (60). Thus, the task of the venter—"a weake breath or two I will writhe into it" (60)—and the profundity of the vent ("desolation") are enough to daunt the secret agent who applies his prose to the wounds of the city. This agent fears the very sins that he describes: "Were it not that in reprouing Contention I might haply seeme contentious, I woulde wade a little farther in thys subiect" (134); and "[e]uen in thys dilatement against Ambition, the deuill seekes to sette in a foote of affected applause and popular fames Ambition in my stile" (87). In addition to a catalogue of punished rebels, Nashe offers an estimate of musicians who have been punished for their "odde fantasticke vaine-glorious" wits (109). While "fantasticke" allows them a spontaneity and imagination prized by Nashe, their fantasias, we are told, are vain. London should learn from Jerusalem's "a whoring after her own inuentions" (16). Both cities should remember the source of their abundance, unlike the householder whose parable Nashe retells.

"Whoring" links stuff and sin even further. When Nashe launches into a diatribe against the *bona roba*, he attacks her cosmetics as well:

> Euen as Angels are painted in Church-windowes with glorious golden fronts besette with Sunne-beames, so beset they theyr fore-heads on eyther side with glorious borrowed gleamy bushes; which, rightly interpreted, shold signifie beauty to sell, since a bushe is not else hanged forth but to inuite men to buy. (137)

We have seen that Jack Wilton associates sex and the *bona roba* with the power of his language. In *Have With You to Saffron-Walden*, Nashe compares the two good stuffs in deriding Harvey. But with the indictment of cosmetics in *Christs Teares*, the stuffer confronts his own giving of face. That prostitutes thrive in the marketplace is no surprise. The analogy between their faces and the "Angels . . . painted in Church-windowes" does, however, give us pause. Poets like George Herbert may believe that stained glass filters the light of grace and affirms a life in which faith and works coincide.[18] But these windows stand, too, for an established church in its fight against those rebels who despise any such ecclesiastical patchwork. Just as the rival factions debate the proper cornerstone and face of the church, so, too, Nashe's own prose must fret its cosmetics—for the orthodox church hired his prose not just for its material force but, in some sense, for its mediating "fronts."

Thus, when Nashe resists his proximity to the *bona roba*, perhaps he sees an unpleasing image on her painted brow—his own. "Neuer was I admitted so neere any of you," he declares, "I dare not meddle with yee, since the Phylosopher that too intentiuely gaz'd on the starres stumbled & fell into a ditch" (138). And yet he goes on and on with the invective, long enough for the distracted reader to recall that Plato derived the cosmetics of a pleasurable rhetoric from the leaky vessel of the soul. We have seen that such a leaky vessel is the stuffer's nightmare; indeed, the *bona roba* takes abuse for venting her body in much the same way that Nashe will for pandering to the city with his own corporeal prose.

Notable Typologies

In a work offering to reform the body and soul of London, then, we find the heightened dilemmas of Nashe's somatic prose. But the proser is not all fear and trembling; he is ready and willing to defend the force and presence of a single word:

> Though all the men that euer God made were hundred handed like *Briareus*, and shoulde all at once take pennes in theyr hundred handes, and doe nothing in a whole age together but sette downe in Figures & characters as many myllions or thousands as they could, so many millions or thousands could they neuer set down as this worde of three sillables, *Eternall*, includeth; an Ocean of yncke would it draw dry to describe it. (169)

"Figures & characters" have little force when compared to the single word. Only with such powerful words can Nashe assume the role of a preacher who conveys with "words of course" (168) the desolation of sin and hell. In other words, the proser who dons the person of Christ cannot afford to "decipher"; no jaded trope or body-wanting mot will do.

But *prosopopeia* asks more of the proser than his most forceful words. For invented speech contributes to the already layered narrative structure of *Chrisis Teares*. To begin with, many Renaissance writers accept the convention of a set speech from the classical historians. Yet, these same writers hold complex views about the relationship between fact and fiction.[19] Some Tudor historians in verse and prose take care in dividing fiction and fact, at least ideally. Others follow the unfortunate traveler in unleashing the outrageous interplay between the two realms. I argue in the next chapter that the vexed relations between fact and fiction affect Nashe's defense of good stuff. In *Chrisis Teares*, however, fact and fiction converge in the fable by which Nashe compares London to Jerusalem. Like Jack Wilton, the narrator of this historical fiction attempts to fashion order and closure with the help of notable discovery.

In *Chrisis Teares*, Nashe relies on historical resources of some complexity. Josephus is not Nashe's primary or immediate source, but his history of the Jewish War gives a clearer picture of the problems in historiography to which Nashe alludes so often in his later works. Josephus confesses to (and was infamous for) venting his emotions over the fall of Jerusalem. But Nashe's favorite historiographer, Bodin, thought Josephus to be faithful to recorded fact.[20] Nashe's account of the destruction of the temple carries the difficulties of historical narration a step further. He is not so worried about separating emotion from fact as he is about closing the gap between sixteenth-century England and the Roman Empire. The schemes with which he proposes to fill this divide are analogy or typology, which lead Nashe to notable discovery. The contemporary historian, William Harrison, once wrote that history features "certaine period[s] of . . . notable alteration."[21] In pursuit of order and closure, Nashe posits a network of comparisons between two such notable periods.

In its most conventional sense, typology draws lines between the notable events of scriptural history. But it also allows for new, fictive relations between myth and non-biblical, historical events. Thus, its discovery of a notable schema intersects with the convergence of fact and fiction or, we might say, of the world and stuff. Now, Nashe's typological schemes are for the most part simple. Christ's tears over Jerusalem reach from both testaments into the future of the New Jerusalem. And the Savior's words are "vnfallibly . . . fulfilled," even as he fulfills the Law (67). But with such a guarantee, Nashe extends the schema of type and anti-type away from its strictly scriptural basis into all of history. As Robert Hollander says of typology in secular literature, this historical license permits the introduction of fictions or "inventions" into the analogical schemes.[22] But typology involves still other variables: according to Barbara Kiefer Lewalski, the position of the author matters, too. For instance, reformed theologians emphasize the individual experience of typology.[23]

Like *prosopopeia*, then, typology entertains the many facets of stuff—truth, fiction, redemption, and the author's own wits. But it does so within the schema of discovery. For this reason, typology serves Nashe in his pursuit of a controlled narrative; indeed, it offers the effects of what one modern critic calls its sequence of "provisional and 'fulfilled' meanings," in contrast with the never-fulfilled cycles of "repressing and reconstructing, of forgetting and remembering" in the Old Testament.[24] Whatever the uncertainties of stuff, Nashe can assert the "period[s] of . . . notable alteration" against the desolation of the city. His recourse to the schemes of discovery may bracket the vexed and troubled relations between stuff, the world, and the author. But as the fustian mounts against the citizens of the world and the world itself, Nashe invokes a veritable army of motifs from Greene's later pamphlets: the "mourning garment" of conversion, the Judgment Day, the watchmen of the city, and even coney-catching. And he understands the editorial demands of "trussing vp" the fable: "The worlde woulde count me the most licentiate loose strayer vnder heauen, if I shoulde vnrippe but halfe so much of their veneriall machiauelisme as I haue lookt into. . . . [w]e haue not English words enough to vnfold it" (153). Here, Nashe links his two most pressing concerns: the reduction of his narrative and the force of his best "English words."

As in *The Unfortunate Traveller*, stuff and discovery aid and abet one another in surviving the fallen world. But they also mirror each other's troubles. "As I haue lookt into": these words remind us that both the stuffer and the discoverer can be charged with too much self-projection. Nashe is prepared to defend his prose for its obedience to the spirit of salvation, and for the materials that it fashions. His main defense appears in a preface to a later edition of *Christs Teares*.[25] When Nashe defends that work and *The Unfortunate Traveller* against his readers, he contrasts deciphering and stuffing in the clearest of terms. But this defense of his material language ushers in a final controversy with Harvey and the authorities, which leads Nashe to revise altogether the worldly status of his prose. In the next chapter, we will look at these apologies, then at the revisions toward a lenten stuff.

5
NASHE'S EMPTY STUFF

In a letter attached to the second edition of *Christs Teares* (1594), Nashe defends his "stuff" against its enemies. In particular, he attacks those readers who distort his texts for political reasons. He calls these readers "new decipherers,"

> that seeke in my *Iacke Wilton* to anagrammatize the name of Wittenberge to one of the Vniuersities of England, that scorn to be counted honest plaine meaning men like their neighbours, for not so much as out of mutton and potage but they wil construe a meaning of Kings and Princes. . . . Infinite number of these phanatical strange hierogliphicks haue these new decipherers framed to them selues, & stretch words on the tenter hooks so miserably. . . . For my part I would wish them not to deceiue them selues with the spirit of inspiration without proofe, or confound Logicke by making no difference betwixt *probabile* and *manifeste verum*. (II.182)

The "new decipherers" are indeed a far cry from Greene's old ones, who simply represented an essence in rhetorical patterns. The new decipherers rewrite narratives in the distorted image of their political interests. They produce readings that, for all their claims on the "spirit of inspiration," amount to torture. Or, to put it another way, Nashe offers a meal ("mutton and potage"), which these guests digest into topical and political matter.

In this chapter, I will look further at the defense of material language set forth in this letter. It just precedes the two works, *Have With You to Saffron-Walden* and *Lenten Stuffe*, in which Nashe retracts his prose from the world. To this end, he questions its veracity—that is, the relations between his texts and "histories." The casual mention of "*probabile* and *manifeste verum*" is only one of the growing number of times in which Nashe invokes the skeptical criteria for historiography. In *Have With You*, Nashe takes a certain madcap pride in his service to history—in the shaping hand that he thrusts into the narrative of the past. But in the same work, he transfers the presumptions of such a service to Harvey, who is awarded with a new muse, the *bona roba*. Thus, *Have With You* prepares us for the revision of "stuff" in *Lenten Stuffe*, where Nashe proposes a fictive void for his inventions. Lenten stuff is conceived as mere play—empty and segregated from the dangerous work of maintaining the kingdom and its narratives.

But in *Lenten Stuffe* the void of fiction is set next to the realm of fact: Nashe draws a line between the history and the myth of a town and its fish. He urges us to believe in this division—one that poets and historians alike were beginning to make and to assume. But the line between fact and fiction—between a record of the world and the invention of myth—is elusive for Nashe. He removes stuff from the world, but the world still speaks in the fiction, and the fiction in the world. Or so the playful rhetoric of *Lenten Stuffe* reminds us against its own stated intentions. Nashe's responses to the problem of his empty stuff are several. For one thing, he takes some parting shots at the new decipherers, never confessing that his new stuff bears some resemblance to the empty stylistics of the old decipherers. For another, he refuses to dwell on the dire consequences that result if his lenten stuff is betrayed by language and politics. But above all, the proser isolates his inventions in a void, not as a sign that he has repudiated the status quo, but at least in part as a show of his submission to their wishes that he leave the world alone. In sum, the dualism between fact and fiction in *Lenten Stuffe* entails a troubled freedom for Nashe and his incarnate prose.

In Defense of New Coinage

The letter attached to the second edition of *Christs Teares* is important for its description of Nashe's material language. But we can appreciate the letter more fully if we take note of Nashe's final assaults on traditional rhetoric. In *Have With You*, Nashe asserts that both kinds of deciphering—that which interprets and that which "depaints"—are political outlets for duplicity. This convergence of the two differs somewhat from the attack on the silly poetics of Surrey and the knights, where any political tension was muted next to the problem of Nashe's misreaders.

In *Have With You*, Carneades is a participant in a dialogue with the embattled "Nashe," and he exhorts the latter not to worry so much about Harvey's "Rhetoricall figure of amplification." Nashe responds:

> Rhetoricall figure? and if I had a hundred sonnes, I had rather haue them disfigur'd, & keep them at home as cyphers, than send them to schoole to learn to figure it after that order. (III.120)

Agreeing with this retort, Carneades assails the political dishonesty that motivates tropes and figures:

> You may haue them worse brought vp, for so you should be sure neuer to haue them counted lyers, since Rhetoricians, though they lye neuer so grosely, are but said to haue a luxurious phrase, to bee eloquent amplifiers, to bee full of their pleasant Hyperboles, or speake by Ironies; and if they raise a slaunder vpon a man of a thing done at home, when hee is a 1000. mile off, it is but Prosopopeya, personae fictio . . . and they will alledge Tully, Demosthenes, Demades, Aeschines, and shew you a whole Talaeus & Ad Herennium of figures for it, foure and fiftie times more licentious. These Arithmetique figurers are such like iugling transformers, lying by Addition and Numeration, making frayes and quarrelling by Diuision, getting wenches with childe by Multiplication, stealing by Substraction. (120)

As Surrey desires the absence of his mistress, so these rhetoricians (and their "cypher" students) claim an empty, if traditional, fiction for their slanders. But their lies resemble bad math—they fool no one but the most foolish of readers. Of course, Nashe aims to set Harvey among these decipherers as a reward for the doctor's "poeticizing" hexameters and jaded themes. It is, moreover, this final attempt to answer Harvey that leads Nashe to the brink of an empty stuff.

As a rival to these traditions of political rhetoric, Nashe must defend the presence and the force of his own honest prose. He bristles at Harvey's suggestion that Nashe's pages are "stufft . . . with hearbs & stones" in the manner of Euphuism, and responds that he would sooner cram feces in Harvey's mouth (132). Indeed, the task of his prose involves just this: venting a stuff that will protect the world from the doctor's lies. However parodic it may be—and Lorna Hutson dismisses the whole issue as such—Nashe returns time and again to the historical dimension of his task. The stuffer is exhorted by his "friends" to set the story straight, even if that means inventing a life of Harvey in which the story is fictive at best, crooked at worst. For Nashe, too, we know, has some familiarity with "Prosopopeya, personae fictio."

From the outset, Nashe's friends remind him that the "reasonable conueyance of historie" (II.201) depends on him: "there is an age to come, which, knowing neither thee nor him, but by your seuerall workes iudging of either, will authorise all hee hath belched forth in thy reproach for sound Gospell" (III.27). Moreover, Nashe considers other historians who have betrayed the future with their dishonesty or neglect. He alludes to the debate over Polydore Vergil's negative evidence for disproving British legends, and to the claim that he "burnt all the ancient Records of the true beginning of this our Ile, after hee had finished his Chronicle" (23). Then there is the more traditional warning about reading histories, that we "bee not nimis credulos aut incredulos, too rash or too slow of beleefe" (23). In addition, he cites a number of historical resources, from Bale's *Acts of the English Votaries* to Bodin's *Methodus ad Historiarum Cognitionem*. And he worries about dilemmas in historiography—for example, the fact that time erases evidence: "Hast thou not heard howe Orpheus wrote in the 2700. age of the world . . . yet his memorie is fresh . . . whereas all the Kings that raignd and suruiude at that time haue not so much as the first letter of their names to posterity commended" (28). These playful references to history prepare us not just for the radical moves of *Lenten Stuffe*, but for the defense of Nashe's wit and language in *Christs Teares* and *Have With You*.

Whether in the name of Christ or against the name of Harvey, Nashe asserts that "witte" and history must help each other to prevail: "I am content my witte should take vppon it antiquitie this once, and nothing else in my defence I will alledge but *Veritas Temporis filia*, it is onely time that reuealeth all things" (28–29). With the passage of time, history always comes true, but wit helps ensure the truth of "antiquitie." The truth may be moral rather than factual, but the close relation between history and stuff leads Nashe to celebrate his own wit as the spontaneous and inventive faculty behind the somatic prose of *Christs Teares* and *Have With You*. The letter added to *Christs Teares* is a major part of this defense.

Having been accused of "prophane eloquence . . . [and] boystrous compound wordes," Nashe appeals in his letter to the "high rauishte" nature of the Christian grand style, then to an *elocutio* that permits "more liberty of Tropes, Figures, and Metaphors, and alleadging Heathen examples and Histories" (II.183). But these colors and instances come too close to the rival poetics of deciphering. So Nashe resorts to defending his "boystrous compound wordes" in material terms. First, he likens his words to a new and bigger mintage, "often coyning of Italionate verbes which end all in Ize" (183). To these coins Nashe adds other materials: "Come, my maisters, inure your mouths to it, and neuer trust me but when you haue tride the commodity of carrying much in a small roome, you will, like the Apothecaries, vse more compounds then simples, and graft wordes as men do their trees to make them more fruitfull" (184). The mercantile and the natural converge in an artificial stuff that returns us to Puttenham's metaphor for decorum, the "graft." But Nashe is grafting one word to another, not meanings to their decorous covers. With one coin welded to another, Nashe can declare in another work that his material language rivals the very best traditions of copia: a heap of epithets for Dick Lichfield shows a "redundance of [Dick's] honorable Familie, and how affluent and copious thy name is in all places, though *Erasmus* in his *Copia verborum* neuer mentions it" (III.6).

Whatever its merits, the alchemy of Nashe's prose has to reckon with its kinship to yet another tribe of rhetorical alchemists—the sophists. The proser has faint praise for those sophists who can make the false seem true: "Singular happie are those that are acquainted with the true mixture of Alchimists musicall gold, and can, with *Platoes Gorgias*, proue vnrighteousnesse true godlinesse with a breath; they shall be prouided for sumptuously, when sooth and verity may walke melancholy in Marke Lane" (II.185). Of course, Nashe aligns his words with "sooth and verity." But, with two alchemists side by side, we wonder if his coin can be exchanged with Gorgias's. At this point it helps to remember that in the *Gorgias*, Plato derived sophistry from the leaky vessel of the soul—from a soul never really gratified by the nexus of cooking, cosmetics, and rhetoric.[1] The fears of the stuffer have always taken the shape of such a leaky vessel, with the risk that his stuff is finally counter to, or at least other than, "sooth and verity." Harvey is such an easy target that Nashe need not ponder the value of his coinage at any awkward length. But the questions of "verity" are not simply a game for Nashe, whose madcap prose has been hired—or has volunteered itself—to salve the scratched face of divinity, the terrors of the night, the desolation of the city, and the damage wrought by the foolish braggart, Gabriel Harvey.

Even when Nashe is most fervent about the power of his prose, he suggests both its triviality and its need for a "ground":

> There is a mountaine in *Cyrenaica* consecrated to the South-wind, which if it be toucht with a mans hand, there arise exceeding boystrous blastes, that tosse and turmoile the sands like waues of the Sea. As great a miracle as that in me is experienst, for let me but touch a peece of paper, there arise such stormes and tempestes about my eares as is admirable. Euen of sands and superficiall bubbles they will make hideous waues and dangerous quicke-sands. This is my last will and Testament: those that tosse at me, ile tosse at them againe if I can, always prouided it bee not a Tennice-play of Pots and Cups, like the Centaurs feast. Diuinity is the

ground-worke of my Booke, no more herein will I doe then shall haue his ground from Diuinity. (II.186)

Not only does Nashe hypothesize the best of his stuff, but he also suggests that, for all its force and "ground," his prose will vanish like bubbles or dreams. What is more, for all his bravado, Nashe is ready to exit from the world in which "Pots and Cups" serve as tennis balls. The removal of "stuff" from the realm of history, verity, and the world at large is the story of *Lenten Stuffe*. But before he divides fact from fiction in that work, he has one more job to do in which history and wit must mingle without shame. He must write the life of a doctor.

Materials for a Life of Doctor Harvey

The "Tennice-play" between Nashe and Harvey grew out of the Marprelate controversy; and it must have seemed difficult as time went on for Tom and Gabriel to decide how much duty called. In *Have With You*, the very title suggests a desire for closure. At a more subtle level, Nashe invokes the same kinds of discovery motifs that offered a scheme of order and closure to *The Unfortunate Traveller* and *Christs Teares*. Not only does Nashe give a "discovery" of Mother Harvey's dreams, but he couches the whole satire in a dialogue and aligns his subject with the "madde trickes" of coney-catchers. And Nashe concedes the importance of editing in a biography that spans "from [Harvey's] infancie to this present 96": "I must haue some further time to get perfect intelligence of his life and conuersation, one true point whereof, well set downe, wil more excruciate & commacerate him, than knocking him about the eares with his owne stile in a hundred sheetes of paper" (29). In other words, Nashe will differ from Harvey because his good stuff ("well set downe") will discover the notorious truth about the doctor. Readers are asked to forgive Nashe for forgetting the "ouer-flowing and numberlesse" details of the "whole piece," whose "[e]uerie circumstance I cannot stand to reckon vp" (92).

What results from Nashe's discoveries is a satirical biography in which fact and fiction—history and stuff—converge in order to tell the truth about Harvey once and for all. Thus, the author moves with dazzling speed between a reporter's offer to "particularize and stake downe the verie words" to some piece of evidence (132), and the outrageous fictions that may be true or apt in some undocumentable sense. For example, Nashe tells us with a straight face about the time when he and Harvey lodged back-to-back in a Cambridge inn. Then he proceeds to burlesque Harvey's arrest in the next room without even the benefit of the peephole through which Jack Wilton witnesses Heraclide's rape. At another point, Nashe mocks his own enterprise of filling out Harvey's life when the "biographer" leaves an empty space on the page for his readers to stuff.

Sometimes, Nashe plays dumb about the merit of his facts: "Whether [his report of the mother's dreams] be verifiable, or onely probably surmised, I am vncertaine" (62). We hear of Hakluyt and Herodotus, whose records dally at the line between the true and the fabulous; we also are reminded of Bodin's attack on Livy for cramming miracles into his Roman chronicles. But Nashe admits that he, too, has "thrust . . . in" the account of the porridge that Harvey is said to have served at Cambridge, although it helps to verify his matriculation there (64). The biographer protests that he has inserted nothing into Harvey's oration, "not so much as a knot to his winding sheete, or corner tip to the smallest seluage of his garments," indeed not "the least shadow of fiction" (42). If the "corner tip" recalls Nashe's earlier defense (in *The Terrors*) of his work on truth's garment, the oration itself is a satirical version of the fiction that is allowed in the invented speech of Christ or any other historical figure. As *prosopopeia*, the "continuat *Tropologicall* speach" (41) reveals the truth about Harvey's character "on my faith and saluation"—and it does so with the best stuff that Nashe can vent.

With every segment of the "life," Nashe weighs his own credibility. The tutor's letter is suspect: although "truth is truth . . . yet I will not positiuely affirme it his Tutors Letter neither, and yet you maye gather more than I am willing to vtter, and what you list not beleeue referre to after Ages, euen as *Paulus Iouius* did in his lying praises of the House of *Medices* . . . or his tempestuous thunderbolt Inuective against *Selimus*" (64–65). Thus, invented speech and stormy invective justify the author when he "thrusts" something in, although that same wit may have to answer to "after Ages." But when he adds the zany progress of Harvey's velvet to the famous Audley incident, Nashe argues from the vantage of Harvey's own humors: "*Nil habeo praeter auditum*, I was not at the cutting it out, nor will I binde your consciences too strictly to embrace it for a truth, but if my iudgement might stand for vp, it is rather likely to be true than false" (74). In some stories we should "settle [our] faith immoueably" (102); in others, a relative trust will do: "x. times more vnfallible than the newes of the Iewes rising vp in armes to take in the Land of promise, or the raining of corne this Summer at *Wakefield*" (74). In still others, Nashe simply confesses that he has fleshed out the narrative or, indeed, the picture of thin, vain Harvey.

With so much talk about the criteria for a true history, Nashe pays little attention to the elusive political status of his attack on Harvey. Even so, he admits (with Machiavelli) that a "singular & vertuous" course can lead to "vtter subuersion" (II.180). When he is not posing as the Janus between history and fiction, the stuffer lets us know that he desires a clean break from this alter ego, this buffoon who has played in the same arena for too long. Even apologies have failed to end the flyting.[2] So it is that Nashe attempts to foist onto Harvey the foolish role of the duteous stuffer who presumes to apply his prose to the gaps and wounds in the established church and state. Such a reversal is always in some measure part of the stuffer's repertoire of moves; but Nashe is so intent this time on extricating himself that he reinvokes his muse, the *bona roba,* and gives her to Harvey.

According to Nashe, Harvey pretends that his prose is honest and plain, but his "vaineglorie (which some take to be his gentlewoman) he hath new painted ouer an inch thicke" (II. 180). With this return to the cosmetics of stuff, Nashe dramatizes the fat muse of prose when he lets Harvey's "vnconscionable vast gorbellied Volume" into his own text: "You may beleeue me if you will, I was faine to lift my chamber doore off the hindges, onely to let it in, it was so fulsome a fat *Bonarobe* and terrible *Rounceuall*" (36). Harvey's stuff, however big or good, fails precisely because it cannot fit the space provided for it. Nashe claims, moreover, that the Harveys always bungle the stuffing of gaps with their trash. For example, the dead, "the most of whose mouthes clods had bungd vp manie *Olimpiades* since, yet seeke [the Harveys] to stifle and choak them again with waste paper" (84–85). The "fat lady," as Patricia Parker calls her, leaves Harvey with the mess of an unauthorized and oversized text.[3]

But Nashe wants his Harvey to get the full force of this political accusation—and so the jaded and self-serving doctor must remain a decipherer despite his new muse. Thus, the doctor's inkhornisms not only presume to defend the established church in facile rhetoric, but they also require "the Queenes Decypherer" (46) to make sense of them.[4] In other words, Harvey's tropes and periods deserve the same kind of malicious reading with which he tortures other books. And at every point there should be no mistake that Harvey is thrusting himself into the service of the Queen—as if the Queen needed that service or, for that matter, enjoyed the doctor's company.

Lest there be any mistake that the stuff of Harvey's texts is really old deciphering writ large, Nashe takes a look at its intestines. No wonder that Harvey's words can fill no holes: they are "[a] Nullitie, a Nullitie" (48). His is a strange and immaterial stuff: "stuft with nought but balder-dash" or, at best, the "excrementall conceipts and stinking kennel-rakt vp inuention" of "Ladie Vanitie" with her "surfetting vomit" (11). Such a verbiage may be useful enough to "mend high wayes," but its tonnage refutes in the oddest of fashions any philosophy about the weight of language:

> But when I came to vnrip and vnbumbast this *Gargantuan* bag-pudding, and found nothing in it but dogs-tripes, swines liuers, oxe galls, and sheepes gutts, I was in a bitterer chafe than anie Cooke at a long Sermon when his meate burnes. Doo the Philosophers (said I to my selfe) hold that letters are no burden, & the lightest and easiest houshold stuffe a man can remooue? (34)

Here, Nashe praises by indirection his own quasi-material prose, light and easy but still the best of all "stuff." But, at Harvey's sermon, Nashe can only feel distraction that his own best prose has been sacrificed. Moreover, Nashe edges his own prose toward sophistry in aligning his stuff with the Socratic nexus of cosmetics, cookery, and false rhetoric. Nonetheless, the satiric emphasis falls still on the gap between the size and merit of Harvey's prose.

Even so, in the middle of his satire, Nashe suggests—perhaps unintentionally—why Harvey might be compelled to fill the world with words. Harvey's book resembles "*Africke*,"

> which being an vnbounded stretcht out Continent, equiualent in greatnes with most Quarters of the Earth, yet neuertheles is (for the most part) ouerspred with barraine sands: so this his Babilonian towre or tome of confutation, swelling in dimension & magnitude aboue all the prodigious commentaries and familiar Epistles that euer he wrote, is, notwithstanding, more drie, barraine, and sandie in substance, than them all. (36)

In this analogy between world and text, two illusions collide against one another: that the voidless world needs no repair (though it is partly barren), and that words can repair it (though they are empty). The face of divinity may be scratched, or the prayer book imperfect, but these defects are merely accidents for which the stuffer can assume little if any responsibility.[5] At the same time, futility does not paralyze Nashe, whose own stuff can (with considerable irony) still assert its force and presence at the expense of Harvey's. For this reason among others, Nashe admits his contamination by the Doctor: "on hys [book] mine hath his whole foundation and dependance, and I doo but paraphrase vpon his text" (123).[6] Although Nashe's kinship to Harvey may compromise his prose, he suggests in this passage that at least his own stuff has a foundation in the world—if not divinity then divinity's worst enemy whom Nashe will expose.

Indeed, Nashe had every reason to ground his stuff and to feign passivity, to look on as "one thing brings on another." After all, Harvey had declared that Nashe claims to "encloseth all within his owne braine, and is a changer, an innouater, a cony-catcher, a rimer, a rayler, that out-faceth heauen and earth" (118). Nashe can return the same names, but he cannot erase Harvey's uncanny connection between the stuffer's own wits and the discoveries of coney-catching. When in doubt about the status of his prose, Nashe proclaims its daimonic power:

> the fire of my wit will not bee spent, till . . . I get it to be worshipt as a god of those whom it most confounds: and as diuers of the *Aethiopians* curse the sunne when it riseth, and worship it when it setteth, so, howeuer they curse and raile vpon mee in the beginning, I will compell them to fall downe and worship mee ere I cease or make an end, crying vpon their knees *Ponuloi nashe;* which is, in the *Russian* tongue, Haue mercie vpon vs. (40)

But Nashe allows his friends to offer some good advice, that he "leaue this big thunder of words, wherein thou vainly spendst thy spirits before the push of the battaile" (40). Thus, they urge the proser to be a good servant, to fight with his big words but to fight with caution. And the friends exhort him to discover only the notable points of Harvey's life—to fashion some semblance of order and closure in the life. But Nashe's friends cannot clarify the lines that are so faintly drawn in *Have With You*—between fact and fiction, duty and play, matter and vacuity, Nashe and Harvey, stuff and deciphering, faith and works. None of these pairs equals any other, but they all motivate Nashe to propose a narrative in which the report of worldly stuff coexists with yet never enters the void where fiction lives, or the void that fiction is. With *Lenten Stuffe,* Nashe looks for a way out of the world, only to imply that stuff is never free from the world that it has so desired to fill.

The Reformation of Stuff

In *Lenten Stuffe,* Nashe offers two realms side by side, one of fact and the other of fiction. For Nashe, this bifold ideal resists the interaction between the world and invention and thus reneges on the materiality of "stuff" in both senses, its makeup and relevance.[7] Whereas the proser draws lines in order to protect his empty fictions, it might be readily argued that any such lines are always already erased. After all, madcap fables and parodies run cheek by jowl with antiquarianism in *Lenten Stuffe,* so that Nashe's factual and fictive herrings might seem too close for comfort at the boundaries drawn between reportage and invention.[8] Many Elizabethan writers were fascinated by the elusive boundaries between fact and myth. But, whether or not it was possible for them (or anyone) to write a factual as against a fictive discourse, Nashe shares in the growing tendency of his day to declare a radical division between the fish that supplies the people of Yarmouth and the fish that provides the stuff of myth.

In *Lenten Stuffe,* then, we have a new and revised ideal for stuff, the failure of which might lead to dire consequences for an author in exile, such as Nashe. For lenten stuff, however much it might celebrate the freedom of prose fiction, is the ultimate concession to the authorities that their world needs no help or commitment from the stuffer. Nashe assures the reader that prose can record the economy of the world, and create its own mythic economy, and that the two can coexist without doing violence against each other. In essence, then, Nashe's lenten solution to his entanglement in the affairs of the world is just as worldly or political as the entanglement itself. But this irony does not prevent him from proclaiming that solution loud and clear.

Nashe prepares for, then announces the fictions of his herring so that the reader will make no mistakes. But at first he assumes the role of a reporter, detailing the facts about Yarmouth, his refuge between the Isle of Dogs scandal and the banning of his books by Whitgift in June 1599. By virtue of its numbers alone, the herring accounts for the abundance of Yarmouth; and in counting his stock, Nashe serves not just Yarmouth but the Queen and her domain. So lenten stuff takes two major steps: the proser reports the plenty of Yarmouth, then he locates his own invented stuff in a void set apart from the materials of the report. Nashe suggests that one must have faith in the distance (without access) between the material world and the myth, between the actual fish and the invented one. As the author should not have to create the world, the town and nation should not rely on him for their moral and economic redemption. Each realm should govern and repair itself in isolation from the other.

In its many contexts, the "lenten" metaphor supports this idealized division. First, there is the Reformation. Harvey once compared Nashe and Luther on account of their powerful words—"neuer anie in their tung writ so forcible" (III.124). As the Euphuists liked to remind us, comparisons are odious. But we have seen that Nashe's prose includes faith and works in its nexus of tropes. Moreover, *Lenten Stuffe* urges a strange but crucial analogy between Protestant soteriology and the red herring. The herring is "lenten": the fish is not just the trivial subject of a mock epic, but it provides the meals during Lent. Here, the herring swims its way into Protestant commentaries on faith and works. Zwingli, among others, considered holiday fasting to be a notorious example of the Roman obsession with works.[9] He argued that eating (or not eating) had nothing whatever to do with salvation, although the believer might feel the need to express or to hone faith by voluntary deprivation. Thus, the herring—in Luther, it is the turbot[10]—has the potential to distract a soul from its justification by faith. Of course, many reformers stressed the importance of works and even admitted the close proximity between faith and deeds, but they insisted that only faith could bring justification.

For "lenten stuff," Nashe urges his readers to accept the radical difference between a saving faith and his indifferent works. But, in his report on Yarmouth, we are supposed to believe not so much in the blood of Christ as in the plenty of God's creation. We are to believe that the world, always abundant, repairs its own defects without the benefit of the author's inventions. In the name of this faith, Nashe aligns his report with the documentary and antiquarian brand of history, for which he praises Camden above all others. Indeed, for Nashe, the new faith and the new history are of a piece.

The kinship between the Protestant scorn for miracle mongering and the antiquarian emphasis on genuine artifacts and documents was proclaimed throughout Tudor and Stuart England. Both movements promised to sweep away error and to restore something true—either faith or history. And with the reformed devotion to the primitive church, the critics of mere works and of mere fables often joined hands. But the union between the Reformers and the antiquarians does not remove, to be sure, the propaganda, invented speeches, and legends that fill the Reformers' own chronicles. Joseph Levine argues that antiquarianism was almost always ancillary to some other interest, whereas Michael McKeon finds the relationship between spiritual and historical reforms so complex that it rivals that between romance and history.[11] It is clear that Nashe wants to simplify these relations, much as Ascham and others would attribute idle romance to the saint-loving monks. But it is equally clear that, if Nashe's "lenten stuff" is simple in its design and faith in the status quo, it is caught in a double bind. If it succeeds, the freedom of Nashe's fictions might perturb the omnipotent gaze of the Queen's decipherers; and if it fails, those fictions are still subjected to that gaze.

What is worse, the status quo is hardly static and monolithic. Yarmouth is and is not typical of the rest of England; the Reformation has and has not "settled" a church in England. Indeed, when it comes to history as against myth, an author might have difficulty deciding whether or not his church ought to believe in the Brute who filled such a gaping hole in the British past. Nashe himself was an apologist for a church whose mediation between extremes could be construed as a slippery ideological pose. All of these variables help explain that, if Nashe intends to free his empty stuff from the world, his "lenten" metaphor must sever the reader's faith in fact from a delight in fiction. With history, then, the reformed contrast between faith and works still holds. Thus, when he offers a documentary history, Nashe endorses a faith in the world's materials with a report that manages to avoid the aridity of some antiquarians who "had rather scrape a peece of copper out of the durt" (I. 182). More to the point, Nashe refuses to follow those antiquarians who fill history's imagined vents: "They will blow their nose in a boxe, & say it is the spettle that *Diogenes* spet in ones face." In sum, the red herring leads us to adjust our faith away from nonsense fictions and toward the economy of Yarmouth.

But the irrepressible energy of Nashe's language still remains: the refusal of aridity, as I called it above. *Lenten Stuffe* is one of Nashe's most inventive works. The chance that his language—or any other—disallows the severance of fact and fiction adds one more footnote to "lenten." In addition to Luther and Camden, Nashe is indebted to the skepticism of Sextus Empiricus, whom he had read in the latest translation. Nashe often dallies with skeptics of one kind or another, especially Agrippa. But Sextus's suspension of judgment is much more useful for lenten stuff than Agrippa's anti-intellectualism ever could be.[12] When the report and the fiction seem too close in the language of the text, Nashe can disclaim all responsibility for deciding their status. He can urge his readers to accept on faith the difference between one fish and the other—between texts full of the world and texts free from (empty of) the same world. Sextus would never resign Nashe's text to an inertia; he counsels only that we suspend judgment because we cannot discern the truth with any certitude. At the impasse between fact and myth, then, the skeptic urges us to act according to our faith in law and sensory immediacy. For these reasons, a skeptical response to the problems of fact and fiction allows Nashe to write an energetic text within orthodox boundaries. That is, it delivers Nashe from error or trespass, even as he promises the textual division between world and fiction, matter and void, faith and works.

It should be clear by now that Nashe's lenten stuff is an unusual, even incongruous, brand of faith. It puts unlikely companions in the same procrustean bed—for instance, Luther and the skeptics. It flouts the usual idioms in which a historian of ideas might discuss nominalism, fideism, or empiricism. For example, fideism distances God's realm from the phenomenal world, describes God in terms of will rather than reason, and denies our knowledge-yielding faculties any access to that God.[13] But Nashe's lenten stuff arranges its realms in an eccentric fashion: it collapses the phenomenal, institutional, and metaphysical realms, and it denies "stuff" access to them all. It encourages us to find new and radical tropes for the empty void of lenten stuff—Epicurean ones, for example. But for all this parody, the main agenda is clear: Nashe wants to dissociate his inventions from the duties of patching and redeeming the world.

We can read this agenda in a number of ways. We can say that Nashe is having recourse to Sidney and the decipherers, who also claim a distant zodiac for wit, be it idealized or empty. Or we can conclude the Nashe is sick and tired of politics—again he attacks the decipherers even as he urges his own freedom from their clutches. Or, at last, we can read lenten stuff as Nashe's one last attempt to please the status quo—this time by abandoning the very duties for which they hired him. But, as *Lenten Stuffe* ranges from the praise of empty and free invention to a kowtowing deference to the authorities that threaten to punish the author, it seems more accurate to read the work as all of these things—gratitude, dismay, and excitement at the voiding of fictions. Ideally, there are two coexistent domains—both full yet independent—so that God's miracle is not challenged by Nashe's, and Nashe's miracle is not "stakt down" to God's material, political, and numinous world. But Nashe's ideals are also his desires, and desire can not save prose from its implication in the very language of the world that it wants to avoid. Therefore, lenten stuff must be justified by the reader's faith and suspension of judgment.

The Facts about Yarmouth

We get some hint in the preface to *Lenten Stuffe* of what later becomes an explicit division between fact and fiction. While Nashe intends to report the things made by agents other than himself, he emphasizes the strictly verbal or stylistic play of his own "light friskin." Not only does his style rival others famous for their big words; but Nashe invokes Ascham's treatment of Cicero's *tragicus orator* (III.152) in order to align Aretino and himself with a rich, even poetic *metaphrasis*. Thus, style extricates Aretino and Nashe from their onetime involvement in politics. Only a pedestrian prose walks "low and soft on foote" (thus Ascham) in its consignment to the quotidian world.[14]

Nashe prepares us, then, for a "lenten argument" that will comprise only the "pure wine of it self" (152). And we are told from time to time that fictions of the herring will be severed from the tour of Yarmouth with which the text begins. Such promises allow Nashe to be at once grateful to his patrons and feckless in his wit. But a reference to the "Isle of Dogs" incident proves to motivate the "not caring" attitude of the proser: "with light cost of rough cast rethoricke it may be tollerablely playstered ouer, if vnder the pardon and priuiledge of incensed higher powers it were lawfully indulgenst me freely to aduocate my owne astrology" (154). Even as Nashe petitions for his "new play" and for the zodiac of his own wit, he recalls in vivid terms the onetime duties of the stuffer who "tollerablely playstered" more than just his own transgressions. The stuffer declares that he is turning his back on politics, but he makes it clear that this move feels the heat of the world.

Rather than expend any more "rough cast rethoricke," Nashe offers to report the history and economy of Yarmouth. We still see grand hypotheses, verbal leviathans, outright parody, and bold coinages; and we can insist that his facts are part and parcel of his myths. But Nashe professes to follow Camden in an antiquarian report as "I saw" the town. For although Camden himself admitted the value of myth—which separates him from John Selden[15]—he is the Elizabethan epitome of the critical historian. Thus, Nashe factualizes his account according to two resources, the reports of Camden (for instance, on the tongue of Yarmouth[16]) and his own eyesight, the latter proof enough that six hundred boats crammed into the harbor "close pestred together as thicke as they could packe" (158). All sources point to Yarmouth's close-packed land and invulnerable economy. Indeed, Yarmouth shows us a perfected venting that works in the service of Elizabeth's little world. If readers cannot believe in the banqueting house of this world, Nashe refers them to the eyewitness who reads over his shoulder. Thus, he appeals to exterior evidence in a report that puts the town and the kingdom in concentric circles, despite the political and rhetorical ironies of its text.

Camden's history of the town's formation by sand maintains that Yarmouth's coast restores its own defects by natural process: "barred and stopped up [by the sand], they wrestle as it were, to their great cost and charges with the maine sea: which to make them amends and to restore what it hath eaten and swallowed up else where in this shore, hath by heaping of earth and sand together, cast up here of late a prety Island."[17] According to Nashe, Yarmouth's trade also relies on a constant restitution because the town is "in so barraine a plot seated" (158). Its unfailing plenty in spite of such infertility is wondrous to Nashe: "[it] egregiously bepuzled and entranced my apprehension" (158). As a reporter, Nashe aims to celebrate the process by which Yarmouth sustains its natural integrity: its windblown sands resemble those that "haue choakt or clamd vp the middle walke or dore of the *Rhene,* and made it as stable a clod-mould, or turffe ground, as any hedger can driue stake in" (160).

Sometimes, the reporter finds occasion to make myth out of big anthropomorphisms. Thus, the sands "would no more liue vnder the yoke of the Sea, or haue their heads washt with his bubbly spume or Barbers balderdash, but clearely quitted, disterminated, and relegated themselues from his inflated Capriciousnesse of playing the Dictator ouer them" (160). His zeal extends to political rulers, although only in hypothesis: he offers to "breake out into a boundlesse race of oratory, in shrill trumpetting and concelebrating the royall magnificence of her gouernement, that for state and strict ciuill ordering scant admitteth any riuals: but I feare it would be a theame displeasant to the graue modesty of the discreet present magistrates; and therefore consultiuely I ouerslip it" (158–59). These are the old promises and strategies of the stuffer: failing any artifacts, he invents them. Thus, in praise of the town, he imagines, again in hypothesis, an archaeological dig. But the process by which he conceives and then retracts such verbiage issues in a very strange text: "a whole moneths minde of reuoluing meditation I raueling out therein, (as raueling out signifies *Penelopes telam retexere,* the vnweauing of a webbe before wouen and contexted)" (168). Nashe undoes his own inventions for reasons that his subtext for Penelope's web, Erasmus's *Adages,* makes clear. For what separates lenten stuff from old stuff is that its creator believes in its emptiness above all other possibilities.

In Erasmus's *Adages, telam retexere* admits the emptiness of labor: "*Penelopes telam retexere, est inanem operam sumere, et rursum destruere quod effeceris*" ("to unweave Penelope's web, is to do futile work, and to destroy in turn what you have accomplished").[18] "To destroy in turn what you have accomplished" is futile work (*"inanem operam"*) in two respects: it undermines the force and presence of the mental creation, and it associates the inventions of the mind with the void that Lucretius called "inane."[19] Such a void is the new place for fiction in Nashe's prose. I would go so far as to argue that the cosmic model for stuff shifts from the voidless world of elements to a Lucretian division of the world into two realms, the material and the void in which matter moves. Each realm excludes the other but allows and even enables the other to exist.[20] In the same fashion, lenten stuff is inane—devoid as well as fictive—and it undoes the notion that Nashe's ventings hold the world together to any considerable extent. Lenten stuff is absent from the indestructible matter of the world: as Lucretius sees fish swimming in water when he envisions the atoms in their void, so Nashe allows the fish of the world and his mythic herring to coexist. And like Yarmouth, the *natura* of Lucretius manages to keep its "sum unimpaired" despite its void.[21] Nashe's own authorial status approaches that of the Lucretian gods, distant from and free of the world and its ravages. Ideally, then, this "inanity" of stuff does not threaten the created world. Indeed, Nashe leaves his imagined dig to report the royal grants and town pedigrees in a fanfare of documentation.

But Nashe is also worried more than ever about his inane readers. Lest his readers fail to observe proper boundaries or get impatient for some fun, the author severs his mock praise of the herring from the walking tour of Yarmouth:

> There be of you, it may be, that will account me a paltrer, for hanging out the signe of the redde Herring in my title page, and no such feast towards for ought you can see. Soft and faire, my maisters, you must walke and talke before dinner an hour or two, the better to whet your appetites to taste of such a dainty dish as the redde Herring; and that you may not thinke the time tedious, I care not if I beare you company, and leade you a sound walke round about Yarmouth, and shew you the length and bredth of it. (159)

The facts can serve the fiction by whetting our appetites for the promised "feast" of invention. Nashe assures us that his signs are no ploy, no mere distraction, but rather the marks by which we can discern the separate realms of his text, reportage and play. These realms are partitioned on the title page as well.

Nashe bolsters the documentary evidence of the walk with some artifacts and antiquities. He refers not just to Camden, but to parchments and a famous "Chronographycal Latine table, which they haue hanging vp in their Guild hall" (161; cf. Camden, 477). This table records for Nashe the "transmutations . . . in a faire text hand texting vnto vs" (161). Not only is its hand clear: the table encourages Nashe to play the reporter to the hilt, defining the date with extreme accuracy, and returning to the "oldest writers" and even to the "visible apparent tokens" (160) in which his readers can witness the past firsthand. He follows the latest historical interest in the Saxons (as against Brute and his party). Indeed, whether Cedric the Saxon jumped or frisked onto shore does not compromise, Nashe suggests, the "scripture verity" (161) of his report. Whereas all historians make their fictions out of speculation, Nashe urges us to keep our eye on data—the details of Yarmouth's size, history, and economy.

The table is more than an artifact. It is a model for the reporter who feigns passivity. The proser becomes a vessel, a follower or mirror, an amanuensis: "My tables are not yet one quarter emptied of my notes out of their Table" (162); their table is "a Sea Rutter diligently kept amongst them from age to age, of all their ebbs and flowes" (162). Nashe's text is guided by this artifact: "I tie my selfe to [it] more precisely, and thus it leadeth on" (162). If the report includes any bombast, say, in its account of royal speech at coronations, Nashe suggests that it records the steady growth of Yarmouth, ever more "well lined and bumbasted" (163). There are risks in elevating the plenty of one town over all others: "It were to be wished that other coasters were so industrious as the Yarmouth, in winning the treasure of fish out of those profundities, and then we should haue twentie egges a pennie, and it would be as plentifull a world as when Abbies stoode; and now, if there be any plentifull world, it is in Yarmouth" (171). Not only does this remark question, even antedate, the abundance of the world; it also renders Yarmouth's own plenty in hypothesis. The strange textual web of *Lenten Stuffe* needs to ensure what it perhaps cannot by virtue of its own inanity: the division of realms in language, and the faith to be placed in the facts of a nation that has given its authors every reason to disbelieve.

Just prior to the gamesome feast of the red herring, then, Nashe pauses to remind us why his tour warrants our faith. He recalls some of his historical authorities, not just in "most recordes" but in his own travels. He sums the entire report as the search for a "correlatiue analagie" of the town; he has striven "to configurate a twinlike image of it" (171). He has canvassed histories from "frierly annals" to Hakluyt's "*Digests* of our English discoueries . . . documentized most locupleatly" (173). Moreover, Nashe asserts that the trade ventings to be found in Hakluyt stand for more than just a stable and sufficient economy; they guarantee the religious faith of the English as well. So it is that one captain Harborne, a Moses to the pagans, embodies the claim that "[n]ot any where is the word seuerer practised, the preacher reuerentlier obserued and honoured" than in Yarmouth (172). In every way, from history to religion, the walking tour is justified by faith. And, whatever the reader's objection to this faith, Nashe moves on from matter to void—from world to fiction where he can play with his food, without fear or pressure from his embattled contexts. Or so he dreams, even while the "webbe before wouen and contexted" keeps creeping in.

The Stuff of Fiction

Leaving the tour behind, Nashe sorts his textual merchandise again: "But of that fraught I must not take in two liberall, in case I want stowage for my red Herring, which I rely vpon as my wealthiest loading" (172). If we are to believe Nashe, there are two kinds of fish in the vessel, the food and the myth. As he turns from one to the other, the *tragicus orator* plays a fanfare on the "huge woords" (152) of his mock epic: "Doe but conuert . . . the slenderest twinckling reflexe of your eie-sight to this flinty ringe that engirtes it . . . then perponder of the red herringes priority and preualence, who . . . hath raisd and begot all this" (174). The author draws a "ringe" around his own performance and, moreover, warns us that this section of the text will be wildly inventive. Separated from his notebooks and topics, Nashe must rely on those "purer intellectuall faculties" that have been "so troubledly bemudded with griefe and care" (175). Now he is alone in the charmed circle of his imagination, although other fictions authorize his praise of the mythic herring: "*Chaucer* preheminentest encomionizeth aboue all iunquetries or confectionaries whatsoeuer" (176). Thus, leviathan words usher in herring fictions.

Nashe proceeds to empty the fish of all political contents, although his first step in this direction suggests that this task may be difficult. The praise of herring takes its place in the long line of paradoxical encomiums where its subversive potential is mitigated by the "famousest schollers of all ages" who have written in the genre (151). But Nashe needs license as his best defense. He aligns himself with the "wast authours" who have "so many heades so many whirlegigs" (178); and he warns the reader that "you must accept of it as the place serues" (176). Some authors have erred, he says, in assuming that they can preserve church and state, for example, by summing up morality with "feare God, and obey the king" (177). Others have been "felloniously suspected" by political powers (178); still others pretend that their empty subjects are important (no one more than the poets of Helen of Troy). But the worst error is made when lenten stuff is treated as a matter of faith. To the contrary, Nashe insists that these encomiums are so incredible that they "bebangeth poore paper in laud of a bag-pudding, as a swizer would not belieue it" (178). The author seeks rights *"Cum gratia & priueligio"* by declaring the irrelevance of his fiction, a *"Terleryginckt . . .* so friuolously of they reckt not what"

(178). Making much of little is distinguished from making up for too little. As Nashe offers another world, not a better one, his work forges a new responsibility by refusing a place in the world governed by his onetime patrons. He celebrates this new stuff for its "pure wine"— "as lieue . . . no cloathes, rather then weare linsey wolsey" (152). In other words, the quality of style has everything to do with its absence from the patchwork of the world.

Thus, the praise of the red herring can proceed when it has rendered unto Elizabeth what is hers. But Nashe has to worry about his readers. They might challenge lenten stuff on the basis of any number of positions—on the belief that language disallows any division of fact and fiction, on the belief that no text can erase itself from the world or the world from itself, or on the basis of the author's own political life. Or lenten stuff can be devalued just because it is empty. Indeed, Nashe defends Varro's style and the herring fishers at the same time against Ascham's charge that both are facile:

> Indian canaos or boats like great beefe trayes or kneading troughs, firking as flight swift thorow the glassy fieldes of *Thetis* as if it were the land of yce, and sliding ouer the boiling desert so earely, and neuer bruise one bubble of it, as though they contended to out-strip the light-foot tripper in the *Metamorphisis*, who would run ouer the ripe-bending eares of corne, and neuer shed or perish one kirnell. (183)

As these "tripper[s]" make no impression on the world, so Nashe values his lenten prose for its light-footed expedition by which nothing bruises. Even this controversy with Ascham falls under the rubric of the herring's "game." Not only are literary rivalries nonpolitical; so, too, are the energies of stuff itself, for its own malleable nature is as harmless as the mythic transformations described by Ovid.

In sum, this ludic stuff is "lenten" precisely because it cannot save the world or the reader. For this simple claim, Nashe provides a Protestant frame of reference. A loss of herring, he explains, would deprive us only of "that word *Quadragesima*, or Lent, [which] might be cleane spung'd out of the Kalender, with Rogation weeks, Saints eues, and the whole Ragmans roule of fasting dayes" (183). Lest we miss the point, Nashe repeats it: "The Rhomish rotten *Pithagoreans* or *Carthusian* friers, that mumpe on nothing but fishe, in what a flegmatique predicament would they be, did not this counterpoyson of the spitting sickenesse . . . patch them out and preserue them" (184). Thus, the rules of fasting epitomize the Romish soteriology of works; these works apply a material plaster to a spiritual lack. The herring, however, joins the *bona roba* Helen of Troy in the category of empty fictions or indifferent works. Whereas Jonathan Crewe has called Nashe's prose "unredeemed,"[22] Nashe himself declares that his lenten stuff is unredeeming.

If the material fish is "vented out of Yarmouth" to supply "all other lands" (192), the herring fiction resembles the *bona roba*, Lais of Corinth, who "will smile vpon no man except he may haue his owne asking" (191). But Nashe must deal with other kinds of misreaders than just those who are irritated by empty subjects. There is a "colony of criticall *Zenos*" who cannot tell the difference between one fish and the other. As far as they are concerned, the language between the two fish, like the sea between Hero and Leander, "diuided them and it diuided them not" (195). These readers misplace their faith: they will "confute and disproue mouing," yet they refuse to suspend belief in the fiction and to believe in the report of that "confluent herring faire" whose plenty, according to Camden, was "incredible" (185). These "new decipherers" cannot be trusted to divide the report from the fiction—the world of Yarmouth from the yarn of Hero.

Nashe gauges his readers—be they foolish, politic, or learned—by testing their credulity in witchcraft, in the quasi-religious dance of the Sun ("you wil say I am no fabler" [189]), and in the coat of the fish: "if a man should tell you that god *Himens* saffron colour'd robe were made of nothing but red herrings skins, you would hardly beleeue him" (189–90). In each case, Nashe scolds those readers who confuse the political, material world with the fiction. Such readers have mangled his texts in the past; he fears the same treatment with the stuff that is so clear about its empty status. But what Nashe does not clarify are the reasons why the readers might have trouble following directions and sorting out one fish from the other. That his own language or the very nature of language might trick them never occurs to the impresario of *Lenten Stuffe*. Bad readers are so to Nashe because their rhetorical training has prepared them for decorous tropes and figures but not for the "rough cast rethoricke" of stuff; or because their ambitions have gotten the best of them.

Whatever the case, Nashe has a variety of strategies for insisting on the fictive nature of his mythic herring. For instance, he poses romance against history.[23] Nashe reduces romance to a fictive residue strained out of histories; to a quixotic counter to what a supposedly critical Froissart records in his chronicles; to the medieval gigantism that overtakes the report of Sir Walter Manny's career; and to gestes (Bevis of Hampton is courteous because the herring made him so). Nashe also stresses the fictive nature of his lenten stuff in a parody of two fables—one of Midas, and the other, of Hero and Leander. For emphasis, the proser marks the end of his Midas fable as the "close of the fiction" (193), and he mocks those readers who find weighty meanings in it. In fact, such readers are analogous to Midas himself, who mistook a fish for "golde in deede" (193). Like Mahomet, they convert the text into a fool's paradise, into a matter of salvation. So it goes in yet another fable, the tale of Jupiter and Dionysius, in which the herring is taken for a golden calf, a false god. But the stuffer would prevent such idolatry: "No such *Iupiter*, no such golden coated image was there; but it was a plaine golden coated red herring, without welt or garde" (194). Even the iconoclast, Dionysius, subjects the herring to religious controversy when he rips it down.[24]

In the extended fable of Hero and Leander, Nashe trades in historical causes for mythic ones: "To recount, *ab ouo,* or from the churchbooke of his birth, howe the Herring first came to be a fish, and then how he came to be king of fishes, and gradationately how from white to red he changed, would require as massie a toombe as Hollinshead" (195). The stuffer prefers a little play derived from the "worke" of Musaeus and Marlowe. Furthermore, Nashe digresses from the tale to redefine the elusive nature of stuff in terms of the familiar analogy between a faith in dreams and a faith in prose. For, if Marlowe pauses to consider the poverty of scholars, Nashe weighs the substance of their dreams: "You may see dreames are not so vaine as they are preached of, though not in vaine Preachers inueigh against them, and bende themselues out of the peoples mindes to exhale their foolish superstition" (197). Dreams are not entirely empty, although too much belief in them is always vain: Protestants and Epicureans agree in rejecting the anxieties of a misplaced faith. But Nashe recedes into metaphors when it comes to the materiality of dreams:

> The labouring mens hands glowe and blister after their dayes worke: the glowing and blistring of our braines after our day labouring cogitations are dreames, and those dreames are reaking vapours of no impression, if our matelesse cowches bee not halfe empty. Hero hoped, and therefore shee dreamed (as all hope is but a dreame). (197)

There are two ways to describe a "halfe empty" bed, and so two approaches to the lenten dream. For those who live half-fulfilled, dreams have "no impression": that is, the dreamers have little need for an imagined filler. For the half-empty, the dream applies a salve to the "glowing and blistring of our braines." Because Hero's bed is half-empty, she mistakes a fish for gold in conjuring away Leander's absence. With lenten stuff, however, we must learn to think of emptiness not as a defect but as a "not halfe empty" void (or vapor) where we dream away the labors of the world in which we strive and toil.

Thus, like Lucretius, Nashe urges us to think of ourselves as full banqueters, not leaky vessels. While Yarmouth supplies the world by day, the reader feasts on a herring in some nocturnal fiction. Surely, we are far from the leaky vessel of the *Gorgias* or the scratched face of divinity. But Lucretius adds to his advice that if life proves a "riddled jar," we should not look for any help from the author, *"nam tibi praeterea quod machiner inveniamque, quod placeat, nil est"* ("for there is nothing else I can devise and invent to please you").[25] There is nothing more indeed, for the voids and fictions exposed by Lucretius have already affirmed the confident and relieved the anxious from what Nashe would call the terrors of the night (Lucretius: *"terrorem animi tenebrasque"* [II.59]). We must learn to stare into the void—or at the herring—with faith that the world will repair itself and without fear of the abyss.

Because there is no leaky vessel, then, there is no sophistry or under-the-table patchwork. The author who writes fictions should not fear punishment; the fables of torment—eternal or political—concern only the ungrateful and guilty dreamer, the "riddled urn," as Lucretius repeats (III.1009). Readers might find Nashe such a dreamer; they might mistake the lenten and the worldly. But Nashe insists that his lenten stuff allows the honest reader—if there is such a one—to refuse the sieve and its horrors and to embrace the void of fiction. The fiction of the herring will not save Yarmouth, while Yarmouth, thanks to its fish, does not need saving. Nashe can only hope that the London gods will agree or turn the other way.

Whatever the official response, Nashe concludes his fable of Hero and Leander with fictions of all kinds: myth ("gods and goddesses all on a rowe, bread and crow, from *Ops* to *Pomona*"); travelers' fables (Mandeville); romance (Palmerin); and legend (Cadwallader). As he tires of his fictions, Nashe refers us to still other fablers; but he pauses to question once and for all our faith in his "notorious" tale. Our faith is implicitly weighed in the fable of the herring's color, in which the pope confuses a fish with God. But, if the papists are too credulous to understand that a fish is simply food, then the biased critics who rave against the incredibility of the fiction miss its point as well: "Euery manne will not clappe hands to this tale; the Norwichers inprimis, who say the first guilding of Herrings was deducted from them" (211). To doubt the fiction is wrongly to make it a matter of belief. One owes doubt or faith to Yarmouth and the nation—the body, soul, and artifice of an England for which the town stands as an idealized part of a suspect whole. Lenten stuff is not, however, of the world.

Toward the end of *Lenten Stuffe*, Nashe derides the confusion of world and fiction with one final attack on the "decipherers." First, he comments forthrightly on the questions of faith, authenticity, fact, and miracle. For those who doubt his fiction, Nashe laughs at their need to "say bo to it" or to disturb the "Queenes peace" because of it (211–12). For the believers, he offers examples of their gullibility: "For a new Messias they are ready to expect of the bedlam hatmakers wife by London bridge, he that proclaymes hymselfe Elias, and sayeth he is inspired wyth mutton and porredge" (212). Such readers mistake the boundaries between jests, foodstuffs, and saving presences. More directly, Nashe warns his readers about confusing his lenten stuff with the real plenty in which they should believe: "Let them looke to themselues as they will, for I am theirs to gull them better than euer I haue done; and this I am sure, I haue destributed gudgeon dole amongst them, as Gods plenty as any stripling of my slender portion of witte, farre or neere" (213). Let the readers beware that the merchandise of fiction is not really the "plenty" that God vented so long ago and merchants still vent.

His readers are prone to still other errors. Some, he complains, turn fiction into their political version of the "truth": of his works, written "carelesly betwixt sleeping and waking . . . [they] absolutely concludeth, it is meant of the Emperour of Ruscia, and that it will vtterly marre the traffike into that country if all the Pamphlets bee not called in and suppressed, wherein that libelling word is mentioned" (213). These "peruerse applications" of his fictive void to worldly vents err in assuming that lenten stuff trades in a material economy. For these readers, language (like reading) shares in too many states, in sleeping and waking, in text and world. The lenten stuffer knows better than this: the readers are "not looking into the text it selfe," the text of no impressions (214). They insist on reading the text as a quasi-materiality with which the author who hopes to patch the world will "vtterly marre" its "traffike."

That Nashe's books were "called in and suppressed" indicates how little the Elizabethan officials believed in the segregation of fictions from the world—of myth from report. In fact, the Elizabethan "settlement" was founded on the entanglement of myth and history at every turn. But Nashe maintains that his words, "mingle mangle cum purre," have not "fisht out such a deepe politique state meaning as if I had al the secrets of court or commonwealth at my fingers endes" (214). He believes that he has acted responsibly, "more boldly, & yet it shall be securelie" (213), in declaring the freedom of his texts, and in the very act of taunting his critics with the absurdity of relevance. Nashe offers nonsense riddles of presence to test their interpretive abilities: "There was a Herring, or there was not" (216). At last, he calls names: "O, for a Legion of mice-eyed decipherers and calculaters vppon characters, now to augurate what I meane by this" (218). The "characters" of deciphering serve now as the words that some reader has distorted into political code. Nashe still would guide his honest reader: "you may imagine, or suppose: or, without supposing or imagining, I will tell you" (217). But the "speciall poynt" of the jests in *Lenten Stuffe* has a larger cause—the liberation of "mine owne stuff" and the author's own wit from the decipherers and their world: "hath it any more sence in it then it should haue" (220). Here, duty ("should") and play converge: "I knew not what to make of [my works] my selfe" (214). The stuffer has both the obligation and the right to mean nothing, for meaning is the domain of the authorities who allow him to play in the lenten void where Leander and the red herring swim.

Of course, the voided fiction is very much a dream. Despite his apologies for lenten stuff, Nashe conveys some uncertainty about the position of his text: "Stay, let me looke about, where am I? in my text, or out of it? not out, for a groate: out, for an angell: nay, I'le lay no wagers, for nowe I perponder more sadlie vppon it, I thinke I am out indeede" (219). As Nashe steers between monetary values and textual boundaries, he returns to the madcap dilemmas of his trade in words. Moreover, lenten stuff—like the patchwork stuff of old—takes us to the very center of the questions that the Elizabethans asked not just about truth, history, and poetry, but about the specific place of prose narrative in these venues. Some questions are obvious: Is it possible to write a lenten text, or an unworldly fiction? Is it possible to divide the page so neatly into parts? In partial answer to these questions, it is not surprising that the exiled and soon-to-vanish Nashe complains about political torture, and that he hastens to modify this complaint by allowing for a vigilant government and its just punishments.

Still, there is one other, more ironic question. To the very end, Nashe challenges all rival literary traditions with his stuff. Against the Greenes, Sidneys, Harveys, and Aschams of old deciphering, Nashe continues to boast that the alchemy of his prose can conjure up words and even fictions with the greatest power. Indeed, the herring revives the stuffer's faith in the protean energy of his prose, for the fish "hath lately beene my ghostly father to conuert me to [the Alchemists'] fayth" (220). These fictions leave the world and its traditions behind with much the same kind of "transfiguration" by which the fish moves "from his duskie tinne hew into a perfit golden blandishment" (220). More and more, the "artificiall" perfection of the herring's fiction rivals the golden world that Sidney's poet delivers from the zodiac of his own wit. But, when we recall that deciphering itself moved from a mysterious position at the very essence of narrative to an absence from essential meaning for the sake of "mere" stylistic play, this rivalry borders on kinship. The ironic question is this: is it possible that Nashe fails to separate his own prose from that of his deciphering rivals, just as surely as he fails to separate it from the world and its deciphering readers? Sidney's poet and Nashe's proser both declare their difference from history and philosophy—both are concerned about the boundaries of their literary endeavors. But clearly, Nashe's rhetoric is not Arcadian in design or execution. For the stuffer, then, the answer to this ironic question is yes and no, because a rivalry like that between Jack and Surrey involves both kinship and alienation. And this twofold answer summarizes the importance of Nashe's stuff for Elizabethan prose narrative: for stuff, lenten and full, is at the center of Elizabethan literary debates, both for what it shares with the decipherers, and for the stopgap place that it stakes for its own quasi-material "rethoricke" in a prose that Nashe's literary fathers cannot write. Stuff may dally with a golden world, but its only apology for Sidney's poesies launches a conception of prose that Astrophil would hardly recognize.

If the dream of the stuffer comes true at last, he can detach his work from the rivalries that compose his worldly inheritance: from the decipherers, Harvey, Martin Marprelate, and the Elizabethan officials. His bifold fish—leaden and golden—is designed to suspend conflict and to receive the reader's faith, even if this "fayth" relies on our distraction from the alchemical tricks by which one word reports while another invents. As the narrator spies land and his nets are trussed, he concludes with signs of yet another faith, with a list of fisher-poets that includes the apostles and Jonah. In this scriptural vein, his final word sets limits on the author, much as the Protestant and the Epicurean would: "No more can I do for you than I haue done, were you my god-children euery one: God make you his children and keepe you from the Dunkerks" (225). The world will not be saved by the fictions of the stuffer, although he might still have to suffer for his onetime involvement in the redemption of the world.

In his introduction to Nashe's works, J. B. Steane culls an allegory from a phrase found in *Lenten Stuffe*, "tossing empty bladders in the ayre." According to Steane, these "empty bladders" refer to nothing less than the "absurd" globe on which we humans live.[26] If such a reading misses the specific proposals of lenten stuff, it understands something of Nashe's motives and, moreover, of his uncertainty about whether stuff has—in or out of the text—done anything at all. With these questions Nashe takes the decipherings and discoverings of

Greene beyond their limits: Nashe stretches Greene out and refashions his prose anew. But it is left to Thomas Dekker to apply Nashe's daimonic style to the end of questioning those discoveries on which Nashe has depended, and those boundaries which Nashe fears no human agent can save from erasure.

6
DEKKER AND NARRATIVE CANT

In the last three chapters, I have traced Thomas Nashe's assault on the "decipherers" who in his view fall short of a forceful and material prose. Thomas Dekker's prose is written in the wake of both Nashe and Greene; but in his plague and coney-catching pamphlets, Dekker focuses his criticism on "notable discovery."[1] In every respect, he unsettles Greene's confidence in a stable plot of notable events. In the daimonic narrator, in the reader's own biased eye, and in the narrative events themselves—in all these cases, Dekker challenges the belief in an inherently typical and remarkable event—that is, in the "notable." Thus, his prose not only picks up where Nashe's left off; but it also employs the stuff of Nashe against the discoveries of Greene.

Dekker's plague and rogue pamphlets do not, however, entail an outright freedom from the conventions of discovery. In fact, he suggests that narratives cannot do without controlling schemes, even if those schemes are merely signs eluding the grasp of any human intention. So Dekker's absorption of discovery—of the very mode that he criticizes—is more subtle than Nashe's rivalry with the decipherers. And this paradox is exactly Dekker's point: in the language of narrative, he suggests, flux and hybridity prevail over the purity of mode and genre. Thus, Dekker's agenda is critical of the whole of Greene's career, even if it fastens on discovery. For this reader of Greene and Nashe writes texts in which deciphering and discovering, romance and roguery are the names or signs with which authors pretend to have mastered the contingencies of their fables and—through fables—of the world.

Dekker's prose features several master tropes in its criticism of discovery. The wounds of the plague are a morbid reminder that notorious signs elude and undo the mortals who so desire to control them. Scattered throughout other works is another series of images—of shops and courts, of labyrinths and puzzles—that serve the same critical purpose as the wounds or "tokens" of disease. Even if these tropes are more local and less chilling than the plague, they imperil the stability of exemplary value in much the same way as debates over Helen in Shakespeare's *Troilus and Cressida*. Between Troilus's "What's aught but as 'tis valued" and Hector's attribution of exemplary value to the thing itself "as well . . . as in the prizer," we have the irreducible debate of Dekker's prose. In one passage, Dekker even compares the frustration of human designs to a strumpet whose value changes from day to night.

But these tropes are only a prelude to Dekker's rewriting of Greene's coney-catching pamphlets. Here, the criticisms of discovery are explicit and thorough. For one thing, Dekker's agents of discovery (the bellmen) are elusive in their daimonic status—a far cry from Greene's officious and respectable converts to the law. For another, the criminals thrive with the help of a language, "cant," that plagues the officers of law and order. What is more, bellmen and criminals alike find themselves in narratives in which golden worlds and criminal dens turn into one another at the wink of an eye. And these affronts to Greene's notable discoveries are energized by Dekker's reading of Nashe, whose material and boisterous style is applied to the transformation of conventions on which Nashe relies.

I am not the first to focus on the critical edge in Dekker's prose. In his two-volume study, Frederick O. Waage argues that the pamphleteer subverts idealized and conventional paradigms for controlling the complexity of experience. In this fashion, Waage locates Dekker in the same world that Francis Bacon inhabits. Whatever the objections to placing Dekker in such high circles, I think Waage is fundamentally right to call Dekker a skeptic, at least in the prose, and to situate Dekker's prose in context. But *skeptic* is a slippery term.[2] For Dekker, it has both conservative and radical effects: the first, a pietism; the second, an unripping or a freeing of prose from its constraints. Whatever its motive, Dekker's skepticism comes down to this point: although he believes that we cannot escape from the normative conventions in our stories, he does not trust them and explicitly challenges their schemes. Thus, his prose is steeped in the very plots that he criticizes: Dekker works in the chief genres of discovery—jest books, plays about honest whores, rogue pamphlets, fables of repentance—but he vexes them beyond the wildest dreams of Greene.

Three studies in particular clarify the larger contexts of Dekker's challenge to discovery. One is Terence Cave's *Recognitions*. As I noted in chapter 2, Cave argues that, in the seventeenth century, there was a growing distrust of recognition scenes on a number of scores—for instance, for their contrivance or their entanglement with desire.[3] Cave's findings about recognition scenes in general support my claim that Dekker challenges Greene's discoveries. The second study is Michael McKeon's book on the origins of the novel.[4] McKeon asserts that the novel emerged from a complex dialectic transforming the representations of truth and of virtue. In the seventeenth century this dialectic is energized beyond recall, as it attempts to negotiate the problems and inconsistencies in epistemology and in status. I am contending that the tightly woven relations between Greene, Nashe, and Dekker contribute to this crucial period for prose narrative, and that they modify to some degree McKeon's claim that nothing in England corresponded to the Cervantean transformation of prose at the outset of the seventeenth century.[5] Like McKeon, J. Paul Hunter argues that old paradigms are absorbed into the new in the production of the novel. In his revisionary reading of Defoe, Hunter shows how much *Robinson Crusoe* derives from the fables of spiritual quest and, therefore, how old resources are transformed in the critical hands of the new.[6] But this transformation is precisely what we see in the transmission of narrative values that stretches from Greene's *Groatsworth of Witte* to Dekker's *Penny-Wise, Pound-Foolish*.

This chapter will proceed in three sections. The first will consider Dekker's plague pamphlets and their deadly affront to discovery. The second will cover the works in which Dekker unsettles the conventions of roguery. In a third section, I look at some of Dekker's contemporaries and successors who participated in the transformation of Renaissance prose. And I glance ahead to the legacy that the Elizabethans and Jacobeans left to their modern readers, who still feel compelled to read them for their "notes"—fallible, wondrous, and strange.

Infected Prose

Thomas Dekker wrote about the wounds or "tokens" of the plague in 1603 and in the 1620s. Although many traditional interpretations of the plague find their way into Dekker's account, he reads the wounds primarily as the unrelieved confusion of all human designs. In his view, the plague cannot be matched for its "Violence, Strength, Incertainty, Suttlety, Catching, Vniuersality, and Desolation" (181).[7] But for Dekker our failure to isolate or to read the wounds of plague indicts the Elizabethan discovery of the notable as well. In other words, an author may claim to regulate the *nodi* of a plot or a disease; but no matter how many treatises attempt to teach him how to predict or even represent the "tokens" of the plague, every accountant must defer to "Incertainty."[8] What this uncertainty means for narrative is clarified when Dekker turns to discuss the "wonder" of the year, 1603, the "cant" used by rogues to elude the authorities, or the ignes fatui that populate Dekker's discovery pamphlets.

Whereas Greene offers the exemplary in the form of the "notable," Dekker focuses instead on the form of "wonder." But "wonder" in Dekker's *The Wonderfull Yeare* (1603) is open to question. Although it might be said to attend the stabilizing effects of "discovery" in Greene's prose, or the heightening effects of romance in Sidney's,[9] "wonder" for Dekker eludes our grasp insofar as it attends breathtaking change:

> Oh it were able to fill a hundred paire of writing tables with notes, but to see the parts plaid in the compasse of one houre on the stage of this newfound world! Vpon Thursday it was treason to cry God saue king *Iames* king of *England,* and vpon Friday hye treason not to cry so. (Wilson, 21)

Wonder results from contingency: citizens can scarcely know whom or what to praise or to admire, yet their uncertainty causes a feeling of wonder. Queen Elizabeth herself is startled when she is summoned to heaven; her virginity, once so prized, now seems mere infertility. The year is a Proteus, epitomizing what "that strange outlandish word *Change* signified" (12). Joy shares the stage with sorrow—over the plague and over the death of a queen. But even James's position shifts from a redeemer—one wonder—to the returning wonders of the plague, for "that wonder begat more." "And last of all," Dekker concludes, "(if that wonder be the last and shut vp the yeare) a most dreadfull plague" (20). If Greene's "notable" events seek to minimize doubt and chance, Dekker's "wonder" depends on them.

The plague itself is a Proteus, assuming in turn the guises of fencer, warrior, and highwayman. What is worse, the plague becomes a demonized "stuff" that fills up the pages of the pamphlet: thus, Dekker "would feede it with no other stuffe for a twelue-moneth and a day than with kindling papers full of lines, that should tell only of the chances, changes, and strange shapes that this Protean Climactericall yeare hath metamorphosed himselfe into" (19). I will have occasion to discuss Nashe's influence on Dekker's somatic prose below[10]; but the plague itself emerges as a somatic writing that always finds the page of the body no matter how many vents are closed: "not a creuis but was stopt, not a mouse-hole left open, for all the holes in the house were most wickedlie dambd vp" (42). The plague enters anyway, and its wounds, although localized in little blue spots, thwart any human attempt to circumscribe them.

We have already seen that the plague destabilizes an already unstable political world—with treason changing its meaning suddenly one day in 1603. At every turn, the narrator encounters the world's instabilities, in his charnel house wit (which measures time by horror), and in economic explanations of the plague (overpopulation, supply and demand), but above all in the jests and tales with which he stipples his account of disease. In these anecdotes, Dekker unsettles with plague some of the most basic plots of discovery.

It should be recalled that anecdotes are a primary resource of notable discovery. But the anecdotes about plague victims thrive on the irony between expected and actual fates. Each item offers the format of a jest, a tale, or a "note," but on the whole they refute any systematic or schematic representation of the lessons of plague. Whatever generic label it might acquire (comic, lamentable, admirable), each tale takes "note vpon what slippery ground life goes" (39). But each "note" slips on its own ground, most obviously in discouraging our confidence in any regular sequence of events. Their whole point is to vex our anticipation of which characters will sicken and die—will drop suddenly, get just rewards, or escape without rhyme or reason. More than this, Dekker acknowledges that "notes" depend in large part on the reader's expectations, and not vice versa. Thus, in one tale, he opts "to rellish the pallat of lickerish expectation" (38). "Note one thing," another tale bids us, but the "one thing" is the biblical epitome of frustrated expectations, the "thief in the night." The plague is such a thief in the night, and so is the whore whose notable conversion to honesty is suspect: "whether this Recantation was true, or whether the steeme of infection, fuming vp (like wine) into her braines, made her talke thus idlely, I leaue it to the Iury" (51) If Dekker wrote *The Meeting of Gallants*, then he composed a fine definition of the assumptions of notable discovery: some tale is "one especially notable and politicke [which] may euen leade you to the rest and driue you into Imagination of many the like" (131). But the "Suttlety" of "wonder" discredits such leadership and disturbs any scheme of narrative values. The book about plague, he tells us, is itself "somewhat infected" (3). As readers, we avoid the wounds of the plague only by chance, not by our own good intentions.

When Dekker returns to the plague in the pamphlets of the 1620s, he focuses on the ironies latent in any attempt to escape the wounds of the epidemic. In *A Rod for Run-awayes*, there are good and bad motives for escaping; but from the country to the city, from the court to the temple, people fool themselves into believing that they can isolate and evade the disease. In recounting this folly, Dekker offers longer anecdotes than those found in *The Wonderfull Yeare*. Some tales moralize death, others leave it uninterpreted, still others rely on puns, but each reminds us of those "little blue Markes, receiued by Haileshot out of a Birding-piece through a mischance" (165). Or so Dekker describes the "tokens" or "Stroke[s] of Contagion." Marks appear ("I am marked," one man cries) and one is plagued: tokens emerge ex nihilo or from previous sores, and so life ebbs or does not according to the "dreadful Accidents" of a slippery world (166). One tale in particular follows the contagious currency of the plague through a long chain of inheritances, "current Money indeed" (169). But all tales suggest that the tokens of the plague defeat any attempt to regulate its value.

In these later pamphlets, Dekker returns to the instability of "wonderful years." Our own perspectives on wonder are biased or mediated, Dekker reminds us: in comparing two notable years (1625 and 1631), we look "through perspectiue-glasses, to make obiects afarre off, appeare as if they were neere you" (186). Dekker is fond of this conceit of the telescope, and of this idea that "discovery" depends upon the agent.[11] What is more, in Dekker's prose, the mediators of discovery are often daimonic, as elusive as the disease itself. So, while years may seem obviously "Climactericall" or "great with Childe of wonder" (178, 176), they are really just another "wonderful mutation" in the "Shifting of the Windes." There is no "certain abyding" from which to "stedfastly fix our Eyes, vpon the Terrible face of that former wonderfull yeare" (184).

There are some radical implications for this "incertaine" world of elusive "tokens." If the wounds of the plague are emblems for the untrustworthy nature of "notes" in general, it follows that narrative itself might be freed like Nashe's lenten stuff from traditional constraints—that it might be "unripped" from conventional modes, to use Dekker's word. But Dekker's interest in wonder also commits him to a faith in transcendence that mocks all human schemes for order.[12] Wonder can lead us to "admire" God when the world cannot be trusted. Thus, as the "spots" or "Carbuncles, Blaynes, and Blisters" multiply, the proser assumes two self-effacing roles. In *London, Looke Backe* he cites the Bible time and again. The word *plague* (*plaga*, stripe) derives, we are told, from *logos,* so that the wounds descend from the Word in which all readers should believe. In *The Black Rode,* Dekker simply counts the deaths, compiling them into tables for annual comparison. In table after table, Dekker follows Nashe's lenten stuffer in devoting himself to the "Incomprehensible" by way of documentation. By citing biblical precedent for counting the peoples, Dekker unites one recourse with the other, faith in God with simple counting, and thus he takes Greene's desire for an index one step further.

But these strategies—trusting, counting—are prayers in the face of the subtle, uncertain "signs . . . at the Doores" of infection. In *The Blacke Rode*, the final prayer hopes for a "Kingdome, where there are no changes of Kings; No alterations of State . . . No Citizens flying for feare of Infection" (217). Thus, the political and the medical changes coincide once more to suggest the instability of wonder. That this instability extends to the Elizabethan tradition of prose discoveries has only been implied thus far. But Dekker wrote coney-catching pamphlets in which he altered Greene's designs in some important ways. These alterations confirm, I think, that the plague pamphlets challenge their readers to isolate or to stabilize the elusive tokens of the world.

The Daimonic Bellmen, 1608–1613

In the plague pamphlets, one of the world's slippery enterprises is language: in our "Negotiations," we "talke in seuerall Languages, And (like the murmuring fall of Waters) in the Hum of seuerall businesses: insomuch that the place seemes Babell, (a Confusion of tongues)" (199). One key way in which Dekker revises Greene's coney-catching tradition lies in his fascination with the "Babell" of the rogues—their "cant." We will return to this most elusive of all languages, one that the police struggle to translate in its daily changes. But I want to begin with Dekker's police themselves, with the bellmen who turn Greene's earnest officers into strange, shadowy daimons. These bellmen encourage less certainty about their discovery of notable cozenage insofar as they destabilize the perspective of the discoverer. Their function is clarified by a series of master tropes in which Dekker emphasizes the bias of the vantage points from which we reconstruct the notable.

From time to time in his prose, Dekker pauses over an image that explores the contingencies of perspective. These tropes suggest that we all judge the "notable" from some biased vantage—that viewers decide in some measure what the notable is. Dekker admits that the "marks" helping the reader through his strange narratives depend to some degree on the reader's position; and he compares what one modern critic calls "rules of notice" to painted chimneys. Titles, for example, deceive a would-be or distant reader who then perceives the deception at close range, or when he enters the book.[13] More elaborately, Dekker compares the "rules of notice" in *A Strange Horse-Race* (1613) to the schemes used by shops and courts to build interest in the buyer and courtier:

> The first step into a Princes Court, treads not in the brauest roomes, but they are reached to, and entred by ascensions, and degrees. This state and complement begetting more obseruance, delectation, astonishment, and reuerence: by the same line are lesser squares drawne. For if you come into a Gold-smiths, or Lapidaries shop, and desire to buy the fairest Iewels: the cunning Artizan tempts you first with slight ones, and then bewitcheth you with costlier, and (for the vp-shot) strikes your eye with admiration, by gazing at the best of all. So that as no man, (how wretched soeuer) can comparatiuely be miserable, because the palsie-lame hand of *Fortune* can throw him to no baseness and deiection so low, but hee shall vpon some other as low as himselfe. Euen likewise on the contrary part, are there no obiects of triumph, (as maskes, presentations, banquets, and such like) how glorious soeuer of themselues, but may haue their splendor and dignity heightned by a comparatiue traducing of things in the same ranke and qualitie. (III. 315-16)

Although this passage allows that some items may have more intrinsic worth than others, it emphasizes the accidents of judgment. These temptations, as Dekker calls them, are explicitly narrative ones—he is talking about the plot of his pamphlet—and they resemble the slippery fortunes of a world with all its political and mercantile cunning. There is always "comparatiue traducing" to consider, even among "things in the same ranke and qualitie."

The readers need, it would seem, a reliable guide through the shop or court of narrative—through the admirable plots in which "wonder" is even more elusive then "notoriety." But in *A Strange Horse-Race*, Dekker warns us that his own guidance is weak and tentative: "The maine plot of my building is a Moral labyrinth; a weake thred guides you in and out: I will shew you how to enter, and how to passe through, and open all the Roomes, and all the priuate walkes, that when you come to them, you may know where you are: and these they be—Yet I will not; I know it is more pleasure to finde out the conceitfull-deceits of a Paire of Tarriers, then to haue them discouered. . . . [t]hat pleasure be yours, the Tarriers are mine" (313). Thus, he denigrates, then offers, then subtracts the map by which readers might proceed through the puzzles or rooms of the tale. We are left without the benefit of stable discovery to see the import of a text not just "wonderful" but "strange."

As just such an elusive guide, the bellman extends his hand to the readers of Dekker's coney-catching pamphlets, in which "wonder" and "strangeness" return at last to Greene's "notable." There is no question that these pamphlets adopt—some would say plagiarize— the aims and strategies of their Elizabethan precursors. We hear the words *notable discovery* and their many variants, and we recognize the criminals and their anecdotes. But the discoverer and the rogues are all decidedly stranger than their counterparts in Greene's prose. The "new discoverer," as Dekker calls him, is daimonic, an ignis fatuus named Cock Wat (and later "bellman") who is nearly invisible, assumes a variety of shapes, and flies to rooftops. He is a Proteus in the tradition of the elusive Black Dog of Newgate, of the devils and fairies. We have seen the protean muse before: Nashe associates his stuff with such shape changers, and Dekker's plague, we recall, was such a one. But with his bellmen Dekker turns Greene's own officer of the law into a parti-color mystery.

When the bellman approaches the scene of the crime, he is identified by several badges at once, an officer of the town but also an "Embleme of wisedome" (66). His instruments (lantern, candle, dog) suggest a range of iconic and literary associations, classical (Diogenes), biblical (Mark 4:21), and fantastic (the man in the moon). Sometimes the narrator has difficulty recognizing him. We look through the narrator's eyes at the approaching bellman, and we are led through a series of "imaginations" about his identity and purpose—including the trumpeter of Judgment Day. The devil's messenger fails to recognize "what [the bellman] was because he went without his *Lanthorne* and some other implements: for the man in the *Moone* was vp the most part of the night and lighted him which way soeuer hee turned: he tooke *him* for some churlish *Hobgoblin,* seeing a long staffe on his necke" (302). Although the bellman is supposed to direct us to the "sufficient notes" of crime in the city, he himself is difficult to "discover" in the "perspective piece" of his narrative.

But it is not just the bellman who lacks a simple shape or identity. His discoveries, sometimes forced on him, are considered "strange" in the half-light of the candle. The criminals are just much more elusive than even the most resourceful of Greene's coney-catchers. The bellman calls them plagues, "such loathsome and such vlcerous impostumes" (168). As infections in the kingdom, they frustrate their captor mainly because of their language—a "cant" that fascinates Dekker more than any of his precursors. It is, moreover, the canting language of the rogues that clinches Dekker's unsettling revision of discovery.

In Dekker's rogue literature, a record of criminal cant replaces Greene's emphasis on "laws" or typical actions. That Dekker sees this shift from action to language as a destabilizing one is made clear by his several accounts of cant's lineage, which includes the "*Wonder* wrought at Babell" (192). In one pamphlet Dekker prefaces his discussion of cant with a myth of the ages that traces the confusion of language, with its dispersion into ambiguity and obscurity. One age is said to give way to another as communication fails to yet a greater degree. But cant out-babbles Babel: after Babel, there remains the hope that each language can communicate with itself; however, the "Rhetorique" of cant defies interpretation or translation of any kind. Even so, the "new discoverer" provides lexicons and sample translations, yet he admits at every turn that cant is always changing, poised as it is between a dialect of English and an entirely different language. One can praise the rogues for their ingenuity: they live "in an Iland very temperate, fruitfull, full of a noble Nation, rarely gouerned" (192). One can derive the word from "canto," and one can speculate on its "kinde of forme." Dekker does all of this and finds time to praise the peculiar merits of each vernacular language to boot. But there is little doubt that cant allows the rogues, like the plague, to escape from a total or lasting domination by officials, daimonic and otherwise. There is just too much "Irregularity" in the "song" of these vagabonds for Greene's notable discovery to drop its net on them.

But Dekker carries this "Irregularity" of cant and discovery a step further. As cant out-vies the dispersion of language into vernaculars, Dekker's criticism of discovery extends beyond that mode to suggest that modes and genres are finally so mixed in language that they are always strange, contaminated, or inextricable. Readers can talk about them separately, perhaps, but they must concede at last that modes resemble the way of the world:

> for this strompet the world hath tricks as wanton as these: he that every night lyes by the sides of one fairer then *Vulcans* wife, hath been taken the next morning in the Sheetes of a Blackamore . . . for (like *Riders* of great horses) all our *Courses* are but *Figures* of 8: the end of one giddie *Circle,* is but a falling into a worse, and that to which on this day we allow a *religious observance,* to morrowe doe we make the selfe-same thing *ridiculous.* (*A Knights Conjuring,* 79)

This passage sounds very much like the unstable judgment of loyalty and wonder in *The Wonderfull Yeare*. And the "*Figures* of 8" resemble the Tarrier puzzles to which Dekker compares *A Strange Horse-Race*. Like the value of Helen in Shakespeare's *Troilus and Cressida,* the values dispensed in the "giddie" world are radically contingent or, at best, mutable. Ideals are, in fact, desires set against the contamination of the world.

Thus, the circles of the world, even the "most perfect Circles of it, [are] drawne so Irregualler awrye" (79–80). If cant is the world's most irregular language, Dekker's prose locates more acceptable literary ideals in the same figure eight. Beyond the language of the rogues, Dekker's prose mixes its resources to such an obvious extent, and with such advertised insistence, that this "irregularity" names his narrative practices as well. It has often been remarked that Dekker's narratives play urban detail against emblems and personification allegory. In his character essays, as in the bellman and London pamphlets, he promotes a slippage between iconic conventions (for instance, the seven deadly sins) and contemporary social reference. Although it is misleading to label Dekker's practices with such titles as "realism," we are encouraged to see in his prose the kind of generic double duty that Cervantes exposes in his works. One example in particular may suffice to illustrate how Dekker's rogue pamphlets endorse the hybridization of genre and counter genre.[14]

In one of the bellman pamphlets, the narrator is escorting us through a myth of the ages, descending from the golden. Dekker often associates the passing of ages with the obfuscation and dispersion of language, but in this case he fuses two very specific conventions from the Elizabethan tradition of prose fiction. The narrator begins in a paradise, the "patterne of that which our first Parents lead (70)." This is the kind of "golden world," its "patterne" the kind of "Idea" that Sidney celebrates for poets of his age. Suddenly, however, the narrator finds himself at the door of a cottage that proves a hideout for coney-catching rogues. We receive no warning that the idealized golden world is giving way to the criminal genres of Greene's discoveries. The narrator himself laments the sublunary changes of his world, replete with Spenserian images of error. In turn, this hideout has its own mythic proportions, for therein lie the emblems of Mammon, Pluto, and their Hell in the best Spenserian vein. But this is no ordinary romance, for in the den live all the rogues that populate the discovery pamphlets of Greene, those "cheefest (both *Hee-Diuels,* and *Shee-Diuels* that daunce in this large circle)" (110). Thus, emblematic patterns and "cheefest" villains dance in the circle together, all part of one strange race through the figures of narrative cant.[15] Indeed, this scene epitomizes the figure eight theory of literary modes and genres: we can invent names to describe what we feel to be discrete strategies or kinds—"romance," "discovery," "allegory," or what have you—but these names only help us negotiate the radical mixtures of what we might call narrative cant.

Dekker's treatment of the great English writers confirms this notion of the two circles, one in parody of the other. Nashe, in particular, was important to Dekker, who inherited, among other things, a critical edge toward the "mystical Hieroglyphick[s]" of some Elizabethan prose. But Dekker found in Nashe's prose effects of more general importance, leaving no doubt that, in theory and in style, his commitment to the inexhaustible energies of language derives from the "stuff" of his precursor. In fact, Nashe appears more than once in Dekker's narratives. In *A Knights Conjuring*, Dekker imagines an Elysium where poets gather in circles. In one circle, the poets form a ring around Chaucer, their eyes fixed on his, their ears tied to his tongue by a golden chain. These are the poets of romance and blazon, the arbiters of what Greene and Nashe would call "deciphering." But Nashe is one of the wits in an alternative circle, among Greene, Marlowe, and Peele who look to him as their center. Nashe stands there inveighing against patrons, unlimited by the oracular circle of poets whose "magic" is grounded in decorum and commonplace. Nashe has opened that circle into another, with new possibilities. Dekker leaves nothing to doubt: in this response to *Pierce Penilesse*, he attributes to Nashe a liberated brilliance, possessed by the "raptures of that fierie and inconfinable *Italian* spirit [Aretino]" (Robbins, 233). This "inconfinable" spirit is said to enter Dekker's text by "*Metempsuchosis*," free to imitate or to refute the golden oratory that binds the servants of Chaucer. So, even if the servants of a "protean Muse"—the ones in Nashe's circle—absorb the very traditions that they parody, their "inconfinable . . . spirit" and its "Metempsuchosis" are cause to celebrate the very qualities of language that the accountant of cant and the plague laments.

In the vein of Nashe, then, Dekker contributes to the skeptical investigation of literary paradigms, and he explores the boundaries of prose narrative. But Greene is still everywhere in this prose, his works appearing time and again in the early part of the century.[16] Indeed, Dekker's *Penny-Wise, Pound-Foolish* (1631) is yet another tale in the lineage of Greene's discoveries, this time in the repentance fables of *Never Too Late* and *Groats-Worth*. If Dekker unsettles the designs of prose narrative advanced by Greene and Nashe, he preserves the vitality of this heritage—the dilemmas of the "continuate" fiction in Greene's two modes, or the worldly restraints on the prose "stuff" with which Nashe explodes traditional poetics and rhetorical *topoi*. Like Nashe, Dekker resists the most radical implications of his own prose, concluding that his prose dreams are "no Pillar for Saluation to leane vpon, to beleeue that there was or was not any such thing, it could (mee thought) be no offence to Perswade it was so, or not so: and the rather, because it was but a Dreame" (*Dekker his Dreame*, III. 48). In another work, Dekker declares that only the mysterious God is such a pillar, and that only the silly almanac-maker claims any ability to read God's signs: to "finde in the Ephemerides of heauen, certain vnlucky, Criticall, and dangerous daies set down, whose fore-heads are full of Plagues" (IV. 188). Again like Nashe, Dekker suggests our inability to escape from the very terms and modes that we criticize—our inability to stop trying to order or to interpret the tales we tell. But Dekker knows better than Nashe that we should never forget how our designs race around that figure eight of which cant and the plague only remind us. In the seventeenth-century "wars of truth," English prose narrative takes its place, however recessive, in the ranks.[17]

Discovering Renaissance Prose Narrative

Whatever their intentions, Nashe and Dekker transformed the strategies of prose narrative that Greene and other Elizabethans called "deciphering" and "discovering." So, while an interest in the "exemplary" or the "notable" tale persists among the "admirable" or "wonderful" narratives of the seventeenth century, other terms appear with more and more regularity.[18] For example, prose writers from John Reynolds to Aphra Behn and William Congreve choose *accident* as the word for the events in their narratives. These "accidents" vary in sense from Aristotle's non-substantial adjunct to our modern notion of an unfortunate mistake. "Accidents" can be ordained by providence, singled out for "especial remembrance," or contrasted (in the case of Congreve) with the heightening effects of romance.[19] For Congreve, the antiromantic "accidents" are familiar yet "odd events," and they are appropriate for "novels." Aphra Behn often calls the events in her stories by the name of "accidents"; and although one gets the impression that some "accidents" are indeed notable, she, like Congreve and others, seems intent on challenging the traditions and paradigms of exemplary narrative passed down from the romancers. "Accidents" epitomize the complexity of narrative paradigms in the seventeenth century: they admit old ways of arranging narrative in the very act of discrediting those ways in favor of new ones.

But it will not do merely to label these new ways "circumstantial realism" or "novelistic." As Michael McKeon has demonstrated, the "origins" of the novel amount to the radical alteration of modes of "cultural signification" in regard to truth and virtue.[20] When the inconsistencies in epistemology and status become "intractable," the novel emerges as the discourse prepared to negotiate, not mirror, what is complex about these realities. For McKeon, the novel absorbs its precursors and intersects with the cultural wars of the seventeenth century; narrative cannot, therefore, be isolated from the social upheavals prior to and during the seventeenth century.

Although McKeon's thesis is a difficult one, he finds in Cervantes's *Don Quixote* its every facet—from romance to "naive empiricism" and onward to "radical skepticism"; from a progressive rebuttal to feudal designs on status to a conservative revision of that progressive challenge.[21] Thus, Cervantes epitomizes in one novel the far-reaching and complex dialectic of more than a century in England. But, although my terms have differed from McKeon's, I think we can see in the prose of Greene, Nashe, and Dekker the assertion and revision of narrative values—indeed, in their own terms. In line with Dekker's criticism of the wonderful or notable, then, Cervantes should also be noticed for another text, his *Novelas ejemplares,* or *Exemplary Stories.* As the translator C. A. Jones has remarked, the label *exemplary* "has been as much a stumbling-block as an aid to understanding."[22] Jones suggests that, failing "the clarity which one might have wished for" in a title, the reader should "draw one's definition as widely as possible." But it seems entirely possible that the author of *Don Quixote* is challenging old paradigms in his *Exemplary Stories* as well—that he is questioning the stability or the value of the exemplary tale, just as he questions the status of romance in *Don Quixote*. Cervantes's preface and the tales, especially "The Deceitful Marriage" and "The Dogs' Colloquy," are self-conscious about the strategies by which a raconteur makes a tale pleasing or memorable to his audience. Some are too preachy, others wish to avoid stretching the narrative, and still others have extensive advice about the production of a "main point" in tales. Or, as one dog says to the other:

> If you're going to be so long in telling me about the habits of the masters you've had . . . we shall have to ask heaven to grant us speech for at least a year; and even then I'm afraid that at the speed you're going, you won't get half-way through your story. And I want to point out to you something which you'll be able to test when I tell you of the adventures of my life; and that is that some stories contain their appeal in themselves, others in the way they are told. In other words there are some which, even without preambles and elegant language, give pleasure; and there are others which need to be decked out with words; and with gestures of the face and hands and changes in the tone of voice, something comes out of nothing, and instead of being weak and feeble they become witty and pleasing. (198–99)

McKeon has shown all the sophistication with which Cervantes challenged paradigms and resources of romance, including its medium of publication. That Cervantes both uses and overturns conventional notions of the "exemplary" suggests that Dekker was not alone in exploring the problems of the notable.

Nor were Dekker and Cervantes the only authors to question discovery. Terence Cave has argued that discovery plots were challenged and sometimes rejected as contrivances throughout seventeenth-century Europe.[23] Congreve admits, for instance, that the discovery plot in his *Incognita* amounts to a "contrivance," even as it imitates a dramatic unity of action. But bad plots, he says, need some contrivance. Thus, in contrasting the romantic and the accidental, Congreve also criticizes those narratives which "begin with an unexpected accident," only to fade into the "insipid." He rebukes such a practice in terms very similar to the images of shops or courts in Dekker. For the reader of such bad tales, who hopes for "a level in the entertainment," is taken upstairs to the dining room, only to be forced "to make a meal in the kitchen" thereafter.[24] In Congreve's preface, notable discovery relies on a set of machinations and contingencies—the identity and hopes of the diner, the sequence by which upstairs and down are visited, and the intent of the server.

Like Congreve or Behn, other successors to the Elizabethan writers of prose narrative were compelled to rethink the emblems and notes by which Greene, Nashe, and Dekker unfolded their tales. It is not surprising to find Daniel Defoe struggling with the causes of the plague—between tokens vertically derived from God, and tokens as the visible network of a radical and horizontal infection:

> This put it out of Question to me, that the Calamity was spread by Infection, that is to say, by some certain Steams, or Fumes, which the Physicians call *Effluvia*, by the Breath, or by the Sweat, or by the Stench of the Sores of the sick Persons, or some other way, perhaps, beyond even the Reach of the Physicians themselves . . . and I cannot but with some Wonder, find some People, now the Contagion is over, talk of its being an immediate Stroke from Heaven, without the Agency of Means, having Commission to strike this and that particular Person, and none other.[25]

In his account, Defoe favors the "accidental" and "particular" as terms for the circumstances or events of the plague. But he shifts between the dispensations of providence and the mere tallies of the dead—between a stable, readable wonder and an elusive, infectious wonder. As Defoe refers to the plagues of the earlier part of the century, from whose accounts he certainly learned, he reminds us that his journal engages an already complex history of affirmation and doubt. In *Roxana* or in *Robinson Crusoe*, Defoe once more inscribes the providential patterns of narrative among the intricate network of accidents known as the novel.[26]

If the immediate heirs of the Elizabethans betoken their own concerns in reacting to the emblems and notes, so do we moderns. But we, too, should at least permit the Renaissance prosers to speak to us in their own language, not in the language of the novel. It is the conviction of this book that, if we are to decode English prose narrative from Lyly to Behn, we need to have a fuller understanding of the terms that they employed time and again. Their terms are lost whenever we universalize their prose, or reject it because the prose seems hardly universal. But if we attend to the vexed and self-referential labors of representing a culture other than ours, we stand to gain a new meditation on our own terms—to learn that "we" is the most slippery node of all.

Thus, with all our contingencies in tow, we discover our own boundaries when we, like the historians, Hayden White and Marilyn Robinson Waldman, debate other cultures and their differences in regard to narrative "explicitness" and the "noteworthy." Above all, as Waldman says, we learn our limitations and biases when we approach the narrative schemes of other cultures: "The presence of so many empty years [in a chronicle] suggests, then, the possibility that the author is establishing a level of significance for included events, a level we do not yet comprehend and which is underscored by the emptinesses."[27] So must we struggle to gauge the "level of significance for included events" when we read through the narrative prose of Shakespeare's contemporaries, a prose that for all its volume can suddenly turn silent on us.

Of moderns and postmoderns alike, perhaps Virginia Woolf knew best what we have to gain from a rediscovery of Elizabethan and Jacobean prose. Fresh from a reading of Gabriel Harvey and others, Woolf wrote of "the strange Elizabethans" that their prose was "almost incapable of fulfilling one of the offices of prose which is to make people talk, simply and naturally, about ordinary things."[28] Woolf herself was in pursuit of a prose in which the ordinary became notable, one closer than the "strange Elizabethans" to the flux of modern life:

> Examine for a moment an ordinary mind on an ordinary day. The mind receives a myriad impressions—trivial, fantastic, evanescent, or engraved with the sharpness of steel. From all sides they come, an incessant shower of innumerable atoms; and as they fall, as they shape themselves into the life of Monday or Tuesday, the accent falls differently from of old; the moment of importance came not here but there. . . . Life is not a series of gig-lamps symmetrically arranged; but a luminous halo, a semi-transparent envelope surrounding us from the beginning of consciousness to the end. Is it not the task of the novelist to convey this varying, this unknown and uncircumscribed spirit, whatever aberration or complexity it may display . . . ? Let us not take it for granted that life exists more

fully in what is commonly thought big than in what is commonly thought small.[29]

With modern prose, the "strange" Elizabethan trust in the notable or exemplary is impossible and undesirable. The proser writes from within the "envelope." But Woolf has absorbed the voices and gestures of Renaissance prose, as surely as T. S. Eliot evoked the poems and plays. Most obviously in *Orlando*, Woolf recreates the "great frosts" of the first decade of the seventeenth century, years portrayed by Dekker in all their wonder.[30] In the same novel, Woolf calls on those strange Elizabethans and Jacobeans to help challenge the complicitous paradigms of gender and narrative. Less obviously, in *The Waves*, we come upon Bernard with his notebook always in hand, and with the rise and fall of the waves suggesting that Woolf herself still strives, in her words, to discover "accent" and "the moment of importance." Woolf denies any equivalence between old and modern prose; but in the Renaissance failures to "talk . . . about ordinary things," she hears the voices and witnesses the dreams of a prose so passing strange.

And she is not alone as a modern who performs new literary tasks with an eye to the old. Literary theorists in our own time debate the multivalence or determinacy of narrative "nodes," distant from the cultural paradigms of the Renaissance and yet, in the case of Foucault, entrenched in its lore.[31] Both Woolf and Foucault, worlds apart, teach us that the rediscovery of Renaissance prose involves two activities. One is the recognition of otherness or "strangeness" in Renaissance texts. The other, however, is the recognition of ourselves wading among all that strange "stuff." Accordingly, it is naive to assume that we simply "find" certain paradigms or tensions in Nashe or, for that matter, in Paracelsus—the one escaping into the fictions that can neither fix nor leave the world, the other applauding the sufficiency of nature that we limited mortals must, nonetheless, always labor to repair.[32] But what we recreate in their texts is not simply our mirror image, either. With their marks of greatness, essence, and wonder, the Elizabethans teach us how to read their narratives, even if recuperation leads us down erroneous paths—toward the assumption that we have healed the gaps in these narratives, that we indeed tell better stories than did they, or that we have had the last, or most notable, word on them.

With Virginia Woolf and Umberto Eco, James Joyce is a modern novelist who invokes strange and old ways of telling tales. It has even been argued that Joyce borrows from Dekkerian cant.[33] A scene from his *Ulysses* provides us with a fit and final parable for the mysteries that await us in the codes of Renaissance narrative. Leopold Bloom has come home from the "wonderstruck" discovery of his son, Rudy, and he undresses on the threshold between that dramatic knot and the endless unfoldings of Molly. Between the two, Leopold fastens on the "medial line of nodes" above and below the "medial line of irregular incrispated black hairs."[34] This is to say that he fingers his buttons and traces his vertebrae. There are other knots to untangle, and so Bloom "disnode[s] the laceknots" (III.1569). Having so divested himself of the discovery along with the clothes, Bloom moves from "irritation" (1567) to "satisfaction" (1571), then onward to irritation in "the visible signs of postsatisfaction" (1627). Between the discovery of Rudy and the unfoldings of Molly, Bloom pauses at the wonder of a narrative that pleases expectations and then takes pleasure away. He pauses, that is, between an elusive "moment of importance" and the (perhaps more important) "ever after," and then he unlaces the knots. As sleep is invoked, Bloom's narrative to Molly, although absent from the text, is questioned for its modifications of reality (positive and negative), its "salient point," and its "limitations" (1628). *Ulysses* is a far cry from the strange Elizabethans, as it is from Homer; and Leopold is an unfortunate traveler in a city that Jack Wilton would not recognize. But Leopold and Molly struggle through their own family romance and its new values and voices in the shadow of narratives past. This sequence in *Ulysses* serves to remind us that, as Woolf knew well, the strange colors of Elizabethan prose still touch the threads by which we weave other, ordinary tales. Volte-face, Elizabethan prose fiction proves to challenge and unsettle the novel rather than to found or originate it.

NOTES

Introduction

1. For "idea and act," see Walter R. Davis, *Idea and Act in Elizabethan Fiction* (Princeton: Princeton University Press, 1969); for "humanism," see Arthur F. Kinney, *Humanist Poetics: Thought, Rhetoric, and Fiction in Sixteenth-Century England* (Amherst: University of Massachusetts Press, 1986).
2. One crossover is the term *convenience*, for which see below.
3. Paul Salzman, *English Prose Fiction, 1558–1700: A Critical History* (Oxford: Clarendon Press, 1985).
4. Renaissance "cultural formations" have been the target of much recent discussion in the work of the so-called "new historicists." See, for instance, the essays by Louis Montrose and Stephen Greenblatt in *Literary Theory/Renaissance Texts*, eds. Patricia Parker and David Quint (Baltimore: Johns Hopkins University Press, 1986).
5. See, for example, Nicholas Storojenko's life of Greene printed in Grosart's edition of the works; John Clark Jordan, *Robert Greene* (New York: Columbia University Press, 1915); and Davis, *Idea and Act*. Salzman comments on this trend that "[b]y René Pruvost, Greene is seen as passing through eleven periods of composition, which Walter Davis sensibly reduces to four" (*English Prose Fiction*, 59). W. W. Barker, "Rhetorical Romance: The 'Frivolous Toyes' of Robert Greene," in *Unfolded Tales: Essays on Renaissance Romance*, eds. George M. Logan and Gordon Teskey (Ithaca: Cornell University Press, 1989), 74–97, finds continuity in Greene's works, but he also sees them moving from one stage to another, in this case from monologism to "greater variety" or "greater complexity."
6. The epigraphs are as follows: "Omne tulit punctum qui miscuit utile dulci" (1584–90), the Horatian poet's creed; "sero sed serio" (1590); and "nascimur pro patria" (1591–92). For recent discussions of Greene's interest in the relation between his career and his works, see Richard Helgerson, *The Elizabethan Prodigals* (Berkeley: University of California Press, 1976), 79–104; and Charles W. Crupi, *Robert Greene* (Boston: Twayne Publishers, 1986). Crupi is typical in seeing "several distinct phases" in Greene's prose (14), but these "phases" need investigation as such. In other words, we need to ask: what does it mean when Greene divides his prose career into stages?
7. Greene's prose attempts to fashion what S. K. Heninger, Jr., has called "*a priori* agreements between author and reader," according to the "forceful orthodox determinant[s] of renaissance thought." But this attempt is a complex and dynamic one. See *Touches of Sweet Harmony: Pythagorean Cosmology and Renaissance Poetics* (San Marino, Calif.: Huntington Library, 1974), xii.
8. The problem of the "author" goes back to Foucault's classic essay, "What Is an Author?" in *Language, Counter-Memory, Practice: Selected Essays and Interviews*, ed. with an introduction by Donald F. Bouchard, trans. Bouchard and Sherry Simon (Ithaca: Cornell University Press, 1977), 113–38. But even the old new-critical disregard for authorial intentions enters into discussions of Greene, who is so emphatic

about his instructions to the reader. Thus, Crupi writes (1): "Indeed, Greene himself often insists on the connection of his works to his life and opinions, demanding a regard for authorial intentions that not all modern readers will concede willingly." Often, such parlance turns into a denial of Greene's didactic value: he claims to teach, the common line goes, but he really wants and manages to delight or to tell stories for their own sake (if the critic isn't prepared to concede delight).

9. Terence Cave's *Cornucopian Text: Problems of Writing in the French Renaissance* (Oxford: Clarendon Press, 1979) investigates this difference at length.

10. Victoria Kahn has labeled the two activities "reconstructive" and "deconstructive." See *Rhetoric, Prudence, and Skepticism in the Renaissance* (Ithaca: Cornell University Press, 1985), 4.

11. The phrase is William J. Kennedy's. See *Rhetorical Norms in Renaissance Literature* (New Haven: Yale University Press, 1978), 13.

12. For licentious fictions, see Lorna Hutson, *Thomas Nashe in Context* (Oxford: Clarendon Press, 1989). See also Helgerson, *Elizabethan Prodigals*. I discuss the claim that tales mean nothing at all toward the end of chapter 1 and throughout chapter 5.

13. I use the term more generally than does Foucault, for whom "convenience" means one kind of resemblance in the Renaissance episteme. See *The Order of Things: An Archaeology of the Human Sciences*, trans. Alan Sheridan (New York: Vintage, 1973).

14. George Puttenham, *The Arte of English Poesie*, in *Elizabethan Critical Essays*, ed. G. Gregory Smith (Oxford: Oxford University Press, 1904), II:174.

15. For the "places" of the mnemonic tradition, see, of course, Frances Yates, *The Art of Memory* (Chicago: University of Chicago Press, 1966). Elizabeth Deeds Ermarth, in *Realism and Consensus in the English Novel* (Princeton: Princeton University Press, 1983), discusses the "discrete" spaces in pre-novelistic art and discourse with reference to Stanley Fish's remark that a sermon by Lancelot Andrewes proceeds by "'merely creating new spaces into which the meaning that is already there expands'" (12).

16. This phrase is, again, William J. Kennedy's. See *Rhetorical Norms*, 3.

17. We might call these guarantors of commonplace meaning the "gathering grounds" of humanist discourse: thus, according to Victoria Kahn, does Ascham describe books as "'containing a certain few fit precepts unto the which should be gathered and applied plenty of examples out of the choiceth authors of both the tongues. This work would stand rather in good diligence for gathering.'" See "Humanism and the Resistance to Theory," in *Literary Theory/Renaissance Texts*, 373–96. The quotation is on 378.

18. There is overlap in the meanings of "deciphering" and "discovering," just as "note" and "place" have some family resemblances. But Greene encourages us to see the difference between the prose of the 1580s and that of the 1590s.

19. This statement is quoted by James Stephens, *Francis Bacon and the Style of Science* (Chicago: University of Chicago Press, 1975), 59, and it pertains to the mind's facile tendency to impose its errant schemes on experience.

20. "Defining Nonfiction Genres," in *Renaissance Genres: Essays on Theory, History, and Interpretation*, ed. Barbara Kiefer Lewalski (Cambridge, Mass.: Harvard University Press, 1986), 45–69.

21. See Kahn, "Humanism and the Resistance to Theory."

22. In the final chapter, I will return to Michael McKeon's important book, *The Origins of the English Novel, 1600–1740* (Baltimore: Johns Hopkins University Press, 1987).

23. For one essay toward the articulation of the negotiations between the modern

critic and Renaissance otherness, see Stephen Greenblatt's essay on psychoanalysis and Renaissance culture in *Literary Theory/Renaissance Texts*.

Chapter 1. Greene Deciphering

1. Not "half" in the parity of years (1580–89, 1590–92), but according to the "conversion" in narrative practice that Greene claims in *Greenes Mourning Garment* (1590). In the same year, *Never Too Late* (parts I and II) appears, and, in the next year, the coney-catching pamphlets begin, all attended by Greene's shift to the term *discovery* as the dominant label for his prose.

2. For Sidney, see Smith, ed., *Elizabethan Critical Essays*, I: 175: "But I am content not onely to decipher [the ideal poet] by his workes . . . but more narrowly will examine his parts"; for James VI, I.211: "sonnet decifring the perfyte poete"; and for Lodge, I.63, 65–66: "Though Aesopes craftie crowe be neuer so deftlye decked, yet is his double dealing esely desiphered"; "Did you neuer reade . . . that vnder the persons of beastes many abuses were dissiphered"; "in the picture of angry Iuno our affections are dissiphered." All of these justifications of "poesy" are germane in their entire arguments to Greene's early prose.

3. *The Complete Works of John Lyly*, ed. R. Warwick Bond (Oxford: Clarendon Press, 1902), I.180.

4. Kinney, in *Humanist Poetics*, 30, differentiates between truthful or icastic prose and fantastic prose (spun by an idle mind of its own materials).

5. See *De Natura Deorum*, trans. H. Rackham (Cambridge, Mass.: Harvard University Press, 1961), I.53–54.

6. Grosart defined *deciphering* as "characterized, or explained, or unfolded" (II.302). This is not a careful gloss, of course, although it does suggest the close relationship between deciphering and unfolding.

7. See Cave, *Cornucopian Text*, Helgerson, *The Elizabethan Prodigals*, Hutson, *Thomas Nashe in Context*, Patricia Parker, *Inescapable Romance: Studies in the Poetics of a Mode* (Princeton: Princeton University Press, 1979) and *Literary Fat Ladies: Rhetoric, Gender, Property* (New York: Methuen, 1987), Jonathan Goldberg, *Endlesse Worke: Spenser and the Structures of Discourse* (Baltimore: Johns Hopkins University Press, 1981), and David Lee Miller, *The Poem's Two Bodies: The Poetics of the 1590 "Fairie Queene"* (Princeton: Princeton University Press, 1988).

8. Seminal work on Euphuism includes Jonas A. Barish, "The Prose Style of John Lyly," *English Literary History* 23 (1956): 14–35; G. K. Hunter, *John Lyly: The Humanist as Courtier* (Cambridge, Mass.: Harvard University Press, 1962); William A. Ringler, Jr., "The Immediate Source of Euphuism," *PMLA* 53 (1938): 678–86; and Bond's introduction to *The Complete Works*.

9. Devon L. Hodges has recently explored the fixity and dispersion of the anatomy genre in *Renaissance Fictions of Anatomy* (Amherst: University of Massachusetts Press, 1985).

10. These are the words of Richard Carew in Gregory Smith's anthology of Elizabethan criticism (II.292).

11. See *Cicero's "Philippics" and Their Demosthenic Model: The Rhetoric of Crisis* (Chapel Hill: University of North Carolina Press, 1983). According to the *ad Herennium*, trans. Harry Caplan (Cambridge, Mass.: Harvard University Press, 1968), 374–75: "Dwelling on the Point occurs when one remains rather long upon, and often returns to, the strongest topic *(in loco firmissimo)* . . . [i]ts use is particularly advantageous [*Hac uti maxime convenit*], and is especially characteristic of the good

orator, for no opportunity is given the hearer to remove his attention from this strongest topic. I have been unable to subjoin a quite appropriate example of the figure, because this topic is not isolated from the whole cause like some limb, but like blood is spread through the whole body of the discourse."

12. Geoffrey of Vinsauf writes in the *Poetria Nova*, trans. Margaret Nims (Toronto: Pontifical Institute, 1967), 61: "[By *commoratio*] I go deeply into one point and linger on in the same place."

13. For the spiritual and affective justifications of rhetoric, see Debora K. Shuger, *Sacred Rhetoric: The Christian Grand Style in the English Renaissance* (Princeton: Princeton University Press, 1988).

14. Cave, *The Cornucopian Text*, 30.

15. Marjorie O'Rourke Boyle shows us Erasmus the editor and philologist who emends *verbum* to *sermo* yet insists that the two words are synonyms (*Erasmus on Language and Method in Theology* [Toronto: University of Toronto Press, 1977], 18–31). In the letter to Dorp, Erasmus explains that the *Moriae Encomium* means "the very same thing" as his other works, but only says it differently (John C. Olin, ed., *Desiderius Erasmus, Christian Humanism and the Reformation* [New York: Harper Torchbooks, 1965], 59). Preference within synonymy persists in Erasmus's defense of his philosophy of Christ: "Christ both taught and presented the same doctrine [as the pagans] so much more fully" (Olin, 101). He claims that he has the "same mind" about Luther as before, and that Luther teaches the "same doctrine as others," though Luther's approach is too radically different (Olin, 157). Finally, Erasmus's defense of the "seamless garment" of the church has him harping on unity in a series of natural similes that connect it to the *Parabolae* and to Euphuism. In his assertion that the "terms differ but the Idea is the same," modern readers, notably Huizinga, find complexity in Erasmus's ways of assertion and non-assertion. See *Erasmus and the Age of Reformation* (New York: Harper, 1957).

16. Janel M. Mueller, *The Native Tongue and the Word: Developments in English Prose Style, 1380–1580* (Chicago: University of Chicago Press, 1984), 382. All further citations will appear in the text.

17. Lawrence D. Green shows a different milieu in which Euphuism acquired its rhetoric of compulsion—John Rainolds's lectures on Aristotle's *Rhetoric*. These lectures are a reputed source for Euphuism and, Green believes, reflect an accepted program at Oxford in which "logical conclusions could never be proven absolutely, but only to a degree of probability . . . only through a cumulative effect, by piling one probable proof upon another, until the sheer weight of probable evidence finally compelled belief on the part of the listener." See *John Rainolds's Oxford Lectures on Aristotle's "Rhetoric"* (Newark: University of Delaware Press, 1986), 75.

18. See the chapter on Greene in *Humanist Poetics*. I return to the problem of wonder in chapter 6. In a recent essay, Robert B. Heilman has studied Greene's Euphuism as essential to a "persistent quest for order," as imposing a "predetermined orderedness" on the romantic tendency to unfold its tales in a wandering fashion. See "Greene's Euphuism and Some Congeneric Styles," in *Unfolded Tales*, 49–73. My quotations are taken from pages 51 and 62.

19. Bond, ed., *The Complete Works*, II.33. All further references appear in the text.

20. See note 1 in this chapter. Two similar paradigms are debated between "Chaucer" and "Gower" in *Greenes Vision* (1592).

21. *The Cast of Character: The Representation of Personality in Ancient and Medieval Literature* (Toronto: University of Toronto Press, 1983), 19.

22. Unless otherwise noted, all references to Greene's works cite Alexander B.

Grosart's edition of *The Life and Complete Works in Prose and Verse of Robert Greene* (New York: Russell & Russell, 1964) by volume and page (here, II.14–15). This seems the best course for the reader's convenience, especially because I am not attempting a study of style. But the reader should be forewarned that Grosart's edition does not meet the modern standards for a critical edition. I cite modern editions or facsimiles where they are available.

23. For Greene's equivalent of the absurdist view of life, see Davis, *Idea and Act*, 138–78. Note that moral chaos is usually linked in Greene's career with the growing fullness of his narratives. But the key words help us to pursue the Renaissance negotiations of these issues rather than simply pronouncing on the moral content of the texts.

24. I refer to her article "Humanism and the Resistance to Theory," cited above. All other references will appear in the text.

25. Some of these works offer very interesting twists to the deciphering-unfolding relations—for instance, *Planetomachia* (1585), *Penelopes Web* (1587), *Euphues His Censure* (1587), and *Pandosto* (1588).

26. This sufficiency of knowledge is in stark contrast with the critical historian's insistence on knowing how a reporter has gained the news of an event. For a summary of this issue, see Barbara J. Shapiro, *Probability and Certainty in Seventeenth-Century England: A Study of the Relationships Between Natural Science, Religion, History, Law, and Literature* (Princeton: Princeton University Press, 1983), chap. 4. For Renaissance myths of the origin of all rivers, see David Quint, *Origin and Originality in Renaissance Literature: Versions of the Source* (New Haven: Yale University Press, 1983).

27. Gabriel Harvey, *Works*, ed. Alexander B. Grosart (New York: AMS Press, 1966), II.39–40. All other references to this edition will appear in the text.

28. Some modern scholars also disparage the humanists—for example, C. S. Lewis in his famous *English Literature in the Sixteenth Century, Excluding Drama* (Oxford: Clarendon Press, 1965), 1–65. For an excellent analysis of humanism, see Victoria Kahn, *Rhetoric, Prudence, and Skepticism in the Renaissance*.

29. This statement is quoted by Wesley Trimpi in *Ben Jonson's Poems, a Study of the Plain Style* (Stanford, Calif.: Stanford University Press, 1962), 33.

30. Barbara J. Shapiro has covered this ground in *Probability and Certainty in Seventeenth-Century England*, 227–46. The quotation is on 236.

31. For quantity as a code that eluded the Elizabethans, see Derek Attridge, *Well-Weighed Syllables: Elizabethan Verse in Classical Metres* (New York: Cambridge University Press, 1974).

32. *Ciceronis Amor*, ed. E. H. Miller (Gainesville, Fla.: Scholars' Facsimiles & Reprints, 1954), A3r. All other citations are in the text.

33. Walter J. Ong, *Rhetoric, Romance, and Technology: Studies in the Interaction of Expression and Culture* (Ithaca: Cornell University Press, 1971).

34. Walter Davis is a good source on this emphasis on style. He notes the experimentation in *Ciceronis Amor*, and he says of *Menaphon* that "[v]ariety of style is always kept foremost in the reader's mind . . . chiefly because its characters are always so much concerned with style, constantly discover things through style, and so frequently comment on each other's style" (*Idea and Act*, 173).

35. Parallels between Greene's *Menaphon* and Sidney's *Arcadia* were first drawn by Samuel Wolff and pursued by others. But Paul Salzman warns us that direct imitation is possible only with the *Old Arcadia* (if Greene saw a manuscript) and "unthinkable" with the *New* (*English Prose Fiction*, 66).

36. As we will see, Nashe uses the word *deciphering* to refer to an empty rhetoric

of mere tropes and figures that also happens to be wily in its politics. He also applies the term to a sneaky kind of topical interpretation that serves political interests. Thus, rhetoric and interpretation converge in the assertion that decipherers only pretend to hide from the world. The politics of interpretation in the Renaissance has been studied in two works by Annabel M. Patterson: *Censorship and Interpretation: The Conditions of Writing and Reading in Early Modern England* (Madison: University of Wisconsin Press, 1984); and "Misinterpretable Donne: The Testimony of the Letters," *John Donne Journal* 1 (1982): 39–53.

37. In a number of works, Greene stages his "farewell to folly," or dons his "mourning garment" for the past. Ronald Levao offers an excellent summary of the general problem of justifying fictions in the Renaissance: there is an "increasing awareness of the mind's power and freedom to create fictional worlds that outstrips its ability to justify them. Critics and poets produced many strategies to defer or contain their unease, but the dilemma emerged with unnerving clarity in the later Renaissance" (*Renaissance Minds and their Fictions: Cusanus, Sidney, Shakespeare* [Berkeley: University of California Press, 1985], 132). For the Elizabethans, this problem is especially acute, I think, among the prosers.

Chapter 2. Greene Discovering

1. Overlap between deciphering and discovering, or between rhetorical places and notes, represents the kind of slippage against which Greene poses tidy schemes. Indeed, these pamphlets of discovery reject any ornament in style, wanting "no eloquent phrases, nor figuratiue conueiance." Yet, we will return to the slippage in chapter 6.

2. The phrase *notable discovery* and its cognates appear so often that Greene can use them as a generic badge. In one emphatic gesture of self-correction, Greene gives us a "discourse, or rather discouery of a Nip" (*Second Part*, 29). In another place, he claims to be "writing this discouery" (40). In the third part of his coney-catching series, an old man delivers "notes of notorious matters" and "notes" of the most "notable villanies discouered" (10–11).

3. The best treatment of the prodigal Greene is Helgerson's in *The Elizabethan Prodigals*.

4. The naturalness of discovery is explored below in the section entitled "The Power of Discovery."

5. See Marvin T. Herrick, *Comic Theory in the Sixteenth Century* (Urbana: University of Illinois Press, 1964); *The Poetics of Aristotle in England* (New Haven: Yale University Press, 1930); and Joel B. Altman, *The Tudor Play of Mind: Rhetorical Inquiry and the Development of Elizabethan Drama* (Berkeley: University of California Press, 1978).

6. For "rules of notice," see Peter J. Rabinowitz, *Before Reading: Narrative Conventions and the Politics of Interpretation* (Ithaca: Cornell University Press, 1987); for synecdoche and "nowness," see the essays by Alan C. Dessen and R. L. Smallwood in the *Cambridge Companion to Shakespeare Studies*, ed. Stanley Wells (Cambridge: Cambridge University Press, 1986). Renaissance writers conceived of different kinds of dialogue, some more anchored in a preconceived truth and others more exploratory within certain guidelines. For dialogue, see Altman and also Kenneth J. Wilson, *Incomplete Fictions: The Formation of English Renaissance Dialogue* (Washington, D.C.: Catholic University of America Press, 1985).

7. See T. W. Baldwin, *William Shakspere's Five-Act Structure* (Urbana: University

of Illinois Press, 1947); and W. W. Greg, *Two Elizabethan Stage Abridgements: "The Battle of Alcazar" & "Orlando Furioso"* (London: Malone Society, 1923).

8. Terence Cave, *Recognitions: A Study in Poetics* (Oxford: Clarendon Press, 1988).

9. See Herrick, *Comic Theory*, 89–129.

10. Herrick, *Comic Theory*, 111.

11. Cave, *Recognitions*, 82.

12. See Marvin T. Herrick, *The Poetics of Aristotle in England*. For Minturno, *De Poeta* (1559), III.283, the word is *agnitione*.

13. *The Scottish History of James the Fourth* (Malone Society Reprints, 1921), sig. K3.2484.

14. David M. Bevington comments on the conflation of discovery spaces and discovery scenes in *Action is Eloquence: Shakespeare's Language of Gesture* (Cambridge, Mass.: Harvard University Press, 1984), 116–17. Bevington is discussing *The Tempest*, and he concludes that the play's discovery space converges with recognition and is "strongly associated with Prospero and his magic."

15. For the synecdochic conventions of stage directions, see Alan C. Dessen, *Elizabethan Stage Conventions and Modern Interpreters* (New York: Cambridge University Press, 1984), 11–13, 103–4, and passim.

16. For a critique of this theory, see Richard Hosley, "The Discovery-Space in Shakespeare's Globe," *Shakespeare Survey* 12 (1959): 35–46.

17. See Dessen, *Elizabethan Stage Conventions*, chapter 5, and notes 8 and 11 (172–73).

18. For Yates, see *The Art of Memory*, 342–67. In addition to Hosley's article, see Andrew Gurr, *The Shakespearean Stage, 1574–1642*, 2d ed. (Cambridge: Cambridge University Press, 1980), 136–46; T. J. King, *Shakespearean Staging, 1599–1642* (Cambridge, Mass.: Harvard University Press, 1971), 3; and Michael Hattaway, *Elizabethan Popular Theatre: Plays in Performance* (Boston: Routledge & Kegan Paul, 1982), 27–29.

19. There is debate about each item in this definition: how many doors? how big an alcove? best seen from what seat in the theater?

20. Hosley, "The Discovery Space," 44–45.

21. Thus, Hamlet and Horatio both express more than we might think when they claim to have "noted" Claudius at the catastrophe of the "Murder of Gonzago." It should be pointed out, too, that it was Greene's St. John's College that led the way in introducing Aristotle's *Poetics* to England, as Herrick tells us in *The Poetics of Aristotle in England*.

22. "Already we have heard many times how various people, with some clever remark or ready retort, or some quick piece of thinking, have been able, by striking at the right moment, to draw the teeth of their antagonists or avert impending dangers." On the next day the narrators will tell of similar "prompt retort[s] or shrewd manoeuvre[s]." See *The Decameron*, trans. G. H. McWilliam (New York: Penguin Books, 1972), 478–79.

23. So did Castelvetro, who illustrates these terms from the *Poetics* with tales from Boccaccio. See *On the Art of Poetry*, trans. Andrew Bongiorno (Binghamton, N.Y.: Medieval and Renaissance Texts & Studies, 1984), III.vi.126–29. According to Cave (*Recognitions*, 82), Giason Denores studied "a story by Boccaccio at great length as a complete paradigm of epic construction within the Aristotelian frame of reference."

24. Jests are frequently adapted in interlude and play, both before and after the printing of jest books in the late fifteenth century. For this information, see Rosemary Woolf, *The English Mystery Plays* (Berkeley: University of California Press, 1972),

188–89. In interludes, jests involve strange intersections between the Vice and coney-catching figures (for example, the Vice as collier, an occupation included among the rogues who dupe innocents). The dramatic use of novellas is well known.

25. This characterization of the novella is Maurice Valency's, who with Harry Levtow edited *The Palace of Pleasure: An Anthology of the Novella* (New York: Capricorn Books, 1960). See pp. 1–3.

26. In the preface to his translation of *Orlando Furioso*, John Harington comments on the multiple notes of the romance when he declares the poem "to be full of *Peripet[e]ia*, which I interpret an agnition of some vn-looked for fortune either good or bad, and a sudden change thereof." See G. Gregory Smith's anthology, II.216.

27. For self-advertising in the pamphlets, see Constance C. Relihan, "The Narrative Strategies of Robert Greene's Coney-Catching Pamphlets," *Cahiers Elisabethains* 37 (1990): 9–15. For the conflict between delight and instruction, see Davis, *Idea and Act* and, more recently, Lorna Hutson, *Thomas Nashe in Context*, chap. 4.

28. The texts for the coney-catching pamphlets are the facsimile editions produced by G. B. Harrison, published by The Bodley Head in 1923–24, republished by Barnes and Noble of New York in 1966.

29. See note 26 above for this phrase.

30. For the requirements and schemes of casting in Tudor drama, see David Bevington, *From "Mankind" to Marlowe: Growth of Structure in the Popular Drama of Tudor England* (Cambridge, Mass.: Harvard University Press, 1962). For other conventions in the literature of roguery, see Sandra Clark, *The Elizabethan Pamphleteers: Popular Moralistic Pamphlets, 1580–1640* (Rutherford, N.J.: Fairleigh Dickinson University Press, 1983).

31. James A. S. McPeek, *The Black Book of Knaves and Unthrifts in Shakespeare and Other Renaissance Authors* (University of Connecticut Publications Series, 1969), 115.

32. See Cave, *Recognitions*, 82. According to Hermogenes, "rapidity" *(gorgotēs)* can have "pointed and clever thoughts," but it usually proceeds with "short clauses that develop the thought quickly" in order "to offset the flatness *(hyptiōtēs)*" in discourse. See *On Types of Style*, trans. Cecil W. Wooten (Chapel Hill: University of North Carolina Press, 1987), 65–70. For "duration," see Gérard Genette, *Narrative Discourse*, trans. Jane Lewin (Ithaca: Cornell University Press, 1980). For "rules of notice," see Rabinowitz, *Before Reading*.

33. There are many examples where Greene entrusts the "rest" of a tale to the reader: for instance, "[i]magine these villaines there in their iollitie, the one reporting point by point his cunning deceipt, and the other (fitting his humour) extolling the deede with no meane commendations" (*Third*, 20); or "what straunge lookes . . . were between him and his wife, I leaue to your supposing" (25).

34. See A. V. Judges, *The Elizabethan Underworld* (London: George Routledge & Sons, 1930), 44.

35. Other examples of present tense are these: "In the dead time of the night, when sound sleep makes ye eare vnapt to heare the verie least noyse, he forsaketh his bed, & hauing gotten all the plate . . . goeth downe into the shop" (*Third*, 19–20); "They go, he lessons the drab in this sorte" (23); "the wily companion calleth . . . wine is brought" (30). At the moment when the trick is turned, "[t]he Citizen not knowing his owne Trunke, but indeede neuer thinking on any such notable deceite: helpes him vp with the Truncke, and so sends him away roundly with his owne goods" (48–49). With the aims of discovery in view, the shift in tenses cannot simply be attributed to the awkward or inept prose of the Elizabethans. The study

that has done the most toward helping us rethink the syntax and structure of Renaissance prose is Janel Mueller's *The Native Tongue and the Word*.

36. See Walter Davis, *Idea and Act*, 183–88. Davis argues that Greene's prose breaks into two styles, one pleasant and the other didactic, and that this "rift" shows that "values or moral states have no contact with reality" (185). David Parker avoids this reductive tendency by invoking Empson in order to emphasize the "complexity" of judgments and values in the literature of roguery. See his contribution to the controversy over the *Defense*, "Robert Greene and 'The Defence of Conny Catching,'" *Notes and Queries*, n.s., 219 (1974): 87–89.

37. For more on the criticism of discovery, see my discussion of Dekker's literature of roguery in chapter 6.

38. These facets of Aristotle's poetics appear in Paul Ricoeur, *Time and Narrative* (Chicago: University of Chicago Press, 1984), I.31–51.

39. Greene often comments on how trustworthy his "notes" are—on how solidly they are "confirmed" by authority or evidence. The "notes" have an ineluctable power and validity.

40. The phrase is Shakespeare's in *The Winter's Tale*, ed. J. H. P. Pafford (New York: Methuen, 1963), 21: "a note infallible/Of breaking honesty." Thus, Leontes's madness prevents him from reading notes aright until, in the final discovery scene, he rediscovers his wife. The word is everywhere in Shakespeare and in the Renaissance as a key term for privileged signs.

41. See Lynn Staley Johnson, "'And Taken Up His Ynne in Fishes Haske,'" *Spenser Newsletter* 18 (1987): 14–15, for the tail of Pisces. According to Calvin's *Institutes*, ed. John T. McNeill, trans. Ford Lewis Battles (Philadelphia: Westminster Press, 1967), II.viii.10, God's providence includes synecdoche as well as typology, election, and conversion.

42. For closets of curiosities, see Steven Mullaney, "Strange Things, Gross Terms, Curious Customs: The Rehearsal of Cultures in the Late Renaissance," in *Representing the English Renaissance*, ed. Stephen Greenblatt (Berkeley: University of California Press, 1988), 65–92. The closets, Mullaney argues, defy category and system, although they are nonetheless categorized as strange (66). For cartography as an ideological battleground, see in the same collection (327–61) Richard Helgerson, "The Land Speaks: Cartography, Chorography, and Subversion in Renaissance England."

43. Michel Foucault, *Discipline and Punish: The Birth of the Prison*, trans. Alan Sheridan (New York: Vintage Books, 1979), 197–98.

44. Stephen Greenblatt begins his definition of "new historicism" in *Genre: The Forms of Power and the Power of Forms in the Renaissance* 15 (1982), 3–6, by focusing on Elizabeth's famous remark about the 1601 performance of *Richard II*. That the performance of the play subverts order is Elizabeth's point; but she makes the point with a "bitter recollection [that] the performance has metasticized: 'this tragedy was played 40tie times in open streets and houses'" (3). It is the "repeatability of the tragedy" outside the walls of the theater and inside the homes and imaginations of the audience that spells trouble for the queen. Like the theater, the conservative ideals of Greene's discoveries propose a "conventional containment" (4) of what it must allow to be repeatable plots.

45. The most important statement of the oppositional voices of the Renaissance stage is Jonathan Dollimore, *Radical Tragedy: Religion, Ideology and Power in the Drama of Shakespeare and his Contemporaries* (Brighton: Harvester Press, 1984). But cf. Lorna Hutson, *Thomas Nashe in Context*, 79: "it was indeed the question of

commercial theatre that condensed all the authorities' fears about the temptations of an opportunistic, improvising lifestyle for the unwary and their would-be deceivers."

46. In Dekker's rogue pamphlets, cant is extremely important as the equivalent to another linguistic plague, Babel. Speculation that Greene had some hand in the *Defence of Conny Catching* began with Grosart, and it was continued by H. C. Hart, I. A. Shapiro, Edwin Haviland Miller, David Parker, and others. Charles W. Crupi (*Robert Greene*, 152) lists the important references and concludes that the puzzle has not been solved. Miller points out, in *Notes and Queries* 197 (1952): 450, that both narrators—the one in Greene's pamphlets and the Cuthbert Coney-Catcher of the *Defence*—want "to preserve the *status quo*," and both rebuke "people like the tailor who strive to rise above their appointed station in a caste society."

47. See *Heterologies: Discourse on the Other*, trans. Brian Massumi (Minneapolis: University of Minnesota Press, 1986), 67–79: "If we are to believe Montaigne, what is near masks a foreignness. Therefore, the 'ordinary' includes 'facts just as wonderful as those that we go collecting in remote countries and centuries.' . . . What Montaigne ponders in this essay is precisely the status of the strange: Who is 'barbarian'? What is a 'savage'? In short, what is the place of the other?" (67).

48. See "Practices of Space," in *On Signs*, ed. Marshall Blonsky (Baltimore: Johns Hopkins University Press, 1985), 127.

49. "Practices of Space," 129.

50. "On the Oppositional Practices of Everyday Life" appears in *Social Text* 3 (1980): 3–43.

51. "Oppositional Practices," 38.

52. See Judges's introduction to *The Elizabethan Underworld*.

53. See "Invisible Bullets," the second chapter of *Shakespearean Negotiations: The Circulation of Social Energy in Renaissance England* (Berkeley: University of California Press, 1988), 49. Greenblatt's text is *A Caveat for Common Cursitors*; his acknowledgment to Michel de Certeau as well as Michel Foucault signals Greenblatt's attempt to modify a monolithic view of power and containment in Tudor England.

54. See the introduction to *The Elizabethan Underworld*. Lorna Hutson offers a contextual reading of the literary and theatrical battlefields on which censorship and transgression fought in the age of Greene and Nashe; see her *Thomas Nashe in Context*.

55. See Craig's *The Enchanted Glass: The Elizabethan Mind in Literature* (Oxford: Basil Blackwell, 1950), 174–75. James McPeek argues that such ineluctable power is part of the pun on "noting" in *Much Ado About Nothing*; see *The Black Book of Knaves*, 205.

56. For notes and noting—affirmed and criticized—in Shakespeare's plays, see (among many examples) the whole of Iago's performance, the prologue to *Henry V*, Hamlet's treatment of the mousetrap scene, and the discussions of value in *Troilus and Cressida*. These examples are in addition to the instances already mentioned from *The Winter's Tale* and *Much Ado About Nothing*.

57. Cave, *Recognitions*, I.3.

58. See Michael McKeon, *The Origins of the English Novel*.

Chapter 3. Nashe and the Stuff of Prose

1. It is Lorna Hutson's concern in her *Thomas Nashe in Context* to study Nashe in his own terms against the humanist conventions that prevailed in his day. All quotations of Nashe are taken from *The Works*, ed. Ronald B. McKerrow (Oxford:

Basil Blackwell, 1966), by volume and page. All dates are taken from Hutson's checklist.

2. See Hutson, *Thomas Nashe in Context*, chaps. 1–5.

3. Nashe's strange relationship to didacticism has led very different critics to the same conclusion—that Nashe's rhetoric is empty of content. For C. S. Lewis, Nashe's prose was "about" nothing. For Jonathan V. Crewe (*Unredeemed Rhetoric: Thomas Nashe and the Scandal of Authorship* [Baltimore: Johns Hopkins University Press, 1982]), rhetoric is always already empty of a transcendental signified—and Nashe only polemicizes the Derridean creed. Hutson contextualizes Nashe's refusal of the conventions of moralizing texts.

4. I am suggesting that the backgrounds of Nashe's spontaneous style are more complex than we might suspect. There is clearly the influence of Martin Marprelate, for which see Raymond A. Anselment, "Rhetoric and the Dramatic Satire of Martin Marprelate," *Studies in English Literature* 10 (1970): 103–19; Donald J. McGinn, "Nashe's Share in the Marprelate Controversy," *PMLA* 59 (1944): 952–84; and Travis L. Summersgill, "The Influence of the Marprelate Controversy upon the Style of Thomas Nashe," *Studies in Philology* 48 (1951): 145–60. Augustine's grand style, as described in *De Doctrina Christiana*, is motivated by a vehement force that seizes its words. For the currency of the Christian grand style in the Renaissance, see Shuger, *Sacred Rhetoric*. One of Nashe's biggest debts, he says, is to Aretino, whose fiery rhetoric feared no prince or magistrate.

5. For "vents," see Nashe's favorite author, Richard Hakluyt, *Voyages and Discoveries*, ed. Jack Beeching (Baltimore: Penguin Books, 1972), 212–14. For "invention," see Gascoigne's oft-quoted defense in *Certayne Notes of Instruction* (in G. Gregory Smith's anthology, I.46–57); and Ronald Levao, *Renaissance Minds*, 114–16. Nashe compares his own prose to boats in the preface to Sidney's *Astrophil and Stella*:

> Onely I can keepe pace with Grauesend barge, and care not if I haue water enough to lande my ship of fooles with the Tearme (the tyde I should say). Now euery man is not of that minde, for some, to goe the lighter away, will take in their fraught of spangled feathers, golden Peebles, Straw, Reedes, Bulrushes, or any thing, and then they beare out their sayles as proudly as if they were balisted with Bulbiefe. Others are so hardly bested for loading that they are faine to retaile the cinders of *Troy*, and the shiuers of broken trunchions, to fill vp their boate that else should goe empty: and if they haue but a pound weight of good Merchandise, it shall be placed at the poope, or pluckt in a thousand peeces to credit their carriage. (III.332)

6. Neil Rhodes, *Elizabethan Grotesque* (Boston: Routledge & Kegan Paul, 1980). Nashe runs cheek by jowl with Falstaff in C. L. Barber's *Shakespeare's Festive Comedy: A Study of Dramatic Form and its Relation to Social Custom* (New York: Meridian Books, 1963). For other attempts to define the materiality of Nashe's prose, see John Berryman's introduction to *The Unfortunate Traveller* (New York: Putnam, 1960); and G. R. Hibbard, *Thomas Nashe: A Critical Introduction* (Cambridge, Mass.: Harvard University Press, 1962), 147: "lively colloquial idiom," "indecorum incarnate," "ordinary conversational speech . . . stamped with Nashe's own personality," a style "relying on his virtuosity as a showman to cover up the gaps." For a survey of the growing humanist interest in the materiality of language, see Martin Elsky, "George Herbert's Pattern Poems and the Materiality of Language: A New Approach to Renaissance Hieroglyphics," *English Literary History* 50 (1983): 245–60. But this materiality is based on writing as the record of sound, and on letters as things.

7. For "performances," see Crewe, 2–3, 22–23, and passim.

8. Leonard Barkan, *The Gods Made Flesh: Metamorphosis and the Pursuit of Pa-

ganism (New Haven: Yale University Press, 1986), 100. For the presence/absence of ghosts in the Renaissance, see Marjorie B. Garber, *Shakespeare's Ghost Writers: Literature as Uncanny Causality* (New York: Methuen, 1987).

9. See *Thomas Nashe in Context*, passim.

10. Other authors have placed Nashe in his humanist contexts. See Kinney, *Humanist Poetics* and Stephen S. Hilliard, *The Singularity of Thomas Nashe* (Lincoln: University of Nebraska Press, 1986).

11. Hutson concedes that she makes Nashe speak in only one voice, and she gets around the un-Bakhtinian implications of her claims by suggesting that the parodic Nashe has many guises. But Hutson is unwilling to dwell on what she calls the "impossibly self-contradictory" tasks (207) of the author who seeks patronage yet is critical of it.

12. See Peter Stallybrass and Allon White, *The Politics and Poetics of Transgression* (Ithaca: Cornell University Press, 1986), 1-26; and Leah S. Marcus, *The Politics of Mirth: Jonson, Herrick, Milton, Marvell, and the Defense of Old Holiday Pastimes* (Chicago: University of Chicago Press, 1986).

13. The quotation appears in *The Returne of . . . Pasquill* (McKerrow, I.92), a work almost certainly not by Nashe yet in the Marprelate controversy.

14. In *The Singularity of Thomas Nashe*, Hilliard has anticipated me in his choice of the term "self-effacing" to describe the strategies by which Nashe attempts to factor out his "singularity." Hilliard argues for a struggle between Nashe the servant of court and ecclesiastical humanism and Nashe the arrogant, inventive wit. He is especially good on the Harvey controversy (see 170 for a summary). But Hilliard's focus on arrogance and cynicism, and his belief that Nashe becomes more and more cynical, are less convincing. Indeed, Hilliard himself concludes that in Nashe we continue to find a mixture of ideologies, orthodox and critical, and that, as such, Nashe's works articulate the skeptical "devolution of Elizabethan idealism more effectively than its outright rejection by later writers" (242).

15. The preface to Sidney is more self-conscious about a mix between deference to Astrophil and promotion of new literary values. Eventually, the rivalry between stuffing and deciphering is dramatized between Jack Wilton and Surrey.

16. Hutson admits that Nashe does approve the traditions of learning in *Pierce Penilesse*. I would argue that most of Nashe's dealings with Elyot and Ascham have an ambivalence about them.

17. Jonson uses the term *decipherer* in several ways in *Every Man Out of his Humour*, but cf. the "narrow-eyed decipherers . . . that will extort strange and abstruse meanings out of any subject" (*The Complete Plays*, ed G. A. Wilkes, vol. 1 [Oxford: Clarendon Press, 1981], 335). Cf. the current phrases "state decypherer, or politic picklock," the "Queen's decipherer," and Nashe's "mice-eyed" decipherer.

18. See *Lazarillo De Tormes*, in *Two Spanish Picaresque Novels*, trans. Michael Alpert (Baltimore: Penguin Books, 1969), 44-45, for the scene in which the starving picaro makes a hole in his master's food chest with the hopes of finding a morsel. The master's discovery of the hole makes him think that there are mice in the house, but the picaro assures him that mice never congregate in such a miserable place (cf. *Pierce Penilesse*). Each day the master fills the holes, and each night they open again, "so quickly that we must have been the originators of the proverb which says, 'Where one hole is closed another opens.'"

19. See Hodges, *Renaissance Fictions of Anatomy*, for Nashe's contaminating process of anatomizing Harvey. The exchange of stuffs required by parody—I empty your text and fill yours with mine, mine with yours—is yet another version of the give-and-take strategy of the stuffer.

20. The relation between faith and works is vexed, even for Luther who wrote that their difference "is easy to be uttered in words, but in use and experience it is very hard . . . [because] these two sorts of righteousness do encounter more near together than you wouldest wish or desire." See *Martin Luther, Selections from his Writings*, ed. John Dillenberger (Garden City, New York: Anchor Books, 1961), 107.

21. C. G. Harlow, "Thomas Nashe, Robert Cotton the Antiquary, and *The Terrors of the Night*," *RES*, n.s., vol. 12 (1961): 7–23.

22. Manfred Weidhorn, *Dreams in Seventeenth-Century English Literature* (The Hague: Mouton, 1970), 24–38.

23. Weidhorn, chap. 1.

24. See Weidhorn, 29–30. For Freud's reading of demonic dreams in the seventeenth century, see his case study of the painter Christoph Haizmann in *The Standard Edition of . . . Freud*, ed. James Strachey, vol. 19 (London: Hogarth Press, 1961), 69–105.

25. Nashe got into trouble over *Christs Teares, Pierce Penilesse, The Isle of Dogs*, and in general for his (and Doctor Harvey's) output. As for the humanists, in *Lenten Stuffe*, Nashe argues with Ascham; in *The Unfortunate Traveller*, Erasmus joins the other somewhat deflated dignitaries; Aretino appears in a number of roles; and in *The Anatomie*, Nashe exposes a rift between the private and public values of Elyot. Yet, Nashe also defends the learned traditions of oratory and poetry. In chapter 5, I will consider Nashe's skepticism and its relation to his cultural positions.

26. Hutson uses the metaphor of solvency to describe the way in which the carnivalesque Nashe breaks didactic materials down into festive pleasure.

27. See Smith's anthology, II.431.

28. For the compromises, see Hodges, *Renaissance Fictions of Anatomy*.

29. Hutson, *Thomas Nashe in Context*, 36.

Chapter 4. The Fortunes of Nashe's Stuff

1. See Hutson, *Thomas Nashe in Context*, chap. 11.

2. Cf. Hutson, 241–42.

3. See Lorna Hutson, "Thomas Nashe's 'Persecution' by the Aldermen in 1593," *Notes and Queries*, n.s., 232 (1987): 199–200.

4. Margaret Ferguson offers a good account of the ambivalence in Jack's treatment of the Leiden massacre. See "Nashe's *The Unfortunate Traveller:* The 'Newes of the Maker' Game," *English Literary Renaissance* 11 (1981): 165–82. Scapegoating seems to epitomize the kind of complex historical phenomenon with which the Renaissance was becoming fascinated. See Lynn White, Jr., "Death and the Devil," in *The Darker Vision of the Renaissance: Beyond the Fields of Reason*, ed. Robert S. Kinsman (Berkeley: University of California Press, 1974), 43: "Heretics, Jews, and at last witches: a generalized hostility toward oneself and one's world must vent itself in torturing and slaying an identifiable and relatively defenseless group which it is culturally not only permissible but even necessary to hate." In *The Jewish War*, trans. G. A. Williamson (New York: Penguin Books, 1969), 21–22, Josephus scolds those historians who "wish to establish the greatness of the Romans while all the time disparaging and deriding the actions of the Jews. But I do not see how men can prove themselves great by overcoming feeble opponents."

5. See Hutson for the dilemmas of the author in Nashe's England. See also Richard A. Lanham, "Tom Nashe and Jack Wilton: Personality as Structure in *The Unfortunate Traveller*," *Studies in Short Fiction* 4 (1966): 207–16.

6. See Arthur F. Kinney, *Humanist Poetics*, 295–303; and Crewe's discussion of humanism-in-crisis in *Unredeemed Rhetoric*, 78.

7. Gordon Braden, "Beyond Frustration: Petrarchan Laurels in the Seventeenth Century," *Studies in English Literature* 26 (1986): 5–23.

8. For studies of style and literary parody in *The Unfortunate Traveller*, see Agnes M. C. Latham, "Satire on Literary Themes and Modes in Nashe's 'The Unfortunate Traveller,'" *English Studies*, n.s., 1 (1948): 85–100; David Kaula, "The Low Style in Nashe's 'The Unfortunate Traveller,'" *Studies in English Literature* 6 (1966): 43–57; and Ann Rosiland Jones, "Inside the Outsider: Nashe's *Unfortunate Traveller* and Bakhtin's Polyphonic Novel," *English Literary History* 50 (1983): 61–81.

9. For the general literary antipathy between fat ladies and the masculinist desire for closure, see Patricia Parker, *Literary Fat Ladies*.

10. See Crewe's discussion of *Christs Teares* in *Unredeemed Rhetoric*, 45–64.

11. Paul de Man, *The Resistance to Theory* (Minneapolis: University of Minnesota Press, 1986), 44.

12. De Man, *Resistance*, 44.

13. *Resistance*, 49.

14. *Resistance*, 41.

15. *Unredeemed Rhetoric*, 45–64.

16. Angus Fletcher, *Allegory: The Theory of a Symbolic Mode* (Ithaca: Cornell University Press, 1964), 86.

17. Abraham Fraunce, *The Arcadian Rhetoric* (Menston, England: Scholar Press, Ltd., 1969), sig. G2r.

18. The Herbert poem is, of course, "The Windows."

19. For a summary of the complex relations between fact and fiction in the Renaissance, see William Nelson, *Fact or Fiction: The Dilemma of the Renaissance Storyteller* (Cambridge, Mass.: Harvard University Press, 1973).

20. Josephus says that, while he "will state the facts accurately and impartially," he must express his "own feelings and emotions; for I must permit myself to bewail my country's tragedy." At another point, he tries to withhold emotions from the account: "[b]ut everyone must interpret the facts in his own way." See *The Jewish War*, 22, 277, 296. For Bodin, see *Method for the Easy Comprehension of History*, trans. Beatrice Reynolds (New York: Columbia University Press, 1945), 81–82.

21. William Harrison, *An Historicall Description of the Iland of Britaine*, in Holinshed's *Chronicles*, vol. 1 (London, 1807), 49.

22. Hollander's article, "Typology and Secular Literature: Some Medieval Problems and Examples," appears in Earl Miner, ed., *Literary Uses of Typology from the Late Middle Ages to the Present* (Princeton: Princeton University Press, 1977), 3–19. Prudentius (quoted by Hollander, 13) actually uses the word *praenotata* in defining typological patterns ("Haec ad figuram praenotata est linea": "This picture has been drawn beforehand to be a model").

23. Lewalski's article, "Typological Symbolism and the 'Progress of the Soul' in Seventeenth-Century Literature," appears in Miner, *Literary Uses*, 79–114.

24. Regina M. Schwartz, "Joseph's Bones and the Resurrection of the Text: Remembering in the Bible," *PMLA* 103 (1988): 114–24.

25. See the discussion of the letter attached to the 1594 (2d) edition of *Christs Teares* below in chapter 5.

Chapter 5. Nashe's Empty Stuff

1. The differences between Platonic and Aristotelian "pleasure" (with the important trope of the leaky vessel) can be traced between *Gorgias* (473–93) and the

Nicomachean Ethics (VII.11–14). As I will argue below, Nashe's lenten stuff is an attempt to remove sophistry from political, historical, and philosophical debates.

2. The chronology of Nashe's thwarted apology to Harvey is surveyed by McKerrow and, more recently, by Charles Nicholl, *A Cup of News: The Life of Thomas Nashe* (Boston: Routledge & Kegan Paul, 1984), 170–73.

3. The phrase is Patricia Parker's from her intertextual study, *Literary Fat Ladies: Rhetoric, Gender, Property*.

4. The Francis Throckemorton ordeal (1584) illustrates the Queen's need for a "decipherer." The treasonous Throckemorton confessed to having sent letters "to the Scottish Queene in Cipher," which letters are of obvious interest to Elizabeth and the High Commission to which Nashe links the Queen's decipherer. Throckemorton confesses further that his letters "were alwaies written in Cipher, and the Cipher with the Nullities and markes for names of Princes and Counsailors." See *Elizabethan Backgrounds: Historical Documents of the Age of Elizabeth I*, ed. with introductions by Arthur F. Kinney (Hamden, Conn.: Archon Books, 1975), 144–63.

5. Although the Church of England periodically revised its prayer book, it could tout such revisions as a sign of refusal to claim Romish infallibility. In other words, the revisions exemplify the excellence of the church in its avoidance of error.

6. Devon Hodges has discussed this fear of contamination in *Renaissance Fictions of Anatomy*.

7. Various readers have read *Lenten Stuffe* as a full-scale attack on the Cobham family, one member of which was responsible for suppressing the theater in line with the wishes of London officials. Lorna Hutson also sees the posing of a festive Yarmouth against a censorious London as the key theme of the work. For the Cobham allusions, see Hutson, *Thomas Nashe in Context*, 251; Nicholl, *A Cup of News*, and Alice Lyle Scoufos, "Nashe, Jonson and the Oldcastle Problem," *Modern Philology* 65 (1968): 307–24.

8. For general studies of the growing segregation between history and fiction, and their residual crossovers in Tudor historiography, see the following: F. J. Levy, *Tudor Historical Thought* (San Marino, Calif.: Huntington Library Press, 1967); William Nelson, *Fact or Fiction;* Joseph M. Levine, *Humanism and History: Origins of Modern English Historiography* (Ithaca: Cornell University Press, 1987); and Wyman H. Herendeen, "Wanton Discourse and the Engines of Time: William Camden—Historian among Poets-Historical," in *Renaissance Rereadings: Intertext and Context*, ed. Maryanne Cline Horowitz et al. (Urbana: University of Illinois Press, 1988), 142–56. In their studies of the sixteenth-century debates about the relation between fiction and history, these scholars bracket (by and large) the theoretical questions raised by Hayden White and others about the rhetoricity of all historical discourse.

9. For Zwingli's "Concerning Choice and Liberty Respecting Food . . .," see *The Latin Works and the Correspondence of Huldreich Zwingli*, ed. Samuel Macauley Jackson, trans. Henry Preble et al., vol. 1 (New York: G. P. Putnam's Sons, 1912), 70–112.

10. In defending the assertion of one's beliefs against the more skeptical Erasmus, Luther says: "Outside that field [the Scriptures], we do not need Erasmus or any other teacher to tell us that over matters which are doubtful, or unprofitable and unnecessary, assertions and contentions are not merely stupid, but positively impious; Paul condemns them often enough! But I do not think you are speaking here about those things, unless like a comic orator you were intending to take up one subject and then deal with another, as the man did over the turbot; or unless you are godless and crazy enough to maintain that the article concerning 'free-will' is doubtful, or unnecessary" (*The Bondage of the Will*, in Dillenberger, 168).

11. See McKeon, *The Origins of the English Novel*, pt. 1, "Questions of Truth."

For Ascham on the romances written by "idle monks or wanton canons," see *The Schoolmaster,* ed. Lawrence V. Ryan (Ithaca: Cornell University Press, 1967), 68.

12. Agrippa makes several appearances in Nashe's earlier works. For Agrippa's "fundamentalist anti-intellectualism" in the context of skepticism, see Richard H. Popkin, *The History of Scepticism from Erasmus to Spinoza* (Berkeley: University of California Press, 1979), 23–26. McKerrow, of course, has done the most toward documenting Nashe's acquaintance with Sextus Empiricus, whom Nashe tells us he has read in the latest translation.

13. *The Oxford Dictionary of the Christian Church* defines fideism as follows: "A term applied to a variety of doctrines which hold in common belief in the incapacity of the intellect to attain to knowledge of divine matters and correspondingly put an excessive emphasis on faith" (eds. F. L. Cross and E. A. Livingstone, 2d ed. [New York: Oxford University Press, 1974]), 511. Although the term is most commonly applied to nineteenth-century trends, the *Sacramentum Mundi* explains that Montaigne and Pascal are fideists insofar as they reject "anything that appears to diminish the supernatural and gratuitous character of faith" (New York: Herder and Herder, 1968), II.336.

14. According to Ascham, *metaphrasis* is the turning of verse into prose, of one meter into another, or of prose into verse. Both Cicero and Ascham question its use by younger students, for it has them putting a matter well expressed into other and (often) more words. In any case, Ascham believes it inferior to his *imitatio;* and in attributing monitory tones to Cicero's *"grandis et tragicus orator,"* he wants to distinguish poetic flights of language ("aloft in poetical terms") from the pedestrian fidelity of a prose that "goeth low and soft on foot" (*The Schoolmaster,* 98–101).

15. Selden's dismissal of fiction from history is best seen in his commentary on Drayton's *Poly-Olbion.* That work, with Daniel's historical fictions and Camden's own *Britannia,* best illustrates the negotiations between history and fiction. A good summary of these matters appears in the article by Wyman H. Herendeen, cited above in note 8.

16. William Camden, *Britain, or A Chorographicall Description of the Most Flourishing Kingdomes, England, Scotland, and Ireland,* trans. Philemon Holland (London, 1610), 476.

17. Camden, 478.

18. See McKerrow's note on the Erasmian source, IV.385.

19. For example, Lucretius, *De Rerum Natura,* trans. W. H. D. Rouse, rev. Martin Ferguson Smith (Cambridge, Mass.: Harvard University Press, 1982), I.330, II.220.

20. Lucretius, I.503f.

21. Lucretius, I.370f.

22. Crewe's term is used to situate the latter's "alleged themelessness" (2) in terms of the critical debate about the "(Western) 'metaphysics of presence'" (6).

23. See McKeon, *The Origins of the English Novel,* pt. 1, "Questions of Truth," where he situates the dialectic between romance and history within the larger epistemological and social crises yielding the novel.

24. Francis Bacon commented on the obsessions and paradoxes of iconoclasm in his essay "Of Superstition": "There is a superstition in avoiding superstition, when men think to do best if they go furthest from the superstition formerly received: therefore care would be had that (as it fareth in ill purgings) the good be not taken away with the bad, which commonly is done, when the people is the reformer" (*The Essays* [New York: Penguin Books, 1985], 112). The complaints against the internal formalisms of the iconoclasts became common in the seventeenth century. For a

recent reading of these issues, see Kenneth Gross, *Spenserian Poetics: Idolatry, Iconoclasm, and Magic* (Ithaca: Cornell University Press, 1985).

25. Lucretius, III.936–37 and 944–45.

26. J. B. Steane, ed., *Thomas Nashe: "The Unfortunate Traveller" and Other Works* (New York: Penguin Books, 1972), 43–44.

Chapter 6. Dekker and Narrative Cant

1. "Whether the prose of Greene or Nash more strongly influenced Dekker's pamphlets, it would be hard to say" (Mary Leland Hunt, *Thomas Dekker: A Study* [New York: Columbia University Press, 1911], 8). "As a writer of pamphlets, Dekker entered the field . . . about eleven years [1592–1603] after the full impact of Thomas Nashe's and Robert Greene's popularity had been felt in London" (George R. Price, *Thomas Dekker* [New York: Twayne Publishers, Inc., 1969], 112). Authors exhumed Greene after his death and put him into their texts—for example, in B. R.'s *Greenes Newes Both From Heaven and Hell* (London, 1593). Dekker provides nearly the same service for Nashe in *Newes from Hell* (1606).

2. See Frederick O. Waage, *Thomas Dekker's Pamphlets, 1603–1609, and Jacobean Popular Literature*, 2 vols. (Salzburg Studies in English Literature, 1977). For mitigated, fideistic, naive, and other varieties of skepticism, see Popkin, *The History of Scepticism*, and McKeon, *The Origins of the English Novel*. The "romantic" Dekker, never very well defined, derives from his expressions of piety, or harmony among the ranks, or of love for the "mother" city, London.

3. See the discussion of Cave's *Recognitions* in chapter 2 above.

4. McKeon's approach corrects the more teleological or evolutionary explanations of the novel.

5. McKeon, *Origins*, 292–94.

6. J. Paul Hunter, *The Reluctant Pilgrim: Defoe's Emblematic Method and Quest for Form in "Robinson Crusoe"* (Baltimore: Johns Hopkins University Press, 1966).

7. The plague pamphlets are quoted from *The Plague Pamphlets of Thomas Dekker*, ed. F. P. Wilson (Oxford: Clarendon Press, 1925). Unless otherwise noted, the text for Dekker's works is *The Non-Dramatic Works of Thomas Dekker*, ed. Alexander B. Grosart (New York: Russell & Russell, 1963). The text for *A Knights Conjuring* is edited by Larry M. Robbins (Paris: Mouton, 1974). For problems with bibliography, see Wilson's introduction; but also see Cyrus Hoy, *Introductions, Notes, and Commentaries to Texts in "The Dramatic Works of Thomas Dekker"*, 4 vols. (Cambridge: Cambridge University Press, 1980); and A. F. Allison, *Thomas Dekker* (London: Dawsons, 1972).

8. One example of a treatise designed to teach readers of the plague is William Bullein's *A Dialogue against the Feuer Pestilence*, ed. Mark W. Bullen and A. H. Bullen (London: EETS, 1888). The word *node* is used in a variety of ways in the seventeenth century, not just for bodily tumors ("inflammatory, malignant" carbunkles [OED]) but also for mental ones. The OED cites Marvell in *The Rehearsall Transpros'd*: "the Mind too hath its Nodes sometimes" (3a). William Harvey shows how "nodes" can be part of a terminology designed to placate old conceptions in the wake of the new. In prefacing his discoveries of the circulation of the blood, he still appeals to cosmic correspondences yet replaces the old gathering of humors with what he calls "knots" or "*nodi*", that is, the valves regulating the flow of blood through the veins. See *Works*, trans. Robert Willis (New York: Johnson Reprint Corporation, 1965), 65–66. At the same time that Harvey was dispersing the humors, literary critics were growing skeptical of the *nodi* and "agnitions" in plots as well.

9. For Greene and wonder, see Arthur F. Kinney, *Humanist Poetics*. For Sidney, see *The Apology* in G. Gregory Smith's anthology, vol. 1: Tragedy has the "affects of admiration and commiseration" (177); poets "drawe with their charming sweetnes the wild vntamed wits to an admiration of knowledge" (151); of the vatic poet, "so farre were [the Romans] carried into the admiration thereof" (154). See also Smith's note for "admiration" (I.392–93).

10. For just one of many possible examples where Dekker imitates the style of Nashe (he also imitates and indeed responds to Nashe's narrative conceptions), consider the following: "The Host had bene a mad Greeke, (mary he could now speake nothing but English,) a goodly fat Burger he was, with a belly Arching out like a Beere-barrell, which made his legges (that were thicke & short like two piles driuen vnder *London*-bridge) to stradle halfe as wide as the toppe of Powles . . . An Antiquary might haue pickt rare matter out of his Nose, but that it was worme-eaten (yet that proued it to be an auncient Nose:) In some corners of it, there were blewish holes, that shonne like shelles of mother of Pearle" (Wilson, 53–54).

11. Timothy J. Reiss argues that the conceit of the telescope becomes prominent when the medieval episteme of "patterning" gives way to the "analytico-referential" episteme of modernity, which articulates an object, a mind, and a mediating instrument (language, the telescope) that shares in neither mind nor object. See *The Discourse of Modernism* (Ithaca: Cornell University Press, 1982).

12. Ruth S. El Saffar finds a similar commitment to a transcendent realm that "serves to obliterate the distinctions in this life" and to leave behind frustrated human designs in Cervantes's *Novelas ejemplares*. See *Novel to Romance: A Study of Cervantes's "Novelas ejemplares"* (Baltimore: Johns Hopkins University Press, 1974), xiii. There is something of this commitment in the faith required of the audience to witness the "notes infallible" of Shakespeare's romances. But there, too, an awareness of the potentially manipulative contrivance of artifice is part of the skeptical edge in these plays. Cave's *Recognitions* is indispensible for any consideration of the critique of discovery in the romances or in any other seventeenth-century text.

13. For "rules of notice," see Rabinowitz, *Before Reading*.

14. For genre and counter genre, see Claudio Guillen, *Literature as System: Essays Toward the Theory of Literary History* (Princeton: Princeton University Press, 1971). For the mixture of genres in the seventeenth century, see Rosalie L. Colie, *The Resources of Kind: Genre-Theory in the Renaissance* (Berkeley: University of California Press, 1973). Good examples of Dekker's strangely mixed allegorical and narrative practices are *The Seven Deadly Sinnes of London*, ed. H. F. B. Brett-Smith (Oxford: Basil Blackwell, 1922), and *Worke for Armorours* (London, 1609). Dekker's character writings take old allegories of character—old decipherings and humors—into new milieus and styles. See W. J. Paylor, ed., *The Overburian Characters* (Oxford: Basil Blackwell, 1936).

15. Waage discusses this scene as typically Dekkerian in upsetting the very expectations that it encourages us to have (*Thomas Dekker's Pamphlets*, I.183–86).

16. The unrivaled popularity of Greene's works through the first half of the seventeenth century is attested by Charles C. Mish's *English Prose Fiction, 1600–1700: A Chronological Checklist* (Charlottesville, Va.: Bibliographical Society of the University of Virginia, 1967).

17. McKeon finds English prose fiction almost entirely dormant at the beginning of the century and in fact uses that dormancy to argue that prose fiction and other social practices are inextricable. For other discussions of the epistemic changes in the seventeenth century, see Foucault, *The Order of Things*, and Reiss, *The Discourse of Modernism*. An older and excellent study of the seventeenth-century "wars of

truth" is Herschel Baker's *The Wars of Truth* (Cambridge, Mass.: Harvard University Press, 1952).

18. In Charles C. Mish's anthology, *Short Fiction of the Seventeenth Century* (New York: Norton, 1963), the reader encounters the "wonderful" in *The Famous and Renowned History of Morindos* (1609); "miraculous discoveries" and "memorable accidents" in John Reynolds's *The Triumphs of God's Revenge* (1635), in which we are asked to "admire . . . [God's] divine decrees" and the "disastrous accident[s]" that follow therefrom (222–23). Also compare Aphra Behn's *The History of the Royal Slave* in *The Novels of Mrs Aphra Behn*, ed. Ernest A. Baker (New York: E. P. Dutton & Co., n.d.), 51, 60: "But it were endless to give an account of all the divers wonderful and strange things that country affords," its many novelties provoking "New admiration." The providential literature of the century is discussed by Hunter in *The Reluctant Pilgrim*, chap. 3.

19. See Congreve's preface to *Incognita*, in *Shorter Novels: Jacobean and Restoration*, with an introduction and notes by Philip Henderson (New York: E. P. Dutton & Co., 1949), II.241, for the difference between romance and novel. For "accidents," see Aphra Behn's introduction to *The Fair Jilt* and *The History of the Royal Slave*. Also see Reynolds, *The Triumphs* (Mish, 222).

20. In *Origins*, 267–70, McKeon clarifies the relationship between questions of truth and of virtue.

21. McKeon, *Origins*, 273.

22. Cervantes, *Exemplary Stories*, trans. C. A. Jones (New York: Penguin Books, 1972), 8–9. For the problems in classifying these tales, see Ruth S. El Saffar, *Novel to Romance*, xii. Cervantes's critical response to Aristotelian poets is the subject of Alban K. Forcione's *Cervantes, Aristotle, and the "Persiles"* (Princeton: Princeton University Press, 1970).

23. See the discussion of Cave's *Recognitions* in chap. 2.

24. Congreve, *Incognita*, (*Shorter Novels*, 242).

25. *Journal of the Plague Year* (Oxford: Basil Blackwell, 1928), 91. For "accidents" in *A Journal*, see, for example, 12 and 23.

26. See Hunter's *Reluctant Pilgrim*.

27. The debate between Hayden White and Marilyn Robinson Waldman appears in W. J. T. Mitchell, ed., *On Narrative* (Chicago: University of Chicago Press, 1981). I quote Waldman from her essay, "'The Otherwise Unnoteworthy Year 711': A Reply to Hayden White," 244.

28. Woolf's essay, "The Strange Elizabethans," appears in vol. 3 of her *Collected Essays* (London: The Hogarth Press, 1967), 32–43. The quotation is on 32.

29. *The Common Reader* (New York: Harcourt, Brace and Co., 1925), 212–13. Woolf criticizes other novelists for writing of "unimportant things"—that is, for failing to perceive anew the ordinary experiences of life (210).

30. See *The Great Frost* and *The Cold Year*, with which there are bibliographical problems that are taken up in A. F. Allison, *Thomas Dekker*. Virginia Woolf's intimate knowledge of Dekker's prose, and her assessment of his strengths and weaknesses, is the subject in part of a recent book by Alice Fox, *Virginia Woolf and the Literature of the English Renaissance* (Oxford: Clarendon Press, 1990), 57, 159–62. In her diary, Woolf once remarked that "'I bathed myself in Dekker last night as in my natural element'" (quoted by Fox, 57). Woolf loved the way in which Dekker could move very quickly from the sonorous to the earthy, but she criticized his typically Elizabethan inability to capture the particular or the ordinary.

31. If commentaries on Terence talked about the "knot" or *nodus* in his plays, literary and cultural theorists are still talking about "nodes." One can find the word

in such diverse critics as Barthes, de Certeau, Lacan, Althusser, Hillis Miller, and Eco. Indeed, the advent of "narratology" has reinvoked some of the schematic concerns of the pre-novel—for instance, in Frank Kermode's *The Sense of an Ending: Studies in the Theory of Fiction* (Oxford: Oxford University Press, 1967), and *The Genesis of Secrecy: On the Interpretation of Narrative* (Cambridge, Mass.: Harvard University Press, 1979). For Foucault on the Renaissance, see *The Order of Things*.

32. See Paracelsus, *Selected Writings*, ed. Jolande Jacobi, trans. Norbert Guterman (Princeton: Princeton University Press, 1973). On the one hand, we must pursue ever new remedies because Nature "does not produce anything that is perfect in itself" (92). On the other, he asks, "[w]hat trousers are the best? Whole ones. Those which are mended and patched are the worst" (90). Indeed, like Nashe's "patchworker," we must realize "that all our affairs are naught, that our knowledge rests upon no firm foundation, and that the truth is not known to us, but that we are inadequate and fragmentary in all ways, and that no ability or knowledge is ours" (81).

33. McPeek, *The Black Book of Knaves*, 42. Eco's novel is, of course, *The Name of the Rose*.

34. *Ulysses*, 3 vols., ed. Hans Walter Gabler et al. (New York: Garland Publishing, Inc., 1984), III.1567. All subsequent references appear in the text.

BIBLIOGRAPHY

Allison, A. F. *Thomas Dekker, c. 1572–1632: A Bibliographical Catalogue of the Early Editions.* London: Dawsons, 1972.

Alpert, Michael, trans. *Two Spanish Picaresque Novels.* Baltimore: Penguin Books, 1969.

Altman, Joel B. *The Tudor Play of Mind: Rhetorical Inquiry and the Development of Elizabethan Drama.* Berkeley: University of California Press, 1978.

Anselment, Raymond A. "Rhetoric and the Dramatic Satire of Martin Marprelate." *Studies in English Literature* 10 (1970): 103–19.

Ascham, Roger. *The Schoolmaster.* Ed. Lawrence V. Ryan. Ithaca: Cornell University Press, 1967.

Attridge, Derek. *Well-Weighed Syllables: Elizabethan Verse in Classical Metres.* New York: Cambridge University Press, 1974.

B. R. *Greenes Newes Both From Heaven and Hell.* London: 1593.

Bacon, Francis. *The Essays.* New York: Penguin Books, 1985.

Baker, Ernest A., ed. *The Novels of Mrs Aphra Behn.* New York: E. P. Dutton & Co., n.d.

Baker, Herschel. *The Wars of Truth.* Cambridge, Mass.: Harvard University Press, 1952.

Baldwin, T. W. *Shakspere's Five-Act Structure.* Urbana: University of Illinois Press, 1947.

Barber, C. L. *Shakespeare's Festive Comedy: A Study of Dramatic Form and Its Relation to Social Custom.* New York: Meridian Books, 1963.

Barish, Jonas A. "The Prose Style of John Lyly." *English Literary History* 23 (1956): 14–35.

Barkan, Leonard. *The Gods Made Flesh: Metamorphosis and the Pursuit of Paganism.* New Haven: Yale University Press, 1986.

Bevington, David M. *Action is Eloquence: Shakespeare's Language of Gesture.* Cambridge, Mass.: Harvard University Press, 1984.

———. *From "Mankind" to Marlowe: Growth of Structure in the Popular Drama of Tudor England.* Cambridge, Mass.: Harvard University Press, 1962.

Blonsky, Marshall, ed. *On Signs.* Baltimore: Johns Hopkins University Press, 1985.

Boccaccio, Giovanni. *The Decameron.* Trans. G. H. McWilliam. New York: Penguin Books, 1972.

Bodin, Jean. *Method for the Easy Comprehension of History.* Trans. Beatrice Reynolds. New York: Columbia University Press, 1945.

Bond, R. Warwick, ed. *The Complete Works of John Lyly.* 3 vols. Oxford: Clarendon Press, 1902.

Boyle, Marjorie O'Rourke. *Erasmus on Language and Method in Theology.* Toronto: University of Toronto Press, 1977.

Braden, Gordon. "Beyond Frustration: Petrarchan Laurels in the Seventeenth Century." *Studies in English Literature* 26 (1986): 5–23.

Bullein, William. *A Dialogue against the Feuer Pestilence.* Ed. Mark W. Bullen and A. H. Bullen. London: EETS, 1888.

Calvin, John. *Institutes of the Christian Religion.* 2 vols. Ed. John T. McNeill; trans. Ford Lewis Battles. Philadelphia: Westminster Press, 1960.

Camden, William. *Britain, or a Chorographicall Description of the Most Flourishing Kingdomes, England, Scotland, and Ireland.* Trans. Philemon Holland. London: 1610.

Castelvetro, Lodovico. *On the Art of Poetry.* Trans. Andrew Bongiorno. Binghamton, N.Y.: Medieval and Renaissance Texts & Studies, 1984.

Cave, Terence. *The Cornucopian Text: Problems of Writing in the French Renaissance.* Oxford: Clarendon Press, 1979.

———. *Recognitions: A Study in Poetics.* Oxford: Clarendon Press, 1988.

Cicero. *De Natura Deorum.* Trans. H. Rackham. Cambridge, Mass.: Harvard University Press, 1961.

Cicero [Pseudo]. *Rhetorica ad Herennium.* Trans. Harry Caplan. Cambridge, Mass.: Harvard University Press, 1968.

Clark, Sandra. *The Elizabethan Pamphleteers: Popular Moralistic Pamphlets, 1580–1640.* Rutherford, N.J.: Fairleigh Dickinson University Press, 1983.

Colie, Rosalie L. *The Resources of Kind: Genre-Theory in the Renaissance.* Berkeley: University of California Press, 1973.

Congreve, William. *Incognita.* In *Shorter Novels: Jacobean and Restoration.* Introduction and Notes by Philip Henderson. New York: E. P. Dutton & Co., 1949.

Craig, Hardin. *The Enchanted Glass: The Elizabethan Mind in Literature.* Oxford: Basil Blackwell, 1950.

Crewe, Jonathan V. *Unredeemed Rhetoric: Thomas Nashe and the Scandal of Authorship.* Baltimore: Johns Hopkins University Press, 1982.

Cross, F. L. and E. A. Livingstone, eds. *The Oxford Dictionary of the Christian Church.* 2d ed. New York: Oxford University Press, 1974.

Crupi, Charles W. *Robert Greene.* Boston: Twayne, 1986.

Davis, Walter R. *Idea and Act in Elizabethan Fiction.* Princeton: Princeton University Press, 1969.

De Certeau, Michel. *Heterologies: Discourse on the Other.* Trans. Brian Massumi. Minneapolis: University of Minnesota Press, 1986.

———. "On the Oppositional Practices of Everyday Life." *Social Text* 3 (1980): 3–43.

Defoe, Daniel. *A Journal of the Plague Year.* Oxford: Basil Blackwell, 1928.

Dekker, Thomas. *A Knights Conjuring.* Ed. Larry M. Robbins. Paris: Mouton, 1974.

———. *The Seven Deadly Sinnes of London.* Ed. H. F. B. Brett-Smith. Oxford: Basil Blackwell, 1922.

De Man, Paul. *The Resistance to Theory.* Minneapolis: University of Minnesota Press, 1986.

Dessen, Alan C. *Elizabethan Stage Conventions and Modern Interpreters.* New York: Cambridge University Press, 1984.

Dillenberger, John, ed. *Martin Luther: Selections from his Writings*. Garden City, N.Y.: Anchor Books, 1961.

Dollimore, Jonathan. *Radical Tragedy: Religion, Ideology and Power in the Drama of Shakespeare and his Contemporaries*. Brighton: Harvester Press, 1984.

El Saffar, Ruth S. *Novel to Romance: A Study of Cervantes's "Novelas Ejemplares"*. Baltimore: Johns Hopkins University Press, 1974.

Elsky, Martin. "George Herbert's Pattern Poems and the Materiality of Language: A New Approach to Renaissance Hieroglyphics." *English Literary History* 50 (1983): 245–60.

Ermarth, Elizabeth Deeds. *Realism and Consensus in the English Novel*. Princeton: Princeton University Press, 1983.

Ferguson, Margaret. "Nashe's *The Unfortunate Traveller:* The 'Newes of the Maker' Game." *English Literary Renaissance* 11 (1981): 165–82.

Fletcher, Angus. *Allegory: The Theory of a Symbolic Mode*. Ithaca: Cornell University Press, 1964.

Forcione, Alban K. *Cervantes, Aristotle, and the "Persiles"*. Princeton: Princeton University Press, 1970.

Foucault, Michel. *Discipline and Punish: The Birth of the Prison*. Trans. Alan Sheridan. New York: Vintage, 1979.

———. *Language, Counter-Memory, Practice: Selected Essays and Interviews*. Ed. Donald F. Bouchard; trans. Donald F. Bouchard and Sherry Simon. Ithaca: Cornell University Press, 1977.

———. *The Order of Things: An Archaeology of the Human Sciences*. Trans. Alan Sheridan. New York: Vintage, 1973.

Fox, Alice. *Virginia Woolf and the Literature of the English Renaissance*. Oxford: Clarendon Press, 1990.

Fraunce, Abraham. *The Arcadian Rhetoric*. Menston, England: Scholar Press, 1969.

Garber, Marjorie B. *Shakespeare's Ghost Writers: Literature as Uncanny Causality*. New York: Methuen, 1987.

Genette, Gérard. *Narrative Discourse*. Trans. Jane E. Lewin. Ithaca: Cornell University Press, 1980.

Geoffrey of Vinsauf. *Poetria Nova*. Trans. Margaret Nims. Toronto: Pontifical Institute, 1967.

Ginsberg, Warren. *The Cast of Character: The Representation of Personality in Ancient and Medieval Literature*. Toronto: University of Toronto Press, 1983.

Goldberg, Jonathan. *Endlesse Worke: Spenser and the Structures of Discourse*. Baltimore: Johns Hopkins University Press, 1981.

Green, Lawrence D, ed. *John Rainolds's Oxford Lectures on Aristotle's "Rhetoric"*. Newark: University of Delaware Press, 1986.

Greenblatt, Stephen, ed. *The Forms of Power and the Power of Forms in the Renaissance*. Genre 15 (1982).

———, ed. *Representing the English Renaissance*. Berkeley: University of California Press, 1988.

———. *Shakespearean Negotiations: The Circulation of Social Energy in Renaissance England*. Berkeley: University of California Press, 1988.

Greene, Robert. *The Blacke Bookes Messenger; The Defence of Conny-catching*. New

York: E. P. Dutton and Company, 1924; reprinted, New York: Barnes and Noble, 1966.

———. *Ciceronis Amor*. Ed. Edwin Haviland Miller. Gainesville, Fla.: Scholars' Facsimiles & Reprints, 1954.

———. *Groats-worth of Witte; The Repentance of Robert Greene*. New York: E. P. Dutton & Company, 1923; reprinted, New York: Barnes and Noble, 1966.

———. *A Notable Discovery of Coosnage; The Second Part of Conny-catching*. Ed. G. B. Harrison. New York: E. P. Dutton and Company, 1923; reprinted, New York: Barnes and Noble, 1966.

———. *The Scottish History of James the Fourth*. London: Malone Society Reprint, 1921.

———. *The Thirde & Last Part of Conny-catching; A Disputation Betweene a Hee Conny-catcher and a Shee Conny-catcher*. London: Bodley Head, 1923; reprinted, New York: Barnes and Noble, 1966.

Greg, W. W. *Two Elizabethan Stage Abridgements: "The Battle of Alcazar" and "Orlando Furioso"*. London: Malone Society, 1923.

Grosart, Alexander B. *The Life and Complete Works in Prose and Verse of Robert Greene*. 15 vols. New York: Russell & Russell, 1964.

———. *The Non-dramatic Works of Thomas Dekker*. 5 vols. New York: Russell & Russell, 1963.

———. *The Works of Gabriel Harvey, D.C.L.*. 3 vols. New York: AMS Press, 1966.

Gross, Kenneth. *Spenserian Poetics: Idolatry, Iconoclasm, and Magic*. Ithaca: Cornell University Press, 1985.

Guillen, Claudio. *Literature as System: Essays Toward the Theory of Literary History*. Princeton: Princeton University Press, 1971.

Gurr, Andrew. *The Shakespearean Stage, 1574–1642*. 2d ed. Cambridge: Cambridge University Press, 1980.

Hakluyt, Richard. *Voyages and Discoveries*. Ed. Jack Beeching. Baltimore: Penguin Books, 1972.

Harlow, C. G. "Thomas Nashe, Robert Cotton the Antiquary, and *The Terrors of the Night*." *RES*, n.s., 12 (1961): 7–23.

Harrison, William. *An Historicall Description of the Iland of Britaine*. In Raphael Holinshed, *The Chronicles of England, Scotlande, and Irelande*. London: J. Johnson et al., 1807–1808.

Harvey, William. *Works*. Trans. Robert Willis. New York: Johnson Reprint Corporation, 1965.

Hattaway, Michael. *Elizabethan Popular Theatre: Plays in Performance*. Boston: Routledge & Kegan Paul, 1982.

Helgerson, Richard. *The Elizabethan Prodigals*. Berkeley: University of California Press, 1976.

Heninger, S. K., Jr. *Touches of Sweet Harmony: Pythagorean Cosmology and Renaissance Poetics*. San Marino, Calif.: Huntington Library, 1974.

Herendeen, Wyman H. "Wanton Discourse and the Engines of Time: William Camden—Historian among Poets-Historical." In *Renaissance Rereadings: Intertext and Context*. Ed. Maryanne Cline Horowitz et al. Urbana: University of Illinois Press, 1988.

Hermogenes. *On Types of Style*. Trans. Cecil W. Wooten. Chapel Hill: University of North Carolina Press, 1987.

Herrick, Marvin T. *Comic Theory in the Sixteenth Century*. Urbana: University of Illinois Press, 1964.

———. *The Poetics of Aristotle in England*. New Haven: Yale University Press, 1930.

Hibbard, G. R. *Thomas Nashe: A Critical Introduction*. Cambridge, Mass.: Harvard University Press, 1962.

Hilliard, Stephen S. *The Singularity of Thomas Nashe*. Lincoln: University of Nebraska Press, 1986.

Hodges, Devon L. *Renaissance Fictions of Anatomy*. Amherst: University of Massachusetts Press, 1985.

Hosley, Richard. "The Discovery-Space in Shakespeare's Globe." *Shakespeare Survey* 12 (1959): 35–46.

Hoy, Cyrus. *Introductions, Notes, and Commentaries to Texts in "The Dramatic Works of Thomas Dekker"*. 4 vols. New York: Cambridge University Press, 1980.

Huizinga, Johan. *Erasmus and the Age of Reformation*. New York: Harper, 1957.

Hunt, Mary Leland. *Thomas Dekker: A Study*. New York: Columbia University Press, 1911.

Hunter, G. K. *John Lyly: The Humanist as Courtier*. Cambridge, Mass.: Harvard University Press, 1962.

Hunter, J. Paul. *The Reluctant Pilgrim: Defoe's Emblematic Method and Quest for Form in "Robinson Crusoe"*. Baltimore: Johns Hopkins University Press, 1966.

Hutson, Lorna. *Thomas Nashe in Context*. Oxford: Clarendon Press, 1989.

———. "Thomas Nashe's 'Persecution' by the Aldermen in 1593." *Notes and Queries*, n.s., 232 (1987): 199–200.

Jackson, Samuel Macauley, ed. *The Latin Works and the Correspondence of Huldreich Zwingli*. Trans. Henry Preble et al. New York: G. P. Putnam's Sons, 1912.

Johnson, Lynn Staley. "'And Taken Up His Ynne in Fishes Haske.'" *Spenser Newsletter*, 18 (1987): 14–15.

Jones, Ann Rosiland. "Inside the Outsider: Nashe's *Unfortunate Traveller* and Bakhtin's Polyphonic Novel." *English Literary History* 50 (1983): 61–81.

Jonson, Ben. *The Complete Plays*. Ed. G. A. Wilkes. 4 vols. Oxford: Clarendon Press, 1981–1982.

Jordan, John Clark. *Robert Greene*. New York: Columbia University Press, 1915.

Josephus. *The Jewish War*. Trans. G. A. Williamson. New York: Penguin Books, 1969.

Joyce, James. *Ulysses*. 3 vols. Ed. Hans Walter Gabler et al. New York: Garland, 1984.

Judges, A. V., ed. *The Elizabethan Underworld*. London: George Routledge & Sons, 1930.

Kahn, Victoria. *Rhetoric, Prudence, and Skepticism in the Renaissance*. Ithaca: Cornell University Press, 1985.

Kaula, David. "The Low Style in Nashe's *The Unfortunate Traveller*." *Studies in English Literature* 6 (1966): 43–57.

Kennedy, William J. *Rhetorical Norms in Renaissance Literature*. New Haven: Yale University Press, 1978.

Kermode, Frank. *The Genesis of Secrecy: On the Interpretation of Narrative*. Cambridge, Mass.: Harvard University Press, 1979.

---. *The Sense of an Ending: Studies in the Theory of Fiction.* New York: Oxford University Press, 1967.

King, T. J. *Shakespearean Staging, 1599–1642.* Cambridge, Mass.: Harvard University Press, 1971.

Kinney, Arthur F., ed. *Elizabethan Backgrounds: Historical Documents of the Age of Elizabeth I.* Hamden, Conn.: Archon Books, 1975.

---. *Humanist Poetics: Thought, Rhetoric, and Fiction in Sixteenth-Century England.* Amherst: University of Massachusetts Press, 1986.

Kinsman, Robert S., ed. *The Darker Vision of the Renaissance: Beyond the Fields of Reason.* Berkeley: University of California Press, 1974.

Lanham, Richard A. "Tom Nashe and Jack Wilton: Personality as Structure in *The Unfortunate Traveller.*" *Studies in Short Fiction* 4 (1966): 207–16.

Latham, Agnes M. C. "Satire on Literary Themes and Modes in Nashe's *The Unfortunate Traveller.*" *English Studies*, n.s., 1 (1948): 85–100.

Levao, Ronald. *Renaissance Minds and their Fictions: Cusanus, Sidney, Shakespeare.* Berkeley: University of California Press, 1985.

Levine, Joseph M. *Humanism and History: Origins of Modern English Historiography.* Ithaca: Cornell University Press, 1987.

Levy, F. J. *Tudor Historical Thought.* San Marino, Calif.: Huntington Library, 1967.

Lewalski, Barbara Kiefer, ed. *Renaissance Genres: Essays on Theory, History, and Interpretation.* Cambridge, Mass.: Harvard University Press, 1986.

Lewis, C. S. *English Literature in the Sixteenth Century, Excluding Drama.* Oxford: Clarendon Press, 1965.

Logan, George M. and Gordon Teskey, eds.. *Unfolded Tales: Essays on Renaissance Romance.* Ithaca: Cornell University Press, 1989.

Lucretius. *De Rerum Natura.* Trans. W. H. D. Rouse; rev. Martin Ferguson Smith. Cambridge, Mass.: Harvard University Press, 1982.

McGinn, Donald J. "Nashe's Share in the Marprelate Controversy." *PMLA* 59 (1944): 952–84.

McKeon, Michael. *The Origins of the English Novel, 1600–1740.* Baltimore: Johns Hopkins University Press, 1987.

McKerrow, Ronald B., ed. *The Works of Thomas Nashe.* 5 vols. Rev. F. P. Wilson. Oxford: Basil Blackwell, 1966.

McPeek, James A. S. *The Black Book of Knaves and Unthrifts in Shakespeare and Other Renaissance Authors.* n.p.: University of Connecticut Publications Series, 1969.

Marcus, Leah S. *The Politics of Mirth: Jonson, Herrick, Milton, Marvell, and the Defense of Old Holiday Pastimes.* Chicago: University of Chicago Press, 1986.

Miller, David Lee. *The Poem's Two Bodies: The Poetics of the 1590 "Fairie Queene".* Princeton: Princeton University Press, 1988.

Miller, Edwin Haviland. "Further Notes on the Authorship of *The Defence of Conycatching* (1592)." *Notes and Queries* 197 (1952): 446–51.

Miner, Earl, ed. *Literary Uses of Typology from the Late Middle Ages to the Present.* Princeton: Princeton University Press, 1977.

Minturno, Antonio. *De Poeta* (Venice: 1559).

Mish, Charles C. *English Prose Fiction, 1600–1700: A Chronological Checklist.* Charlottesville: Bibliographical Society of the University of Virginia, 1967.

———, ed. *Short Fiction of the Seventeenth Century*. New York: Norton, 1963.
Mitchell, W. J. T., ed. *On Narrative*. Chicago: University of Chicago Press, 1981.
Mueller, Janel M. *The Native Tongue and the Word: Developments in English Prose Style, 1380–1580*. Chicago: University of Chicago Press, 1984.
Nashe, Thomas. *The Unfortunate Traveller*. Intro. John Berryman. New York: Putnam, 1960.
Nelson, William. *Fact or Fiction: The Dilemma of the Renaissance Storyteller*. Cambridge, Mass.: Harvard University Press, 1973.
Nicholl, Charles. *A Cup of News: The Life of Thomas Nashe*. Boston: Routledge & Kegan Paul, 1984.
Olin, John C., ed. *Desiderius Erasmus: Christian Humanism and the Reformation: Selected Writings*. New York: Harper, 1965.
Ong, Walter J. *Rhetoric, Romance, and Technology: Studies in the Interaction of Expression and Culture*. Ithaca: Cornell University Press, 1971.
Paracelsus. *Selected Writings*. Ed. Jolande Jacobi; trans. Norbert Guterman. Princeton: Princeton University Press, 1973.
Parker, David. "Robert Greene and 'The Defence of Conny Catching.'" *Notes and Queries*, n.s., 219 (1974): 87–89.
Parker, Patricia. *Inescapable Romance: Studies in the Poetics of a Mode*. Princeton: Princeton University Press, 1979.
———. *Literary Fat Ladies: Rhetoric, Gender, Property*. New York: Methuen, 1987.
Parker, Patricia and David Quint, eds. *Literary Theory/Renaissance Texts*. Baltimore: Johns Hopkins University Press, 1986.
Patterson, Annabel M. *Censorship and Interpretation: The Conditions of Writing and Reading in Early Modern England*. Madison: University of Wisconsin Press, 1984.
———. "Misinterpretable Donne: The Testimony of the Letters." *John Donne Journal* 1 (1982): 39–53.
Paylor, W. J., ed. *The Overburian Characters*. Oxford: Basil Blackwell, 1936.
Popkin, Richard H. *The History of Scepticism from Erasmus to Spinoza*. Berkeley: University of California Press, 1979.
Price, George R. *Thomas Dekker*. New York: Twayne, 1969.
Quint, David. *Origin and Originality in Renaissance Literature: Versions of the Source*. New Haven: Yale University Press, 1983.
Rabinowitz, Peter J. *Before Reading: Narrative Conventions and the Politics of Interpretation*. Ithaca: Cornell University Press, 1987.
Reiss, Timothy J. *The Discourse of Modernism*. Ithaca: Cornell University Press, 1982.
Relihan, Constance C. "The Narrative Strategies of Robert Greene's Cony-catching Pamphlets." *Cahiers Elisabethains* 37 (1990): 9–15.
Rhodes, Neil. *Elizabethan Grotesque*. Boston: Routledge & Kegan Paul, 1980.
Ricoeur, Paul. *Time and Narrative*. Vol. 1. Chicago: University of Chicago Press, 1984.
Ringler, William A., Jr. "The Immediate Source of Euphuism." *PMLA* 53 (1938): 678–86.
Sacramentum Mundi: An Encyclopedia of Theology. Ed. Karl Rahner et al. New York: Herder and Herder, 1968.
Salzman, Paul. *English Prose Fiction, 1558–1700: A Critical History*. Oxford: Clarendon Press, 1985.

Schwartz, Regina M. "Joseph's Bones and the Resurrection of the Text: Remembering in the Bible." *PMLA* 103 (1988): 114–24.

Scoufos, Alice Lyle. "Nashe, Jonson and the Oldcastle Problem." *Modern Philology* 65 (1968): 307–24.

Shakespeare, William. *The Winter's Tale*. Ed. J. H. P. Paffored. New York: Methuen, 1963.

Shapiro, Barbara J. *Probability and Certainty in Seventeenth-Century England: A Study of the Relationships Between Natural Science, Religion, History, Law, and Literature.* Princeton: Princeton University Press, 1983.

Shuger, Debora K. *Sacred Rhetoric: The Christian Grand Style in the English Renaissance*. Princeton: Princeton University Press, 1988.

Smith, G. Gregory, ed. *Elizabethan Critical Essays*. 2 vols. Oxford: Oxford University Press, 1904.

Stallybrass, Peter and Allon White. *The Politics and Poetics of Transgression*. Ithaca: Cornell University Press, 1986.

Steane, J. B., ed. *Thomas Nashe: "The Unfortunate Traveller" and Other Works*. New York: Penguin Books, 1972.

Stephens, James. *Francis Bacon and the Style of Science*. Chicago: University of Chicago Press, 1975.

Strachey, James, ed. *The Standard Edition of the Complete Psychological Works of Sigmund Freud*. 24 vols. London: Hogarth Press, 1953–1974.

Summersgill, Travis L. "The Influence of the Marprelate Controversy upon the Style of Thomas Nashe." *Studies in Philology* 48 (1951): 145–60.

Trimpi, Wesley. *Ben Jonson's Poems: A Study of the Plain Style*. Stanford: Stanford University Press, 1962.

Valency, Maurice and Harry Levtow, eds. *The Palace of Pleasure: An Anthology of the Novella*. New York: Capricorn Books, 1960.

Waage, Frederick O. *Thomas Dekker's Pamphlets, 1603–1609, and Jacobean Popular Literature*. 2 vols. Salzburg: Salzburg Studies in English Literature, 1977.

Weidhorn, Manfred. *Dreams in Seventeenth-Century English Literature*. The Hague: Mouton, 1970.

Wells, Stanley, ed. *The Cambridge Companion to Shakespeare Studies*. New York: Cambridge University Press, 1986.

Wilson, F. P., ed. *The Plague Pamphlets of Thomas Dekker*. Oxford: Clarendon Press, 1925.

Wilson, Kenneth J. *Incomplete Fictions: The Formation of English Renaissance Dialogue*. Washington, D.C.: Catholic University of America Press, 1985.

Woolf, Rosemary. *The English Mystery Plays*. Berkeley: University of California Press, 1972.

Woolf, Virginia. *Collected Essays*. London: The Hogarth Press, 1967.

———. *The Common Reader*. New York: Harcourt, Brace and Co., 1925.

Wooten, Cecil W. *Cicero's "Philippics" and Their Demosthenic Model: The Rhetoric of Crisis*. Chapel Hill: University of North Carolina Press, 1983.

Yates, Frances. *The Art of Memory*. Chicago: University of Chicago Press, 1966.

INDEX

Agrippa von Nettesheim, Henricus Cornelius, 112, 160
Andrewes, Lancelot, 146
Aretino, Pietro, 66, 113, 138, 155, 157
Aristotle, 45–46, 48–49, 148, 151
Ascham, Roger, 37–38, 72, 111, 113–14, 119, 124, 156–57, 160
Augustine of Hippo, 155

Bacon, Francis, 128, 160; on deduction, 18; on words and things, 38
Bakhtin, M. M., 70
Bale, John, 103
Barkan, Leonard, 68
Behn, Aphra, 139, 141–42
Boccaccio, Giovanni, 31, 39, 48
Bodin, Jean, 98, 103, 106
Braden, Gordon, 85
Browne, Thomas, 56

Camden, William, 78, 111–12, 114, 116, 120, 160
Castelvetro, Lodovico, 46
Cave, Terence, 23, 25, 46, 51, 55, 63, 71, 128, 141
Cervantes, Miguel, 129, 137, 140–41
Chaucer, Geoffrey, 138
Cheke, Sir John, 37
Cicero, 23, 25, 39–40, 85, 113, 160
Coney-catching, 18, 49–60, 128, 133–39
Congreve, William, 139, 141
Convenience, 15–16
Copia, 23, 25, 104
Craig, Hardin, 60
Crewe, Jonathan V., 94, 120
Cyropaedia, 40

Daniel, Samuel, 160
Davis, Walter, 30
Decameron, The, 31, 39, 48–49
de Certeau, Michel, 57–58, 154
Deciphering, 13–16, 18, 147, 149–50; in Greene, 21–42; Nashe's criticism of, 64, 72–73, 79, 81, 84–88, 98, 100–102, 107–8, 123–25

Decorum, 16, 19, 32
Defence of Conny Catching, The, 60
Defoe, Daniel, 129, 141
Dekker, Thomas, 13, 20, 64, 126, 127–44; cant in, 18, 128, 135–36, 143, 154; critic of Greene, 14–19, 62–63, 127–28, 130, 132; Nashe's influence on, 128, 130, 132, 138–39, 161–62; plague in, 127, 129–33, 135, 161; rogue literature of, 127, 133–39; skepticism in, 18, 161. Works: *Black Rode*, 132–33; *Dekker his Dreame*, 138; *Honest Whore*, 60; *Knights Conjuring*, 136, 138; *London, Looke Backe*, 132; *Meeting of Gallants*, 131; *Penny-Wise, Pound-Foolish*, 129, 138; *Rod for Run-awayes*, 131; *Strange Horse-Race*, 133–34, 136; *Wonderfull Yeare*, 130, 132, 136
de Man, Paul, 94–95
Demosthenes, 25
Dessen, Alan C., 47
Discovery, 13–14, 16, 33, 150; Dekker's criticism of, 127–39; in Greene, 43–63; in Nashe, 18, 82–83, 88–90, 97–99, 105
Donatus, 45
Drayton, Michael, 160

Eco, Umberto, 143, 164
Eliot, T. S., 143
Elizabeth I, 18, 153, 157
Elyot, Sir Thomas, 157
Empson, William, 153
Erasmus, Desiderius, 25; *De copia*, 104, 115, 148, 159
Euphuism, 21, 24–27, 29, 40, 102, 147–48
Evanthius, 46

Foucault, Michel, 57, 143, 154
Fraunce, Abraham, 95
Freud, Sigmund, 157
Froissart, John, 120

173

Galileo, 56
Genette, Gerard, 51
Geoffrey of Vinsauf, 25
Ginsburg, Warren, 27
Gosson, Stephen, 38
Greenblatt, Stephen, 59
Greene, Robert, 13–14, 20, 64–65, 67, 72, 81, 124, 126–29, 132–35, 137–38, 140; *commoratio* in, 25, 147–48; convention in, 15–16; conversion narratives of, 60–62; deciphering in, 17, 21–42, 79, 147; discovering in, 17, 43–63; dramatic models in, 45–49; Euphuism in, 21, 24–27, 29, 33, 40; experimentation with style and verse, 37–42; ideology in, 56–60; myth of origins in, 35–37; notable signs in, 44–45; Ovid and, 35–36, pastoral romances of, 39–41; rogue literature of, 49–60; "uncritical character" of, 18. Works: *Alcida*, 35–37; *Arbasto*, 29–30; *Blacke Bookes Messenger*, 49, 55; *Ciceronis Amor*, 37–40, 85; *Disputation*, 49, 53, 55; *Greenes Mourning Garment*, 41; *Groats-Worth of Witte*, 60–62, 129, 138; *Mamillia*, 27–29; *Menaphon*, 37, 40–41; *Morando*, 30–35; *Never Too Late*, 138; *Notable Discovery*, 49; *Orlando Furioso*, 45; *Orpharion*, 41; *Perimedes*, 37–38; *Scottish History*, 47; *Second Part*, 49; *Thirde Part*, 49

Hakluyt, Richard, 66, 106, 117
Harlow, C. G., 74
Harrison, William, 98
Harvey, Gabriel, 37, 39, 61, 73, 75, 80–81, 97, 101–10, 124–25, 142, 156–57, 159
Harvey, William, 161
Helgerson, Richard, 23
Herbert, George, 97
Hilliard, Stephen S., 71, 156
Hollander, Robert, 99
Hosley, Richard, 48
Humanism, 37–38, 65, 72
Hunter, J. Paul, 129
Hutson, Lorna, 23, 65, 69–72, 74, 81–82, 102, 154

Imbrie, Ann E., 19

James VI and I, 22
Jones, C. A., 140
Jonson, Ben, 73, 156
Josephus, 98, 157–58
Joyce, James, 19, 143–44
Judges, A. V., 59

Kahn, Victoria, 19, 32–33
Kinney, Arthur F., 26

Levine, Joseph, 111
Lewalski, Barbara Kiefer, 99
Livy, 106
Lodge, Thomas, 22
Lucretius, 115–16, 122
Luther, Martin, 110–13, 157, 159
Lyly, John, 13, 22, 65, 142; Euphuism in, 24–27. Works: *Euphues and his England*, 26, 29; *Euphues, the Anatomy of Wit*, 24

Machiavelli, Niccolò, 107
McKeon, Michael, 111, 129, 139–40, 161–62
McPeek, James A. S., 51
Mandeville, John, 122
Manifest Detection, A, 52, 54
Marlowe, Christopher, 62, 121, 138
Marvell, Andrew, 161
Minturno, Antonio, 48
Mish, Charles C., 17
Montaigne, Michel de, 58, 154
Mueller, Janel M., 25–26
Mussaeus, 121

Nashe, Thomas, 13, 20, 24, 30, 32, 34, 41, 64–126, 127–30, 132, 138–39; attack on deciphering, 18, 27, 64, 72–73, 81, 84–88, 98, 100–102, 107–8, 123–25, 149–50, 156; critic of Greene, 14–19, 62–63, 72; Epicureanism in, 113, 115–16, 121–22, 125; extemporal vein of, 65–68; faith and works in, 87, 111, 113, 119–21, 125, 157, 160; fiction and, 118–26; Harvey and, 61, 73, 75, 80–81, 97, 99, 101–9, 110, 156–57, 159; history in, 98, 100, 103, 106–7, 110–12, 114–18, 159; humanism and, 65, 72, 156–57; Martin Marprelate and, 70, 79, 125, 155; materiality and, 66–68, 71, 75–76, 88–89, 91–95,

INDEX

100–105, 108, 121, 155; patrons of, 69–70, 74, 78; picaresque in, 73, 156; *prosopopeia* in, 83, 92–95, 98, 102, 106; "stuff" as major trope of, 13, 18, 64–126; uses of Greene's discovery, 18, 82–83, 88–90, 97–99, 105; skepticism in, 112, 160; venting and, 66–68, 88–89, 91, 155. Works: *Anatomie*, 65, 72; *Christs Teares*, 65–66, 69, 80–83, 90–101, 103–5; *Have With You*, 65–66, 69, 100–109; *Lenten Stuffe*, 64–65, 70, 75, 91, 100, 103, 105, 109–26; *Pierce Penilesse*, 65, 72–74; preface to Greene, 64–65; preface to Sidney, 65, 72; *Strange Newes*, 75, 80; *Summers Last Will*, 70; *Terrors of the Night*, 65, 68–69, 73–81, 106

Ong, Walter, S.J., 39

Paracelsus, 143
Parker, Patricia, 107
Peele, George, 138
Pettie, George, 25
Plato, 97, 104
Prudentius, 158
Puttenham, George, 13, 15–16, 23, 27, 32, 104

Quintilian, 33

Rainolds, John, 148
Reynolds, John, 139
Rhetorica ad Herennium, 25–26
Rhodes, Neil, 66
Rich, Barnaby, 13
Riffaterre, Michael, 94

Salzman, Paul, 13
Saussure, F. de, 94
Seiden, John, 114, 160
Sextus Empiricus, 112, 160
Shakespeare, William, 13, 25, 47, 62, 128, 136, 142, 153–54, 162
Shapiro, Barbara J., 38
Sidney, Sir Philip, 13, 22, 39, 41, 72, 124–25, 149, 156
Skepticism: in Dekker, 16, 128, 161; in Nashe, 112
Smith, G. Gregory, 22, 80
Spenser, Edmund, 39, 137
Sprat, Thomas, 38
Stanyhurst, Richard, 39
Steane, J. B., 125
Stuff, 13, 18, 64–126

Terence, 45, 163
Throckemorton, Francis, 159
Typology, 56, 59, 97–99, 158

Varro, 119
Vergil, Polydore, 103

Waage, Frederick O., 128
Waldman, Marilyn Robinson, 142
White, Hayden, 142
Whitgift, John, 110
Wilson, Thomas, 26
Wolff, Samuel, 149
Wonder: in Dekker, 18, 130, 132, 134; in Greene, 26, 162
Woolf, Virginia, 19, 142–44, 163
Wooten, Cecil W., 25

Yates, Frances, 48

Zwingli, Huldreich, 111